KU-029-448

Research Methods for Law

RESEARCH METHODS FOR THE ARTS AND HUMANITIES

Published Titles

Research Methods for English Studies
Edited by Gabrielle Griffin

Forthcoming Titles in the Series

Textual Editing in English Studies
Research Methods for History
Research Methods for Practice-based Research
Research Methods for Film Studios
Research Methods for Linguistics
Research Methods in Theatre Studies
Research Methods for Geography
Research Methods in Cultural Studies
Research Methods for Education

Advisory Board

Professor Geoffrey Crossick, Chief Executive, AHRB

Professor Warwick Gould, Director, Institute of English Studies, London

Professor David Bradby, Theatre Studies, Royal Holloway, London

Professor Angela McRobbie, Media and Communication Studies, Goldsmith's, London

Professor Robert Morris, History, Edinburgh University

Professor Harold Short, Director of the Centre for Computing in the Humanities (CCH) at King's College London

Research Methods for Law

Edited by Mike McConville and Wing Hong Chui

Edinburgh University Press

© in this edition, Edinburgh University Press, 2007
© in the individual contributions is retained by the authors

Edinburgh University Press Ltd
22 George Square, Edinburgh

Reprinted 2012, 2014

Typeset in 11/13 Ehrhardt by
Servis Filmsetting Ltd, Manchester, and
printed and bound by
CPI Group (UK) Ltd, Croydon, CR0 4YY

A CIP record for this book is available from the British Library

ISBN 978 0 7486 3357 9 (hardback)
ISBN 978 0 7486 3358 6 (paperback)

The right of the contributors
to be identified as authors of this work
has been asserted in accordance with
the Copyright, Designs and Patents Act 1988.

Contents

Preface and Acknowledgements

Legal research may be carried out for varied reasons. Some use it to identify the sources of law applicable to understanding a legal problem, and then find a solution to the problem that has been identified. It is apparent that practising lawyers are expected to conduct factual and legal research in an effective manner because of the cost implications for their client. Others would use research as a tool to extend our knowledge on aspects of law and the operation of the legal system that are of great interest. Research may also be driven by the policy considerations promoted by bodies such as law reform commissions to investigate social, political and economic implications of current and proposed legislation. Increasingly, students are required to engage in research themselves and no longer have their studies confined to textbooks.

No one denies that research in the real world is of increasing importance and that conducting legal research is a complex business. Nevertheless, how far are law students, graduates, the legal profession and academic lawyers equipped to undertake legal research? How are their research skills comparable to researchers with a medical science, social science or humanities backgrounds? What pitfalls await the new researcher and can these be avoided or addressed through careful planning? These are indeed very difficult questions, and it is not the intention of this edited volume to look for a complete answer. Rather, it offers general and practical guidance to those who are interested in learning how to use legal research in order to expand the knowledge of legal processes, improve understanding of specific legal problems, and produce findings of significance for society, and it sets out questions that a serious researcher needs to ask before embarking upon any important project.

The primary aim of the book is, then, to introduce some of the essential methodologies, approaches and tools of research in relation to different fields of law. Each chapter introduces generic research skills by examining qualitative or quantitative methodologies relevant to all areas of legal research or through engagement with a variety of areas such as international law, intellectual property, public law, comparative law and criminal justice which are used to illuminate the application of particular skills. It is hoped that this will be a cutting-edge volume advancing our knowledge of three specific kinds of legal research, including black-letter legal research, empirical research, and international and comparative legal research.

Given the complexities of each of these research methodologies, it is impossible to cover all approaches or methods of research within one text. However, we make it clear in our introductory chapter why some approaches will be elaborated in subsequent chapters, and others will be introduced briefly and readers will be directed to further reading. The book has been designed to reach a wide audience including black-letter lawyers, socio-legal researchers and those in related disciplines such as sociology, political science and psychology.

Last but not least, we wish to thank all the contributors for their willingness to play a part in putting together this book, and of course, for their excellent work. We are indebted to Chuo University for kind permission to reproduce the chapter by Geoffrey Wilson. We are also grateful to Eastman Chan at the Chinese University of Hong Kong for her patience in preparing the script for publication; to Alice Chan Ka-yee of the Chinese University of Hong Kong for her technical help and support; the Series Editor of Research Methods for the Arts and Humanities, Gabriele Griffin, for her constructive comments and support in the book project; and to Jackie Jones of the Edinburgh University Press for her commitment to the project.

Mike McConville and Wing Hong Chui

Introduction and Overview

Mike McConville and Wing Hong Chui

Legal scholarship has historically followed two broad traditions. The first, commonly called 'black-letter law', focuses heavily, if not exclusively, upon the law itself as an internal self-sustaining set of principles which can be accessed through reading court judgments and statutes with little or no reference to the world outside the law. Deriving principles and values from decided cases and re-assembling decided cases into a coherent framework in the search for order, rationality and theoretical cohesion has been the fodder of traditional legal scholarship.

A second legal tradition which emerged in the late 1960s is referred to as 'law in context'. In this approach, the starting point is not law but problems in society which are likely to be generalised or generalisable. Here, law itself becomes problematic both in the sense that it may be a contributor to or the cause of the social problem, and in the sense that whilst law may provide a solution or part of a solution, other non-law solutions, including political and social re-arrangement, are not precluded and may indeed be preferred. The law in context approach has given an extra dimension to legal studies that has been taken up in every higher education institution.

Apart from these broad traditions, however, legal scholarship has also undergone significant transformations and is facing significant challenges. One is the increasingly global character of legal life. This is seen in the ready access that can now be secured to materials describing and analysing legal systems across the world (previously inaccessible to most researchers) and requiring, at the least, that research and scholarship pay attention to alternative perspectives and consider their relevance to the local situation. Additionally, it is now inescapable that transjurisdictional instruments, such as Conventions relating to human rights, increasingly penetrate domestic legal systems and stimulate those responsible for operating or interrogating national systems to have regard to wider considerations than was possible when the world was considerably larger and less easily navigated.

Additionally, the teaching of law has moved decisively a way from a teaching-focused system of rote learning tested through examinations to a learning environment in which students are encouraged to assume more responsibility for their own education and in which research tested through coursework assignments plays a more prominent role. Law students are now more research-based than ever before, and research is an integral part of the undergraduate curriculum, no longer the preserve of postgraduate students. This means, at the least, that legal research and scholarship is much more pervasive, complex and demanding than ever before and those engaging in research have more possible pathways to travel and require a greater range of skills and competences than their law-focused predecessors.

AIMS OF THE BOOK

Every law school offers instruction on legal research to equip students with skills of identifying the sources of law and relevant legal materials, and advanced methodology courses to support not only postgraduate students but also those writing dissertations in later undergraduate years. Undeniably legal research is a complex business, and it 'is not merely a search for information; it is primarily a struggle of understanding.'[1] Both academic and practising lawyers are required to think deeply about information recovered and discovered and what are the best methods of collecting, analysing, and presenting information and data. In many respects, strong legal research and writing skills are fundamental tools for legal practice and scholarship. Based on his experience as a lawyer and research student, Nicholas Hancox draws our attention to the distinctive differences in terms of their perceived use of law and legal research between academics and practising lawyers. Some of the observations are: 'academic lawyers want to understand the way that law works and how it affects people and organisations, but practitioners are not interested in *why* the law says what it says'; 'only academic lawyers are interested in how things are done abroad'; 'academics are often less interested in what they (alone) call black letter law'; and 'for academic lawyers, getting published is very important, but practitioners ought never to have time to write books'.[2] While acknowledging these as his subjective observations, the divide is somehow inevitable because of the different expectations among the two sets of lawyers. It is apparent that scholarly legal research is comprehensive and directed towards conclusions whereas practising lawyers are accountable to their clients who seek their professional advice and knowledge on the matter of legal rules, authorities and procedures. Thus, the way academic and practising lawyers see the meaning of law and legal research is diverse. Nonetheless, in order to advance legal scholarship, students, lawyers and academics are recommended to be open-minded and flexible in terms of choosing the best method of understanding and investigating a matter of concern.[3]

This edited volume seeks to provide law students at all levels with exposure to available methods of research – legalistic, empirical, comparative and theoretical – in an accessible, grounded but demanding and hopefully inspirational way, thereby enabling them to pursue research from a variety of perspectives, as they will be expected to engage in during their studies. It offers a pluralistic view of methodological issues and research techniques as opposed to adopting a narrow parameter of traditional legal research. More specifically, three major types of legal research, namely empirical legal research, international and comparative legal research, and doctrinal research will be examined in the collection. In so doing, a variety of research methodologies adapted from law and social sciences will be introduced to investigate legal phenomena such as doing research in the field, criminal justice, international law, and intellectual property law.[4]

At the outset it should be acknowledged that this collection by no means covers all existing legal methodologies but contains selected examples of research based upon the contributors' research experience.[5] It puts great emphasis on the reasons for the choice of research methods, the importance of practical research experience and an examination of dilemmas and problems encountered during the research process. One consistent theme highlighted in each chapter is that while there are procedures or steps to be followed when embarking upon a research project, the researcher is reminded of the need to be reflective and reflexive during the research process and to question whether the chosen methodology is the most appropriate for researching the chosen topic.[6]

TYPES OF LEGAL RESEARCH

Doctrinal Research

A number of titles on legal research are available and have been adopted as textbooks for legal research courses across the world.[7] Admittedly most of these texts on research methods for law are targeted exclusively at 'black-letter law' rather than non-traditional, interdisciplinary research projects. These texts are able to equip students with basic research skills including the knowledge of the sources of legal authority, locating cases and statutes, the use of indexes and citators, and the use of computer information retrieval systems such as Westlaw and LexisNexis. In a word, the 'black-letter law' approach or doctrinal research relies extensively on using court judgments and statutes to explain law:

> Most [law departments / schools] have their own specialized libraries full of raw materials for textual analysis: the law texts, case law, legislation, and increasingly, materials via the internet. There is no need to go outside and research the material realities of people's everyday lives.[8]

The 'black-letter' research aims to systematise, rectify and clarify the law on any particular topic by a distinctive mode of analysis to authoritative texts that consist of primary and secondary sources. One of its assumptions is that 'the character of legal scholarship is derived from law itself'.[9] David Stott articulates a range of skills of legal research to be covered and taught in the Legal Practice Course in the United Kingdom. They are as follows:

- to determine the objectives of the lawyer or client;
- to identify and analyse factual material;
- to identify the legal context in which factual issues arise;
- to identify sources for investigating relevant facts;
- to determine when further facts are required;
- to identify and analyse legal issues;
- to apply relevant legal provisions to facts;
- to relate the central legal and factual issues to each other;
- to identify the legal, factual and other issues presented by documents;
- to analyse a client's instructions and be able to identify legal, factual and other issues presented to them; and,
- to present the results of research in a clear, useful and reliable form.[10]

The above list is not exhaustive but summarises the skills component of the methods classes mainly for the first-year undergraduate students. It is generally agreed that these skills of conducting library legal research and computer legal research must be imparted to law students and new lawyers. Teaching legal research is not always an easy task especially from the law librarian's perspective, and training should not solely focus on finding information but should promote students' understanding of legal doctrine.[11] In many respects, as far as law students are concerned, it remains the case that the majority of undergraduate and LLM-level dissertations are 'black-letter', using interpretative tools or legal reasoning to evaluate legal rules and suggest recommendations for further development of the law.[12]

Empirical Legal Scholarship / Socio-legal Studies

In recent years, several commentators have criticised pure doctrinal analysis for its 'intellectually rigid, inflexible and inward-looking' approach of understanding law and the operation of the legal system.[13] There is evidence that law schools in the United Kingdom, the United States and elsewhere are offering new postgraduate programmes (such as socio-legal studies, feminist legal studies, critical legal studies and new approaches to international law) that encourage an interdisciplinary approach to the study of law.[14] A number of legal educators have drawn attention to the emergence of empirical legal research as well as socio-legal research:

> British university law schools are undergoing a radical change in the
> nature of legal research and scholarship. They were once dominated by
> pure doctrinal analysis but new generation of legal scholars are either
> abandoning doctrinal work or infusing it with techniques and
> approaches drawn from the humanities and the social sciences. . . .
> [T]his change will lead to a greater ability to provide law students with
> a truly liberal education and will also enable the law school to take a
> much greater part in the intellectual debates to be found elsewhere in
> the university.[15]

The non-doctrinal approaches represent a new approach of studying law in the broader social and political context with the use of a range of other methods taken from disciplines in the social sciences and humanities. Socio-legal scholars point to the limitations of doctrinal research as being too narrow in its scope and application of understanding law by reference primarily to case law. This traditional legal method fails to prepare students and legal professionals to attend to non-doctrinal questions.[16] Roger Cotterrell comments:

> All the centuries of purely doctrinal writing on law have produced less
> valuable knowledge about what law is, as a social phenomenon, and
> what it does than the relatively few decades of work in sophisticated
> modern empirical socio-legal studies . . . [17]

The merits and relevance of using other disciplines such as sociology, political science, economics, psychology, history and feminism as aids to legal research have been widely recognised. Interdisciplinary or socio-legal research broadens legal discourse in terms of its theoretical and conceptual framework which guide the direction of the studies and its specific research methodologies are able to generate empirical evidence to answer research questions. In the 1960s and 1970s, legal realists and socio-legal scholars started the law and society movement, and pointed to the importance of understanding the gap between 'law in books' and 'law in action', and the operation of law in society. They were interested in examining the legal system in terms of whether legal reform brings about beneficial social effects and protects the interests of the public.[18] Similarly, in the 1980s critical legal studies integrated ideas and methods found in disciplines such as sociology, anthropology and literary theory.[19] On the whole, these approaches to legal scholarship not only provide an alternative to the traditional legal analysis but also encouraged lawyers to engage in critical and cutting-edge research to examine the relationship between law and gender, social class, ethnicity, religion and other social relations of power.[20] At a more practical level, the promise of interdisciplinary legal research is:

> In purely pragmatic terms, interdisciplinarity offers an opportunity for product differentiation in an increasingly competitive academic environment: an 'interdisciplinary perspective' may help a researcher place his or her work with a more prestigious academic journal or publishing house. Interdisciplinary research is perceived to be popular with research funding bodies, and for legal academics in particular it provides access to research grants of a magnitude not usually available for 'pure' legal research.[21]

What is more, socio-legal scholarship employs a wide range of applied social science methods including quantitative and qualitative research.[22] These methods aim to decipher the workings of legal, social and cultural processes. For instance, Dave Cowan and his colleagues employ a socio-legal analysis to study the role of adjudication or decision-making processes within the local authority in influencing the implementation of homelessness law.[23] Grounded in both quantitative and qualitative data, his research team confirms that despite the implementation of the homelessness law provisions in the Housing Act 1996, local authorities have chosen to exercise discretion in making decisions during the internal review, and obstacles were posed to most aggrieved applicants for reviewing the decisions. Their study demonstrates how hard data are collected to examine how one legal institution operated and whether legal reform achieved its intended outcomes, thereby pointing to further policy and legal reform. It is important to note that empirical legal scholarship is complementary to doctrinal research and both methodologies can be used simultaneously to examine a legal issue, as advocated by academic lawyers.[24] Nonetheless, doubts have been cast on whether the present-day law schools put enough emphasis on the social policy of law, and provide students with sufficient training on the application of applied social sciences to legal research. To fill this gap, this book demonstrates that empirical research can transform how law can be understood and studied.

International and Comparative Legal Research

The third type of legal research covered in the book is international and comparative legal research. The reason for its inclusion is mainly because of the increasing influence of international and supra-national legal materials, and the increasing need for legal scholars to refer to materials from a variety of jurisdictions, together with the demands made by contemporary law schools upon their students to engage in critical thinking. This type of research crosses traditional categories of law, integrating public and private international law with domestic law, European law and the comparative method. It aims to facilitate our understanding of the operation of international law and legal systems and its impact on the formulation of public policy in an era of global interdependence.

STRUCTURE OF THE BOOK

The book is structured into nine chapters. Each of these chapters covers a particular research method within law, and uses actual research projects as illustrative examples to discuss the innovative ideas for conducting legal research. The limitations of each methodology are also highlighted. A selected bibliography of relevant research methodological literature is provided as further reading at the end of each chapter.

Chapters 1 to 3 provide an overview of qualitative and quantitative research methods which lay a foundation for fieldwork in the legal arena. In Chapter 1, Ian Dobinson and Francis Johns define qualitative legal research as simply non-numerical, and contrast it as such with quantitative (numerical) research. Four broad divisions are identified: doctrinal, problem, policy and law reform. Regardless of whether the research done is doctrinal, problem, policy or law reform (or a combination of these), various qualitative approaches should be taken. The researcher's aim should be to reach certain conclusions (or inferences) based on what is found. In this sense, legal research is no different to other forms of academic or scholarly research, and rigorous empirical methods should be used. Using such empirical methods, however, requires a level of academic thoroughness and it is here, according to others, that much of the legal research which has been undertaken falls short. This chapter seeks to alert the would-be legal researcher to such issues and, consequentially, by reference to research examples, how best to undertake qualitative legal research in a more robust and structured manner.

The principal task of Chapter 2 is to examine the nature and applications of quantitative research methods in socio-legal studies. Wing Hong Chui begins with an overview of the aims and core features of quantitative methods, whilst contrasting these with qualitative methods. The role of theory in quantitative research is examined. A range of research designs such as measurements of concepts and sampling strategies available for empirical research are also described. Illustrated with examples from classic and contemporary quantitative studies, the chapter then focuses on main data collection techniques such as surveys, experiments and secondary data analysis. Particular emphasis is placed on unpacking the rationales, strengths and weaknesses of each technique. This chapter ends with a discussion of quantitative data analysis and a review of the key ethical issues in quantitative research.

Chapter 3 identifies the key characteristics of ethnographic research, and explains how Masters and PhD students can make an invaluable contribution to maintaining this socio-legal tradition. Valuable insights are provided into the role of theory in qualitative research, the difficulties of formulating research questions, and the multi-faceted nature of gaining and maintaining access. Satnam Choongh uses his own experience of conducting research for his DPhil thesis into procedural fairness at police stations to give practical guidance on how and where to interview, how to structure interviews so as to extract the experiences and views of those being studied, and how to observe, record and analyse everyday interaction and occurrences in a manner which provides legal and sociological insight.

The growing importance of global legal studies is addressed in Chapters 4 to 6. Geoffrey Wilson raises fundamental questions as to the purpose and objectives of comparative legal study in Chapter 4. Comparative law has usually been seen as an extension of the study of national law and justified in terms of the benefits it brings to the national legal system. This chapter illustrates how an expanded view of comparativism can open up a range of exciting opportunities for legal researchers. The potential opened up by the Columbia experiment is re-considered in the context of a comparativist approach directed towards dealing with major problems facing individuals and society and making plain the links between law and real life. Beyond this, Chapter 4 considers some of the differences made by the information revolution and possible responses to this through comparative research.

Mark Findlay and Ralph Henham illustrate one way in which complex legal theory may be generated by cross-jurisdictional research. By interrogating fundamental issues of context, comparison, interaction and interpretation, Chapter 5 lays the essential foundations for the theory and methodology of comparative contextual analysis. In this case the chapter analyses criminal trials in different procedural contexts in order to speculate on the possible synthesis of trial decision-making in an international context. The conceptual framework of one case-study analysis provides a set of organising and interpretative constructs which are capable of identifying elements and processes crucial to the application of rules and resources by participants during the course of the criminal trial. The theoretical grounding is developed to recognise structural, organisational and interactive levels of analysis within each chosen context and in so doing provides a suitable framework against which to model the major dimensions of decision-making in the criminal trial. In the end Chapter 5 maps out the importance of theoretical foundations for case-study methodology and subsequent modelling which are recurrent technologies in socio-legal research. The chapter argues for the crucial utility of theory as the foundation phase and prevailing influence for successful research methodology. Much of this remains implicit in legal research and the chapter provides a capacity to expose theorising and demonstrates its utility.

In Chapter 6, George Meszaros illustrates important questions relating to researcher identity, assimilation, and the collection and processing of information and how comparative research can combine law, politics and theory whilst overcoming difficult problems of access. Conflict is a central feature of law and thereby of much socio-legal enquiry. This raises important methodological issues for researchers in all parts of the world. However, the juxtaposition of precarious legal institutions alongside massive social pressures so characteristic of developing countries places its own set of demands upon researchers. While issues of researcher identity, identification with research subjects, accessing information, handling information, and so on are not unique to developing countries, they are routinely magnified and intensified. High stakes means that the life-blood of research, the gathering and processing of information, rapidly acquires political overtones. This chapter addresses these issues against the background of what, at first glance, looks like a worst-case scenario: a research project that looked at different sides of a land conflict in which dozens of people are killed every year. The research, set in Brazil, had to move between militants occupying land, and judges, prosecutors, and those in charge of state security who routinely locked them up. While this raised unique difficulties, it also raised the sorts of problems and dilemmas with which researchers in developing countries are routinely faced, and for which aspiring researchers ought to be prepared.

In unique contributions, Chapters 7 and 8 give guidance, not elsewhere available, on how to undertake doctrinal research (the staple of many undergraduate research projects) and how to research in the increasingly popular areas of intellectual property and international law. To be more specific, Michael Pendleton, in Chapter 7, expresses concern that contemporary legal research has become predominately empirical or quantitative. He argues that this global trend is largely dictated by university funding models which by and large adopt the science model for funding the humanities, social sciences and law. While criticising this development, the author asks what is traditional non-empirical legal research, what are its merits and how does one go about doing it. Examples of traditional doctrinal legal analysis and criticism are used to illuminate this doctrinal approach.

In Chapter 8, Stephen Hall argues that International Law has, for more than a decade, been a significant growth area in legal scholarship. This growth is largely due to the acceleration of international interdependence, usually known as 'globalisation' and the new post-Cold War threats to international peace and security. The methodologies for scholarship in this field are unavoidably shaped by the nature of International Law's 'sources', which lawyers from other fields frequently find to be notably idiosyncratic. This feature of International Law's sources results from the fact that they emerge unavoidably from the decentralised and mainly consensual nature of the international legal system. This chapter looks at each of these sources with a view to identifying methodological pitfalls into which inexperienced researchers sometimes fall and the means of avoiding them. It also identifies a non-exhaustive range of broad topics which provide potential for young researchers looking for a fertile area to explore.

The final chapter reviews a thirty-year-long project as it evolved and metamorphosed to bring out many of the threads linking the other contributions and to provide a guide to the challenges and possibilities of legal research. Mike McConville reviews a variety of approaches that may be taken in undertaking research illustrating basic principles with worked examples. Taking the issue of negotiated justice, the chapter traces the evolution in approach from 'revelatory' research to meta-theory grounded in detailed data collection. The narrative picks up issues in the chapters and looks at comparativism, 'top-down' and 'bottom-up' theory building, issues of access, assimilation and researcher identity, as well as the ethics and politics of research.

FURTHER READING

Doctrinal Research

C. M. Bast and M. Hawkins, *Foundations of Legal Research and Writing* (3rd edn) (Clifton Park, NY: Thomson/Delmar Learning, 2006).

C. Chatterjee, *Methods of Research in Law* (2nd edn) (Horsmonden, Kent: Old Bailey Press, 2000).

P. Clinch, *Using a Law Library: A Student's Guide to Legal Research Skills* (2nd edn) (London: Blackstone, 2001).

G. Holburn, *Butterworths Legal Research* (2nd edn) (London: Butterworths, 2001).

W. H. Putman, *Legal Research, Analysis, and Writing* (Clifton Park, NY: Thomson/Delmar Learning, 2005).

D. Stott, *Legal Research* (2nd edn) (London: Cavendish Publishing, 1999).

Empirical Legal Scholarship

C. Bell, 'A Note on Participant Observation' (1969) 3 *Sociology* 417.

N. L. Channels, *Social Science Methods in the Legal Process* (Totowa, NJ: Rowman & Littlefield, 1985).

M. Clarke, 'Survival in the Field: Implications of Personal Experience in Field Work' (1975) 2 *Theory and Society* 95.

S. Cohen and L. Taylor, 'Prison Research: A Cautionary Tale' (1975) 31 *New Society* 253.

M. O. Finkelstein, *Quantitative Methods in Law: Studies in the Application of Mathematical Probability and Statistics to Legal Problems* (New York: Free Press, 1978).

Journal of Empirical Legal Studies (Oxford: Blackwell).

J. H. Schlegel, *American Legal Realism and Empirical Social Science* (Chapel Hill: University of North Carolina Press, 1995).

Socio-legal Studies

A. Bradney, *Conversations, Choices and Chances: The Liberal Law School in the Twenty-first Century* (Oxford: Hart Publishing, 2003).

R. Banakar and M. Travers (eds), *Theory and Method in Socio-legal Research* (Oxford: Hart Publishing, 2005).

R. Collier, '"We're All Socio-legal Now"? Law Schools and the Knowledge Economy – Reflections on the UK Experience' (2004) 26 *Sydney Law Review* 503.

D. J. Galligan (ed.), *Socio-legal Studies in Context: The Oxford Centre Past and Present* (Oxford: Blackwell, 1995).

I. Horowitz (ed.), *The Rise and Fall of Project Camelot* (Cambridge, MA: MIT Press, 1967).

L. Humphreys, *Tearoom Trade* (London: Duckworth, 1970).

Journal of Law and Society (Oxford: Blackwell).

Law and Society Review (Oxford: Blackwell).

P. Thomas, *Socio-legal Studies* (Aldershot: Dartmouth, 1997).

A. Vidich, J. Bensman and M. Stein (eds), *Reflections on Community Studies* (New York: Wiley, 1964).

International and Comparative Legal Research

Asian Journal of Comparative Law (The Berkeley Electronic Press) (http://www.bepress.com/asjd/).

U. Drobnig, 'The International Encyclopedia of Comparative Law: Efforts toward a world wide comparison of law' (1972) *Cornell International Law Journal* 5(2): 113.

Electronic Journal of Comparative Law (http://www.ejcl.org/index.html).

G. Frankenburg, 'How to Do Projects with Comparative Law – Notes of An Expedition to the Common Core' (2006) 6 *Global Jurist Advances* 1.

J. Husa, 'Melodies on Comparative Law: A Review Essay' (2005) 74 *Nordic Journal of International Law* 161.

O. Kahn-Freund, 'Comparative Law as an Academic Subject' (1966) 82 *Law Quarterly Review* 40.

R. Peerenboom, C. J. Petersen and A. H. Y. Chen, *Human Rights in Asia: A Comparative Legal Study of Twelve Asian Jurisdictions, France and the USA* (London: Routledge, 2006).

M. Rheinstein, 'Comparative Law – Its Functions, Methods and Usages' (1968) 22 *Arkansas Law Review* 415.

J. Stone, 'The End to Be Served by Comparative Law' (1968) 25 *Tulane Law Review* 325.

R. Zimmermann and M. Reimann (eds), *The Oxford Handbook of Comparative Law* (Oxford: Oxford University Press, 2006).

Historical Research in Law

J. B. Ames, *Lectures on Legal History and Miscellaneous Legal Essays* (Cambridge, MA: Harvard University Press, 1913).

D. Cairns, *Advocacy and the Making of the Adversarial Criminal Trial 1800–1865* (Oxford: Oxford University Press 1999).

D. Ibbetson, 'Historical Research in Law' in P. Cane and M. Tushnet (eds), *The Oxford Handbook of Legal Studies* (Oxford: Oxford University Press, 2003).

Journal of Legal History (Abingdon: Taylor and Francis).

J. Langbein, *The Origins of Adversary Trial* (Oxford: Oxford University Press, 2005).

Law and History Review (Chicago: University of Illinois Press).

Legal History Connections (Professor Bernard Hibbitts of the University of Pittsburg at http://www.law.pitt.edu/hibbitts/connect.html).

M. McConville and C. Mirsky, *Jury Trials and Plea Bargaining* (Oxford: Hart Publishing, 2005).

F. W. Maitland, *English Law and the Renaissance: With Some Notes* (Cambridge: Cambridge University Press, 1901).

The Legal History Review (Martinus Nijhoff).

S. F. C. Milsom, *Historical Foundations of the Common Law* (2nd edn) (London: Butterworths, 1981).

Feminist Legal Research

K. T. Barlett, 'Feminist Legal Methods' (1990) 103 *Harvard Law Review* 829.

Columbia Journal of Gender and Law (http://www.law.columbia.edu/current_student/student_service/Law_Journals/gender_law).

J. Conaghan, 'Reassessing the Feminist Theoretical Project in Law' (2000) 27 *Journal of Law and Society* 351.

Feminist Legal Studies (Springer Netherlands).

Harvard Women's Law Journal (http://www.law.harvard.edu/students/orgs/jlg/).

F. Heidensohn, *Women and Crime* (Basingstoke: Macmillan, 1996).

S. Hesse-Biber, C. Gilmartin and R. Lydenberg (eds), *Feminist Approaches to Theory and Methodology: An Interdisciplinary Reader* (New York: Oxford University Press, 1999).

L. Smith, 'What is Feminist Legal Research' in W. Tomm (ed.), *The Effects of Feminist Approaches on Research Methodologies* (Waterloo, ONT: Wilfrid Laurier University Press for the Calgary Institute for the Humanities, 1989).

NOTES

1. M. J. Lynch, 'An Impossible Task but Everybody Has to Do It – Teaching Legal Research in Law Methods' (1997) 89 *Law Library Journal* 415.
2. N. Hancox, 'What Lawyers Want: Comparing Academics with Practitioners', paper presented at the 7th Annual Conference of the Learning in the Law Conference, 7th January 2005, University of Warwick. Available at: http://www.ukcle.ac.uk/interact/lili/2005/contributions/hancox.html
3. T. Hutchinson, *Researching and Writing in Law* (2nd edn) (Pyrmont, NSW: Lawbook Co., 2006) 7.
4. Authors in this edited collection have experience of the type of research on which they write, and they attempt to use various classic and contemporary examples to illustrate their more theoretical discussion and give practical guidance to the reader.
5. For instance, historical research in law and feminist legal methodology is not covered extensively in this edited collection. Readers are recommended to consult texts elsewhere (see a list of further reading at the end of the chapter).
6. D. A. Schon, *The Reflective Practitioner: How Professionals Think in Action* (New York: Basic Books, 1983); J. Mason, *Qualitative Researching* (London: Sage, 2002).
7. See, for example, D. Stott, *Legal Research* (2nd edn) (London: Cavendish, 1999); I. Nemes and G. Coss, *Effective Legal Research* (2nd edn) (Chatswood, NSW: Butterworths, 2001); P. Clinch, M. Barber, C. Jackson and N. Wakefield, *Teaching Legal Research* (2nd edn) (Warwick: UK

Centre for Legal Education, 2006); T. Hutchinson, *Researching and Writing in Law* (2nd edn) (Pyrmont, NSW: Lawbook, 2006). Please also consult a list of further reading at the end of this chapter.

8. P. Hillyard, 'Invoking Indignation: Reflections on Future Directions of Socio-legal Studies' (2002) 29 *Journal of Law and Society* 650.

9. E. L. Rubin, 'Law and the Methodology of Law' (1997) *Wisconsin Law Review* 525.

10. D. Stott, *Legal Research* (2nd edn) (London: Cavendish, 1999) 3.

11. R. K. Mills, 'Legal Research Instruction in Law School, the State of the Art or, Why Law School Graduates Do Not Know How to Find the Law' (1977) 70 *Law Library Journal* 343; D. J. Dunn, 'Why Legal Research Skills Declined, or When Two Rights Make a Wrong' (1993) 85 *Law Library Journal* 49; Lynch, note 1 above, 428.

12. This observation is based on the editors' extensive teaching experience in different countries, including England, Hong Kong, Australia and the United States.

13. D. W. Vick, 'Interdisciplinary and the Discipline of Law' (2004) 31 *Journal of Law and Society* 164.

14. See, for example, R. W. Gordon, 'Lawyers, Scholars, and the "Middle Ground"' (1993) 91 *Michigan Law Review* 2075; R. Banakar and M. Travers (eds), *Theory and Method in Socio-legal Research* (Oxford: Hart Publishing, 2005).

15. A. Bradney, 'Law as a Parasitic Discipline' (1998) 25 *Journal of Law and Society* 71.

16. P. Goodrich, 'Of Blackstone's Tower: Metaphors of Distance and Histories of the English Law School' in P. B. H. Birks (ed.), *Pressing Problems in Law What are Law Schools For?* (Vol. 2) (Oxford: Oxford University Press, 1996) 59.

17. R. Cotterrell, *Law's Community: Legal Theory in Sociological Perspective* (Oxford: Oxford University Press, 1995) 296. Also cited in Bradney, see note 15 above, 73. However, some scholars hold the view that the identity of legal discipline is under threat because of the increasing number of socio-legal studies which borrow concepts, theories and research methods from non-law disciplines. See, for example, G. Jones, '"Traditional" Legal Scholarship: A Personal View' in Birks, see note 18 above, 14.

18. See, for example, J. H. Schlegel, *American Legal Realism and Empirical Social Science* (Chapel Hill: University of North Carolina Press, 1995); Banakar and Travers, see note 14 above.

19. Vick, see note 13 above, 184.

20. R. Collier, 'The Law School, the Legal Academy and the "Global Knowledge Economy" – Reflections on a Growing Debate: Introduction' (2005) 14 *Social & Legal Studies* 259.

21. Vick, see note 13 above, 171.
22. T. E. George, 'An Empirical Study of Empirical Legal Scholarship: The Top Law Schools' (2006) 81 *Indiana Law Journal* 141; R. Banakar and M. Travers, 'Law, Sociology and Method', in R. Banakar and M. Travers, see note 14 above, 17.
23. D. Cowan, S. Halliday and C. Hunter, 'Adjudicating the Implementation of Homelessness Law: The Promise of Socio-legal Studies' (2006) 21 *Housing Studies* 382.
24. J. Baldwin and G. Davis, 'Empirical Research in Law' in P. Cane and M. Tushnet (eds), *The Oxford Handbook of Legal Studies* (Oxford: Oxford University Press, 2003) 881.

CHAPTER I

Qualitative Legal Research

Ian Dobinson and Francis Johns

INTRODUCTION

In 2002 a lively exchange took place in the *University of Chicago Law Review* between two eminent social scientists on one side[1] and a distinguished law professor on the other.[2] The substance of the debate centred on the assertion by the social scientists that:

> Although the term 'empirical research' has become commonplace in legal scholarship over the past two decades, law professors . . . appear to have been proceeding with little awareness of, much less compliance with, many of the rules of inference, and without paying heed to the key lessons of the revolution in empirical analysis that has been taking place over the last century in other disciplines.[3]

The two social scientists had analysed all American law review articles published between 1990 and 2000 which had the word 'empirical' in the title. The conclusions, they said, were discouraging, with every single one breaching what they contend are basic rules of empirical research.[4]

The law professor, whose research had been specifically criticised by the social scientists, responded by saying that:

> Epstein and King state in no uncertain terms that empirical legal scholarship is wholly unconcerned with questions of methodology, and that no law review article – not a single one – is concerned with 'understanding, explicating, or adapting the rules of inference.' Perhaps not surprisingly, given the sweeping and incautious nature of their claim, the authors are simply wrong.[5]

Manderson and Mohr raise associated issues which reflect what they see as:

> a strange disjunction between, on the one hand, the limited notion of 'legal research' as it is understood in text-books and, on the other, the rich and complex world of research presented . . . in graduate seminar rooms, and in the academy.[6]

The above observations raise important questions regarding legal research but it is not the purpose of this chapter to join or analyse the Chicago debate or to consider the types of legal research being undertaken in law schools. Having said this, however, Epstein and King do raise an important issue in terms of the quality of legal research which has been, and continues to be, undertaken at law schools by both graduate students and academics.[7] Their contention is that many law academics are simply untrained and lacking in experience when it comes to empirical research and the general rules applicable to such research. This is largely due to a deficiency in their education as graduate research students. Many academics are accordingly limited in the extent to which they can train future graduate students in the requirements of empirical research. This, they rightly say, is of considerable concern given the importance of legal research in informing policy and law reform. As noted, their conclusions are contentious but there is likely substance in what they say.

The principal aim of this chapter is to consider how to best do qualitative legal research. As part of this 'best or good practice' approach, however, there is a need to first identify the fundamentals of our topic. We start by identifying, in a broad sense, categories which could be considered as covering the majority of legal research that is currently carried out.[8] Two categories are identified: doctrinal and non-doctrinal. Qualitative legal research we define as simply non-numerical and contrasted as such with quantitative (numerical) research (see Chapter 2 of this volume). We also differentiate between academic legal research, that is, that carried out by academics and students, as compared to legal research for professional (legal practice) purposes or research by government[9] and non-government agencies. It is all legal research in both a quantitative and qualitative sense but there will be significant differences between the scholarly research endeavours of a student or academic and that undertaken by a law reform commission. Not the least of these differences will be the resources available at the university level and that which might be provided by the government. Given the purpose of this text, the focus is on graduate research undertaken at the law school level. Having said this, however, much can be learnt in terms of correct approach from non-law school research, and some of the research examples referred to later have been done by government research agencies. Their use is not as a benchmark but rather to highlight examples of good practice, the purpose being to inform and guide graduate law students and teachers involved in research degree programmes.

We accept Epstein and King's assertion that both qualitative and quantitative legal research is empirical research.

> What makes research empirical is that it is based on observations of the world, in other words, data, which is just a term for facts about the world. These facts may be historical or contemporary, or based on legislation or case law, the results of interviews or surveys, or the outcomes of secondary archival research or primary data collection. Data can be precise or vague, relatively certain or very uncertain, directly observed or indirect proxies, and they can be anthropological, interpretive, sociological, economic, legal, political, biological, physical, or natural. As long as the facts have something to do with the world, they are data, and as long as research involves data that is observed or desired, it is empirical.[10]

This is an extremely broad definition and it is arguable that it is perhaps too broad. By comparison, legal research, as taught in many law schools, is far too narrow in its outlook. So-called legal research texts demonstrate this, most being only concerned with very narrowly defined doctrinal research. In commenting on legal research in Australian law schools, Manderson and Mohr see this as an oxymoron particularly in light of the research done by law school academics and postgraduate law students.

> According to a survey of postgraduate research in Australian law schools recently undertaken by one of us, only 20 per cent of all doctoral research projects might happily be described as 'doctrinal'. A further 20 per cent were characterised as 'law reform' work, which might embody, from a more socially normative perspective, a similar approach to the exegetical 'intricacies' of legal scholarship. On the other hand, reflecting the great burgeoning of work in the law and society movement, on post-colonialism, human rights, and globalisation, and drawing on legal realist, critical legal, and post-structural studies in law (Manderson 2001; Goldring 1998: 168–71) 17 per cent were said to be 'theoretical' in orientation, and a further 17 per cent 'interdisciplinary'. The remaining 26 per cent were described as 'international or comparative'.[11]

DOCTRINAL RESEARCH

Much past and current legal research could be placed under this heading. Doctrinal or theoretical legal research can be defined in simple terms as research which asks what the law is in a particular area. The researcher seeks to collect and then analyse a body of case law, together with any relevant legislation (so-called primary sources). This is often done from a historical perspective and may also include secondary sources such as journal articles or other written commentaries on the case law and legislation. The researcher's principal or even sole aim is to describe a body of law and how it applies. In doing so, the researcher may also provide an analysis of the law to demonstrate how it has developed in terms of judicial reasoning and legislative enactment. In this regard, the research can be seen as normative or purely theoretical.

King and Epstein state that purely theoretical research is not empirical.[12] We are not like minded and it is arguable that all doctrinal research is qualitative simply because it is non-numerical. Such labelling, however, is somewhat meaningless, particularly when one's objective is to consider legal research from a best or good practice perspective. In engaging in doctrinal research, it is important to acknowledge the law researcher's dilemma. While legal sources can be accessed to determine what the law is, in terms of case law and legislation, the application of the law is contentious. Indeed, this may be the very reason for why the research was undertaken in the first place. A piece of doctrinal research may not involve empirical method but this does not mean that inferences will not be drawn from what is found.

Many legal researchers, however, do not readily distinguish between research directed at finding a specific statement of the law and an in-depth analysis of the process of legal reasoning. In the standard legal education text, *Learning the Law*,[13] Glanville Williams identifies two types of legal research:[14] one being 'the task of ascertaining the precise state of the law on a particular point'; the other being 'the sort of work undertaken by lawyers (often but not always academic lawyers) who wish to explore at greater length some implications of the state of the law . . . '. Williams may in fact be describing one sort of research which only differs in degree, that being doctrinal research. The methodology involved would be common to both approaches.

The overriding objective of this chapter is accordingly to help legal researchers understand the importance of acknowledging the type of research they are doing, and approach it in a structured way which enables the most effective research outcomes.

NON-DOCTRINAL RESEARCH

All other legal research can be generally grouped within three categories: problem, policy and law reform based research. It is accepted that these categories are not mutually exclusive and are identified in terms of an assessment of what a piece of research is largely about. They can be considered together because of the often occurring link between them. In fact, all four categories of research, doctrinal, problem, policy and law reform, could be part of a large-scale research project. A researcher, for example, could begin by determining the existing law in a particular area (doctrinal). This may then be followed by a consideration of the problems currently affecting the law and the policy underpinning the existing law, highlighting, for example, the flaws in such policy. This in turn may lead the researcher to propose changes to the law (law reform).

While the doctrinal component of the above example could be seen as non-empirical, the assessment of the problem, evaluation of the policy and the need for law reform would require an empirical approach which could be quantitative, qualitative or a combination of the two. By its very nature, such research is inferential. Even in the most descriptive of forms, policy research on legislation, for example, would seek to provide some level of explanation as to why particular laws were enacted. Other research may seek to explain this historically and could include consideration of the effect of relevant appellant court cases on the development of such policy leading to the enactment of the legislation concerned.

Other research may simply seek to outline an existing legal problem. As noted, this could lead to law reform which itself could then be subject to evaluative research. Such research might begin by collecting all relevant case law in order to demonstrate how a particular law is not working. Alternatively, a researcher may observe a number of cases to assess whether there are existing procedural problems in the way in which certain parts of a trial are carried out. Based on this, the researcher could reach a tentative conclusion that the current law needs amendment, repeal, or there is a need for new law.

Problem, policy and law reform research often includes a consideration of the social factors involved and/or the social impact of current law and practice. In this regard, the type of research done might include surveys and interviews with various individuals and groups affected. Such research is often referred to as socio-legal research. As a generic category, socio-legal research encompasses a huge range of different types of research. It is beyond the scope of this chapter to describe and analyse this type of research in detail.[15] As such, a more general approach is taken to so-called non-doctrinal research which encompasses both legal and socio-legal studies. Regardless of whether the research done is legal or socio-legal or a combination of the two, various qualitative approaches should be taken. The researcher's aim should be to reach certain conclusions (or inferences) based on what is found. In this sense, legal research is no different to all other forms of academic or scholarly research. Where there is difference is in the empirical method used. Using such empirical method, however, requires a level of academic rigour and it is here, according to King and Epstein,[16] that much legal research falls down. This chapter seeks to alert the would-be legal researcher to such pitfalls. In addition, it will discuss, by reference to examples, how to best undertake qualitative legal research.

IS DOCTRINAL RESEARCH QUALITATIVE RESEARCH?

If the law can simply be discovered using a systematic approach and the same law would be found no matter who was carrying out the research then it could be argued that doctrinal research was quantitative. Hutchinson describes doctrinal research as though it was equivalent to quantitative research or at least does not categorise it as qualitative research.[17] She describes the reluctance and inability of lawyers to move beyond the doctrinal in their research and to broaden their approach to adopt social science methodologies. She describes qualitative research as an exploration of 'social relations and reality as experience'[18] rather than 'dealing in specific cases'.[19] The characterisation of doctrinal research as not being qualitative is interesting because it reveals the established paradigm of legal research: that there is somehow an objective approach to finding the law.

This assumption about the law is at odds with the type of reasoning that judges apply. Judges reason inductively, analysing a range of authorities relevant to the facts, deriving a general principle of law from these authorities and applying it to the facts in front of them. The dynamic relationship between law and facts has been defined as the 'stepping stone approach'.[20] A common law lawyer applies a process of distinguishing cases on their facts until what is left is an applicable principle. This is a process of elimination which is an application of the inductive reasoning where the principle is gleaned from a detailed analysis of all relevant precedent. Returning to the social science perspective, it can be argued that judicial inductive reasoning, which is what a doctrinal researcher does, must be qualitative in its research methodology.

> In summary, theory produced as part of qualitative data analysis is typically a statement or a set of statements about relationships between variables or concepts that focus on meanings and interpretations. Theories influence how qualitative analysis is conducted. The qualitative researcher attempts to elaborate or develop a theory to provide a more useful understanding of the phenomenon. The focus on meanings makes qualitative research difficult to do well, because meanings are more 'slippery' than quantitative statistics.[21]

Ultimately law may be knowable but it is not necessarily predictable. Doctrinal research is not simply a case of finding the correct legislation and the relevant cases and making a statement of the law which is objectively verifiable. It is a process of selecting and weighing materials taking into account hierarchy and authority as well as understanding social context and interpretation. For this reason it can be argued that doctrinal research is qualitative.

However, lawyers are not trained to admit this. They will rely on the hierarchy and authority to support a particular principle. Doctrinal legal research traditionally proceeds on the basis that the law can be found without enquiry into meaning or origins.[22] Epstein and King contrast the approach of a lawyer and a science PhD where the lawyer is encouraged to research from the perspective of the client whereas the science PhD has to acknowledge contrary positions. 'An attorney who treats a client like a hypothesis would be disbarred; a PhD who advocates a hypothesis like a client would be ignored'.[23]

QUALITATIVE DOCTRINAL LEGAL RESEARCH

To describe doctrinal legal research as qualitative recognises that law is reasoned and not found. It is important also to recognise that lawyers are not trained in a research methodology that acknowledges that the law cannot be objectively isolated. The aim here is to establish a doctrinal legal research methodology which takes into account the nature of law. Social science can be referred to again to get a sense of the objectives of a research methodology:

> These three elements – the techniques, the research community and the methodological rules – together constitute a methodological domain through which all research must pass in order for it to achieve certain standards of integrity and validity. It acts as a mediator between the researcher's subjective beliefs and opinions and the data and evidence that he or she produces through research. If this domain is functioning properly, it acts as something like a filter which prevents bad research from passing through.[24]

This analysis is referring to research generally. With legal doctrinal research the methodology is going to be very specific. The identification of relevant legislation, cases and secondary materials in law can be seen as analogous to a social science literature review. Fink defines a literature review as being 'a systematic, explicit and reproducible method for identifying, evaluating and synthesising the existing body of completed and recorded work produced by researchers, scholars and practitioners'.[25] More specifically, Fink's requirements for a thorough literature review are listed below.[26]

1. Selecting research questions
2. Selecting bibliographic or article databases

3. Choosing search terms
4. Applying practical screening criteria
5. Applying methodological screening criteria
6. Doing the review
7. Synthesising the results

For the purposes of this chapter Fink is used as a template because it reflects the discipline of social science research and, being focused on literature, provides a model which can be adapted to law. What is described below is by no means a definitive methodology for legal research but might be a departure point for developing a research discipline within law. The question is whether these requirements can be applied to doctrinal legal research. It is useful to look at these steps point by point and see how they can be applied to legal research. The emphasis will be on the first five points. These elements, when considered in the context of legal research, should be the foundation of a comprehensive approach. The last two are not so relevant to law as they related to the correlation and comparative analysis of literature that focuses on field research results, which is not what legal literature covers.

Requirement 1: Selecting research questions

For doctrinal research the question is going arise from a search for law which is applicable to a given set of circumstances. Unlike policy research there are no apparent value judgments to be made. The established assumption will be that the law is there to be found. A research methodology, however, should aim to eliminate the possibility of selectivity. Manderson and Mohr[27] warn that the natural predisposition of the legally trained is to research as an advocate and not as an academic. It is also important to acknowledge that the law is there to be derived from the reasoning applied to the sources found.

Requirement 2: Selecting bibliographic or article databases

For doctrinal legal research this is perhaps the most important step. Doctrinal law is based on authority and hierarchy. The objective will always be to base any statements about what the law is, on primary authority: that is, either legislation or case law. Secondary sources such as journal articles or textbooks may be useful in supporting a particular interpretation but they cannot replace primary sources.

In doctrinal legal research where the aim should be to research as an academic rather than as an advocate, the methodology should be thorough, systematic, justifiable and reproducible. There may be a number of approaches depending on the nature of the search. Below are listed a number of research tools and an overview of their respective utility. This chapter is not going to describe how to use these sources, rather why they should be used, their value, and where they fit into a methodology.

- Encyclopaedic works – where the research question is regarding the law which can be applied in a specific circumstances, then the starting point could be an encyclopaedic work. The term 'encyclopaedic work' does not mean simply legal encyclopaedias but reference publications that attempt to cover the law of a jurisdiction so the discussion will include a broad range of works.
- Legal encyclopaedias – the most famous common law legal encyclopaedia is *Halsbury's Laws of England*. It is published in the United Kingdom (UK) by LexisNexis Butterworths. In the context of a research methodology, it is essential to understand its underlying rationale. It is written in propositional style which means that it comprises a series of statements or propositions of law where every statement is supported by primary authority, that is, legislation or case law. *Halsbury* does not attempt to look at the history of the law or examine its social context. *Halsbury* will not express an opinion about the law. If a legal principle cannot be supported by primary authority, then it will not appear. In the context of choosing a data source in a discipline which relies on authority then, *Halsbury* is a useful starting point. While *Halsbury* is regularly cited in court, it is not in itself a source of law. The work is used to find authority and the next step must always be to consult the original source of law.

  There are *Halsbury*-style encyclopaedias in other jurisdictions which can be used the same way. There are currently *The Laws of Scotland: Stair Memorial Encyclopaedia*, *Halsbury's Laws of Australia*, *Halsbury's Laws of Hong Kong*, *Halsbury's Laws of India* and *Laws of New Zealand*, all published by local LexisNexis companies. In Australia there is also a *Laws of Australia* legal encyclopaedia published by Thomson which, although it purports to be written in propositional style, does not cover all topic areas in as much depth as *Halsbury*, and does not apply the so-called propositional style with the same level of discipline.

  In the United States the parallel black-letter law works are *American Jurisprudence* and *Corpus Juris Secundum: Complete Restatement of the Entire American Law as Developed by All Reported Cases*, both published by Thomson. There are also some state-based *Jurisprudence* works which follow the same structure.

  It would be a mistake to assume that the traditional legal encyclopaedias were an objective approach to the law as it stands. There are two possible criticisms of legal encyclopaedias. One is that despite the reputation developed by their strict black-letter law approach, there is still authorial involvement in selecting which cases are selected to represent the law. Also, law should not be seen as strictly black-letter. The way in which law is applied may be determined by policy.

Nevertheless, as part of a methodology, these works are a necessary starting point. They have a long tradition and a stable publication history and are accessible either online or in hard copy in major law libraries. Any research using these legal encyclopaedias as a starting point can be seen as a credible and reproducible stage of a methodology.

• Case digests – other encyclopaedic law resources include case digests. These publications do not provide an overview of an area of law but instead digest case facts and holdings, and categorise them under a comprehensive legal topic classification system, or what could be described as a legal taxonomy. These works assume knowledge of the area of law being researched. The expectation is that while the researcher knows the topic, the circumstances that have generated the need for research are slightly unusual and the researcher needs to look through a number of cases to find either relevant law or a parallel fact situation to see how the law might be applied.

In the UK the key work is *The Digest* formerly known as the *English and Empire Digest* and published by LexisNexis Butterworths. It includes not only English case digests but also digests of important cases from other Commonwealth countries as well as Europe.

In Australia Thomson publish *The Australian Digest* which is set out the same way as *The Digest*. The cases digested are Australian only but cover all states and territories as well as the federal jurisdictions. *The Australian Digest* is available online in a form which combines the content of the work with a current awareness service and case citator in a product called *FirstPoint*.

In New Zealand case digests can be found in the *Abridgement of New Zealand Case Law* which digests cases reported in the *New Zealand Law Reports* only.

The leading legal encyclopaedic works in Canada are the *Canadian Encyclopedic Digest* and the *Canadian Abridgement* published by Carswell. The former is a legal encyclopaedia published in several editions corresponding to regions, whereas the latter is a case digest.

In the United States Westlaw publishes the *American Digest System*. Note that this is not a consolidated work but comprises discrete multi-volume editions which require research by jurisdiction and year of the case.

As a starting point a legal encyclopaedia will provide an overview of an area of law with a case list and relevant legislation; a case digest will provide judicial authority carefully categorised under the topic area being researched. An advocate would select the authority that supports the position being argued. For an academic researcher all authority must be considered. Nor is this the end of the research steps. Case law and legislation need to be checked for currency and further judicial consideration.

• Case citators are most often used to find the correct citation or parallel citations for a case. Their main purpose, however, is to enable a researcher to check the status of a case and to find other cases which have discussed the legal principles expressed in that case.

Checking the status of a case means tracking the subsequent treatment of a case to see if it is good law. It also means understanding the fine distinctions between the annotations used to characterise the cases, for example the terms *followed*, *applied* and *distinguished*. If a case has been followed, the expectation is that the subsequent case has similar facts; if the case has been *applied*, then the principal of law has been relied upon in different factual circumstances. Clearly, law from a case which has subsequently been consistently *applied* rather than *followed* is going to represent a more fundamental and significant legal principal. If a case has been subsequently *distinguished*, it can be two things. Either the case was simply not relevant or the legal principal relied upon is narrow and should be confined to the circumstances of the original case.

The use of a case citator to check any cases derived from an encyclopaedic search is essential to determine the relative value of case authority that the researcher wishes to rely upon.

For UK law use the *Current Law Case Citator* published by Sweet & Maxwell. This work is available in four separate volumes current until 2004. It is also available online on *CLI Online*.[28] LexisNexis Butterworths UK has recently launched *CaseSearch* which is an exclusively online service.

For Australian cases the available online citators are *CaseBase*, *FirstPoint* (which combines the *Australian Digest* and the *Australian Case Citator*) and *Keycite* on Westlaw. *Keycite* covers United States, United Kingdom, Canada and Hong Kong cases. *CaseBase* cites leading US and UK judgments where they have been referred to in Australian judgments. The *Australian Case Citator* is a multi-volume hard copy work published by Lawbook Co.

For Canadian cases the online citator is QuickCITE on LexisNexis Quicklaw. Carslaw publishes a hard copy citator, *Canadian Case Citations*, which is a companion to the *Canadian Abridgement*.

For US cases *Shepard's* can be accessed on Lexis.com and *Keycite* can be accessed using Westlaw.

LexisNexis Hong Kong publishes the *Hong Kong Case Citator (1905–2002)* which covers all reported Hong Kong cases.

An advocate will use a case citator to find authority which supports a proposition. An academic should use a case citator to ensure that every aspect of interpretation or application of the law has been canvassed.

- Legislation – where an area is governed by legislation, finding the relevant source is generally straightforward. However, it is essential to check currency and judicial consideration. Checking currency is a routine technical process. Checking if there has been judicial consideration of an act or section ensures that any personal assumptions about interpretation or application are not misdirected. It may also be useful to examine the context in which the legislation was created, for example the relevant parliamentary debates and, specifically, second reading speeches.
- Statute annotators – one way to do that is by using a statute annotator. These publications track changes to legislation over time including listing amending legislation and identifying commencement dates of any changes. A statute annotator also indicates where there has been judicial consideration. Most annotators list cases that have considered an act or regulation generally, and also list where specific sections have been subject to judicial consideration.

  Once the researcher has updated relevant legislation and found useful case references, then the cases should be checked in a citator to see if there has been subsequent treatment of the issues involved.

  In Australia both LexisNexis Butterworths and Thomsons Legal publish statute annotators for the major Australian jurisdictions.

  In the UK the Sweet & Maxwell service *Current Law Legislation Citator* identifies where an act has been judicially considered.

  Canada Law Book publishes the *Canada Statute Citator* which covers federal legislation. There are also citators for the major provinces.

  In the US there are comprehensively annotated versions of the US code and many of the state codes. Examples are the *United States Code Service*, *United States Code Annotated*, *Deering's California Codes Annotated* and *LexisNexis Florida Annotated Statutes*.
- Current awareness services – where it is important to be completely up to date with changes in legislation and case law, current awareness services provide monthly updates of amendments and case digests.

  In Australia the key publications are *Australian Current Law* and the *Australian Legal Monthly Digest*.

  In the UK Sweet & Maxwell publish monthly digests as a component of their *Current Law* work.

  When updating US state or federal legislation, look for online bill tracking services provided by LexisNexis or Westlaw.
- Hansard – a thorough approach to legislation may involve research into the circumstances of the creation of the legislation. Some jurisdictions have statutory interpretation provisions which enable reliance on extrinsic sources to help determine the meaning of a section. This may include second reading speeches.[29]

When researching legislation, it may be useful to refer to the respective parliament's Hansard in order to understand the objectives of the legislation. Whether or not Hansard may legitimately be applied to the interpretation of the legislation, a second reading speech can be useful for getting a concise overview of an act.

- Secondary sources – the overview so far has focused on tracking developments in primary sources. Secondary materials can also be important in developing approaches to how a doctrinal legal issue might be analysed. They enable the researcher to know who the leaders in a particular field are. In-depth doctrinal research must acknowledge work that has been done previously in the area.
- Textbooks – a doctrinal research methodology would be incomplete if leading textbooks were not consulted. While not authoritative, they may be persuasive. They often represent the standard form of expression of particular areas of law.[30] Long established texts will entrench the author's association with a legal area – for example, *Cross on Evidence*, *Palmer on Bailment*, *Nimmer on Copyright*, *Bowstead on Agency*, *Chisum on Patents*, *Wigmore on Evidence* and *Corbin on Contracts*. The name will have such value that new editions may outlive the author.
- Periodicals are regularly published subscription works that may contain articles which are thematically linked: for example, the *Journal of Legal Education* or the *Journal of Contract Law*.

  Periodicals may be in the form of law journals or law reviews. It is important to distinguish between law journals and law reviews. Law journals tend to be published by professional organisations such as law societies or bar associations and comprise short articles focusing on the practical application of current law. Law reviews are usually published by universities and contain in-depth articles emphasising a theoretical rather than practical approach, and they may be peer reviewed. Beware that this is not a hard and fast rule. The terms 'journal' and 'review' may be used loosely, nevertheless there is a consistent distinction between practice and academic periodicals.

  In the preparation of a research methodology for doctrinal research, it is important to choose between a practice and an academic approach. If the doctrinal research is simply asking a question relating to finding the relevant applicable law, researching journals may be sufficient. However, if the purpose of the doctrinal research is a critique of whatever law is found, then perhaps a researcher should look to academic law reviews to develop a theoretical basis for analysing the law.
- Finding articles – to find relevant articles a researcher can do a free text search on an online legal information aggregator such as LexisNexis, Westlaw or Heinonline. However, the researcher is limited by the holdings of the respective service and their Boolean searching skills (see below).

Before searching online it may be useful to refer to a legal journal index. The most useful journal index for legal publications is publisher HW Wilson's *Index to Legal Periodicals* which is usually abbreviated to *ILP*. This product indexes law journals from the US, Canada, UK, Ireland, Australia, and New Zealand. It is important to understand that this index is not simply a list but that every article entered has been read and indexed by legally qualified indexers. This means that by commencing with an index search, every journal article related to a particular topic can be found. *ILP* is available online or in hard copy.

Other indexes include the online-only *Legal Resource Index* (or *LegalTrac*) published by IAC, and the Australian Government's *Attorney-General's Information Service* (*AGIS*) which indexes Australian, New Zealand and Pacific legal periodicals.

For doctrinal research, then a possible methodology for doctrinal legal research in relation to selecting sources would be to (1) consult a legal encyclopaedia to establish an overview of the law and gather an initial list of authorities; (2) refer to a case digest to see if there is any other authority which might be useful to include; (3) check with a current awareness service to add the latest cases; (4) use a case citator to check the status of any authority that will be relied on and as a way of discovering further authority; (5) if legislation is relevant, check the currency using a current awareness service; check for judicial consideration using a statute annotator; and check if parliamentary sources are useful if ambiguity exists in the text; and (6) conduct a survey of secondary sources to compare approaches of other researchers in the field.

The detail in these steps for a research task should be documented so they can be reproduced. The outcomes may of course change over time because law is dynamic and the treatment of issues may be qualified in subsequent law or commentary.

Requirement 3: Choosing search terms

Legal research has been transformed by the easy access to vast databases of online materials. It has been argued that the change of medium has changed the nature of legal research – that outside the context of the library, legal research is now less structured which challenges the emphasis on authority.

> We no longer live in a universe where absolutes can be discovered
> through judicious reading of common law precedents . . . For the
> modern Supreme Court there is no final primary authority, only a
> kaleidoscope of sources that one can shift to provide any of a number of
> pictures . . . [31]

Fink emphasises the importance of constructing a Boolean search when using an online service. However it should be acknowledged that because of the volume of legal materials available online, Boolean or free text searching may not be the most efficient way to proceed.[32]

Online services should be approached with an understanding that they are designed to be either *browsed* or *searched*. *Browsing* means relying on the structure of a database, where navigation is done by using an alphabetical list, a table of contents, a date range or an index, simply using mouse clicks to find a particular document. *Searching* means using Boolean search logic to find documents. The disadvantages of a Boolean search include either finding too many hits or finding relevant hits, but with the uncertainty of not knowing whether every relevant document has been found.

Browsing allows a researcher to approach a search with a more systematic step-by-step methodology. For example, in this context it is important to emphasise the importance of an index. Indexes are conceptual and hierarchical. A user can search by drilling down from broad to more specialised topics or be cross referred to areas which may be more relevant. There may be an assumption that Boolean searching obviates the need for an index. But the opposite is true. The more overwhelming the information available online, the more important the proper indexing of a database.

When searching online, if the information provider has structured databases that enable browsing, it can be a more thorough approach to finding information than a Boolean search. If there is no choice but to do a Boolean search across a database, then it is essential that care is taken in selecting search terms. From teaching legal research for a number of years to both students and practitioners, it is clear that there is an element of talent involved in successful Boolean searching. There is a balance between understanding the relative weight of legal terms and the operation of the logical connection between the terms that many users find difficult or impossible to grasp. The other dilemma is that Boolean searching can improve with experience; however, many researchers do not do enough Boolean searching to become experts.

Regular Internet users who are familiar with Google are often frustrated that Boolean searches in their law databases do not provide the same levels of success. Most users of Google do not understand that Google works by providing a hit list which is relevance-ranked according to a combination of the search terms and in order of other web pages which point to that document. Google's hit lists are dynamic and determined by the importance given to specific web pages by the Internet community. This ensures that any search in a way second-guesses the information a researcher is looking for.

Legal information providers do not have this level of sophistication and interactivity. Search outcomes are based solely on the application of the terms and logical relationship between them constructed by the researcher.

Given that the majority of users may not employ anything more complex than using the AND connector or a phrase search, it is essential that the terms used in a search are productive. This is not the place for a lesson on Boolean logic. However, here is a hint which ties in closely with the notion of a systematic legal research methodology. In common law countries, case names can be seen as encapsulating the essence of a legal principle. In the common law profession, the case name *Donoghue v Stevenson* needs no introduction or explanation. Other jurisdictions have their equivalents in each area of law: *Roe v Wade*; *Delgamuukw v British Columbia*; *Associated Provincial Picture Houses v Wednesbury*; *ACLU v Reno*; *Waltons v Maher*. Without any complex logic, a search can be structured to include a name of a case that must be referred to in another case or article. It is a very effective method of narrowing down a search without unwittingly excluding important hits.

The same can be done with the names of leading authors. A search which includes 'Glanville Williams' will retrieve legal education documents; a search which includes 'Stanley Fish' will retrieve documents relating to law, language and culture. In the context of a legal research, such searches recognise there are leading cases as well as leading authors in the respective fields, which is an essential element in developing a credible legal research methodology.

Requirements 4 and 5: Applying practical screening criteria and methodological screening criteria

These requirements are placed together because legal literature is unique. In a way relevant documents are self-selecting because law is precedential and hierarchical. A superior court judgment is going to be preferable to an inferior court's judgment. However, as Manderson and Mohr warn, lawyers are trained to be advocates and may be tempted to be selective in a literature review.[33] Whether the screening of sources is based on quality or relevance, it should not be screened on the basis of whether they support the researcher's legal position.

The difficulty for common lawyers is the relationship between the law and the facts. The current facts determine the relevant law, which law is relevant is determined by the facts within the case that a researcher seeks to rely on. The researcher is proceeding by fact analogy and principles of law.[34] This process has been discussed above. The reasoning applied here is part of the screening process.

Requirements 6 and 7: Doing the review and synthesising the results

As mentioned above, these final steps in Fink's list apply to literature reviews of field research done in a social science context. A legal research literature review is based on primary sources which state the law or secondary sources which analyse the law. In legal research the process of reviewing the documents and synthesising results is a process of inductive reasoning. Authorities are summarised and acknowledged and an overall principle derived from the survey. This inductive approach is the process of judicial reasoning.

At this stage the difference between the application of these steps in conventional legal research and legal research based on a more thorough and systematic methodology is that the outcome should have more credibility.

In summary, the preceding paragraphs have set out a comprehensive approach to legal research that establishes a methodology which relies on key resources to ensure that all possible relevant documents are discovered. The research is not done on the basis of proving a point but by applying a systematic approach which can be documented and duplicated. The social science model cannot be wholly applied to legal research because the source documents are derived in a different way. But the discipline of a thorough unbiased and reproducible methodology can be applied.

As for the resources themselves, the examples provided above should be seen as simply a list of useful works with an attempt to give a sense of their value and where they would fit in a legal research methodology. They do not pretend to be totally comprehensive. A complete overview of relevant sources for each jurisdiction and how to use them is covered in other publications.[35]

When looking at doctrinal research, there are two points. The first is that law is not objectively ascertainable, it is not there to be found; and the second is that lawyers are not trained in an effective research methodology. Acknowledging that legal research is qualitative is the first step to developing a credible doctrinal legal research methodology.

NON-DOCTRINAL RESEARCH − PROBLEMS, POLICY AND LAW REFORM

Qualitative research under this heading can be divided into two general types: descriptive and evaluative. It is arguable that graduate research could never be purely descriptive but such research may contain a descriptive component. Undertaking this part or stage of a research project would often be in the form of a literature review and might even be doctrinal. In this regard it would rely on the guidelines specified in the first part of this chapter in terms of researching the law as well as the relevant literature.

A consideration of whether the research is descriptive or evaluative, or a combination of the two, is useful from a researcher's perspective in first identifying what his or her objectives are. This in turn determines the research questions and methodology adopted.

All good legal research should begin by identifying the specific goal or goals which the researcher wishes to achieve. The research then undertaken must follow some general rules. Fink specifies five requirements:

1. Specific research questions
2. Defined and justified sample
3. Valid data collection
4. Appropriate analytic methods
5. Interpretations based on the data[36]

King and Epstein suggest four rules 'that are, regardless of whether the research is qualitative or quantitative, essential to reaching valid inferences: (1) identify the population of interest; (2) collect as much data as is feasible; (3) record the process by which data come to be observed; and (4) collect data in a manner that avoids selection bias.'[37]

The analysis that follows considers a number of randomly selected pieces of qualitative legal research using Fink's five requirements.

Requirement 1: Specific research questions

The researcher should begin by identifying the specific research questions. In an article on organised crime and illegal migration in Australia, for example, the author (a PhD student),[38] begins by stating his general objective, that being to 'compile and analyse the fragmentary knowledge on trafficking in migrants in Australia and the Asia-Pacific Region'. The four essential research questions he poses are:

- What exactly is the phenomenon known as trafficking in migrants?
- Why does migrant trafficking exist and prosper?
- How do criminal organisations respond to the demand for illegal migration?
- Where do these activities take place?[39]

This is a good start but the problem faced by this researcher is that there is virtually no prospect of his actually answering such questions, and at best he is restricted to considering information which relates to them. The paper itself is an analysis of certain literature on illegal migration and organised crime. This does not diminish the value of this research but the author is on much safer ground by acknowledging that his research considers certain available information which assists in an initial consideration of various issues relevant to answering these essential questions. To say that the paper answers these questions to any real extent is misleading.

Contrastingly, the authors of a paper on the commercial sexual exploitation of children take a much more cautious approach.[40] They begin by acknowledging the lack of research and information on sexual exploitation in Australia.

The appropriate methodology and starting point in beginning to define the 'problem', they state, was to carry out a comprehensive literature review and to undertake a 'stock-take' and analysis of all Australian legislation, policy and programmes on the sexual exploitation of children. In addition to this, the researchers carried out a series of interviews with people who worked directly with children in a variety of fields, some of these children being possible victims of sexual exploitation.

Considerable care and thought is required in determining the specific research questions. Resource issues, such as funding and time, may limit the scope of these questions particularly in light of the appropriate methodologies required to answer such questions. In this regard, a student and academic supervisor may need to consider the research being undertaken in stages. This would certainly be the case for the first study considered which sought to analyse the involvement of organised crime in migrant trafficking.[41] Answering the research questions posed in this article may have been the ultimate goal but the researcher would have been better advised to take a similar approach to the study on child sexual exploitation[42] in terms of a literature review and so-called 'stock-take' and analysis of all Australian legislation and policy.

Requirement 2: Defined and justified sample

In an article on the delivery of legal services to women in North Queensland, the author (an academic) seeks to partially consider the extent to which such services should be provided to women by women and whether it is appropriate for males to advise women in relation to matters that are essentially female in nature.[43] As a specific research question, this is adequate but it is unclear as to whether there is a problem in terms of the legal services currently available to women in North Queensland. The research question arose as part of concerns expressed by the provision of legal advice to women by both male and female law students undertaking a clinical legal studies course involving work at a community law centre. The author implies that there is a problem arising from the socio-economic circumstances of women using various legal and non-legal services and their subsequent lack of choice in terms of the gender of the service advisor. This may well be true but the research does not address this in terms of any data as to the numbers of cases where female clients are advised by males.

The author states that the project 'is an exploratory though essentially descriptive study which seeks the opinions of workers at Women's Community Legal Services in Queensland and various other community organizations/services/groups, as to the provision of legal (and non-legal) services for women'.[44] In this regard, the study was restricted to interviews with workers employed by a variety of organisations/services/groups. A total of fifteen persons were interviewed.

The author acknowledges the limitations of the study, in particular that it would have been beneficial to interview all workers as well as a number of clients. Such additional research, however, was not possible owing to insufficient resources.[45] In a study of this nature, and given that the total number of those employed in this area may not have been great, then it would have been better to interview all workers. Alternatively, all workers could have been sent the questionnaire and asked to complete it. Failure to interview any clients at all to seek their views as to the preferred gender of those providing the service certainly detracts from the significance of any findings.

An example of a more structured study is that by three American researchers on how family factors influence juvenile justice processes and sanctions.[46] The study was carried out at a number of juvenile courts in a midwestern state in the US. The problem (research question) identified by the researchers was the extent to which the familial qualities of youths appearing before the courts were being appropriately considered.

In their article outlining the study, the researchers begin with a review of the literature including previous research. This is followed by a description of the methodology and data collection. The data was derived from a series of face-to-face interviews with various court personnel across seven counties in the state. The courts chosen were located in high-density urban, suburban and rural areas. There were ninety-four interviews conducted with judges, referees, supervisors, intake staff and probation officers. In addition to questions concerning the factors important in their decision-making, interviewees were asked to make a hypothetical determination on a case involving a felony scenario.

Returning to King and Epstein's four basic rules for legal research, the first two were: (1) identify the population of interest; and (2) collect as much data as is feasible.[47] In the study on legal services for women, the two populations of interest were the providers of such legal services and the clients.[48] While the author acknowledges that the study was only partial and limited by the resources available, data collected from only fifteen service providers falls well short of what was needed and feasible, especially in terms of the so-called findings from the study. This can be compared to the American juvenile justice study.[49] While the resources available to the American research team were obviously much greater than for the women's legal services study, the conclusions drawn from the American research are, comparatively, much more valid and ultimately important because of the scope and depth of the research.

At this point, it must be acknowledged that an inability to collect as much data as is feasible, and necessary, should call into question the undertaking of the actual research proposed. This does not mean that the research be abandoned altogether but that there is certainly a need to review the specific research questions and the consequent methodology. Attempting to draw conclusions where the research is deficient in terms of the data collected calls into question the very validity of any so-called findings.

Requirements 3 and 4: Valid data collection and appropriate analytical method

The study on the delivery of legal services to women used a combination of face-to-face interviews and a posted questionnaire, while that on how family factors influence juvenile justice processes and sanctions was based on face-to-face interviews only. Both methodologies are appropriate in terms of the research undertaken. The problem with the study on legal services for women is again the extremely small and limited sample surveyed. In this regard, the methodology can be considered as acceptable but the data collected was limited. As discussed later, this will inevitably restrict the conclusions reached.

The following two studies are examples of policy or law reform evaluations. They are similar in that they seek to evaluate specialist court functions designed in one case to deal with a certain category of case (child sexual abuse) and in the other to deal with specific offenders (indigenous Australians). The two examples are also useful in demonstrating the constraints placed on research by the resources available and the expertise of those carrying out the research. In the study concerning child sexual abuse cases, the research was carried out by researchers employed by a government research agency,[50] while that concerning indigenous offenders was undertaken by an undergraduate law student.[51]

The child sexual abuse study involved an evaluation of a 2003 pilot scheme which created a specialist jurisdiction for child sexual assault matters in the Sydney West District Court Registry.

> The aim of the specialist jurisdiction was to address the difficulties in prosecuting child sexual assault matters and to improve the experience of child sexual assault complainants. This report outlines the results of the evaluation of this pilot.[52]

The research questions addressed by this evaluation were:

1. To what extent were the features of the specialist jurisdiction implemented?
   (a) Does the chosen venue for the specialist child sexual assault court have the appropriate facilities?
   (b) Has the appropriate technology been installed in the courtroom? Is it working properly?
   (c) Was the training given to relevant staff sufficient and appropriate?
2. Has the advent of the specialist child sexual assault jurisdiction had any effect on the conviction rate?

3. Has the advent of the specialist child sexual assault jurisdiction resulted in more expeditious handling of child sexual assault matters? For example, has it resulted in fewer mentions / quicker disposition of the case / less time in court for witnesses?

4. Is the physical environment and the way in which evidence is given in child sexual assault prosecutions less intimidating for child witnesses since the advent of the specialist jurisdiction? To what extent has the use of special technological measures (such as CCTV and the electronic recording of the child's investigative interview) played a role in this?

5. To what extent has the specialist jurisdiction improved the way child witnesses are treated at court? Has it resulted in more sensitive handling by judges and others?[53]

The methodology adopted included a comparative analysis of sexual abuse cases at the courts involved in the Child Sexual Assault Specialist Jurisdiction and a court centre which did not. Data was collected by way of (1) observation of trials in court; (2) court transcripts; (3) interviews with child complainants; (4) interviews with the child's non-offending parents/guardians; (5) interviews with legal professionals and court staff; and (6) juror surveys.[54]

The second research example involved a limited evaluation of Koori Court Division of the Victorian Magistrates' Court. The article outlining the research is divided into two main parts. The first part deals with the development of the division. This is followed by an assessment of the stated aims which resulted from the development process.

The methodology adopted by the author was a combination of court observations and interviews. The author states that she attended two Koori courts on six occasions and interviewed the Aboriginal justice officers at both courts, a police prosecutor, a corrections officer, a client services manager and a magistrate (a total of six interviews). No offenders were interviewed and the author acknowledges that this, together with the limited number of times she was able to observe court cases, was 'not adequate to definitively answer the questions outlined earlier and can only be used as an indicator of the Koori Court Division's success or lack thereof in fulfilling its aims'.[55] Having said this, however, the author contends that 'this is balanced by the analysis of the potential of the Division'.[56]

Requirement 5: Interpretations based on the data

It is here that much legal research falls down.[57] Many conclusions are simply not justified by the data collected. In the study on organised crime and migrant trafficking, the author is quite cautious in his conclusions despite the very broad initial research questions posed.

The findings suggest that for purposes of the examination and elaboration of existing and future countermeasures it is necessary to recognize the economic dimension of organized crime and consider trafficking in migrants as a business conducted by transnational criminal organizations.[58]

In the article on the delivery of legal services to women in North Queensland, however, the author was not so cautious in her conclusions. The principal finding of the study was that:

A female solicitor with feminist beliefs and a client-centred approach is the best person to provide legal assistance to a woman, where the matter is sensitive and essentially female in nature.[59]

This may be correct but the research, as a result of its methodological limitations, is only able to conclude that this was the opinion of a number of those interviewed. No mention is even made of any gender differences amongst those surveyed. If, for example, the majority of workers surveyed were female, then this would certainly have required consideration in terms of their statements that they, as females themselves, were best suited to deal with female clients.

In the study of juvenile justice processes and sanctions, the researchers' findings were that court staff gave considerable weight to family characteristics, such as caregiver control and family structure, in determining intake decisions, case processing, disposition and placement.[60] Such consideration, however, appeared to be based on 'the traditional two-parent functional model of family life, with assigned roles and responsibility', a model, the researchers noted, that had 'to a large extent been abandoned by family researchers and scholars.'[61]

The recommendation made by the researchers was that the courts should give greater consideration to parental competency rather than focusing on traditional views on family structure and parental control.

This could include an evaluation of the caregiver's abilities to negotiate their own complex environment while at the same time establishing linkages and networks that provide legitimate opportunities and mentorships for their children.[62]

The extent to which these findings are valid would involve a detailed analysis of the research, the methodology, the data collected and any statistical analysis involved. Such a review may find problems with the research but, on the face of it, the methodology adopted and the data provides initial support for the conclusions reached. This is in stark contrast to the study on the delivery of legal services to women.

A similar conclusion is reached when comparing the two studies that sought to evaluate certain specialist court functions. In the study on the evaluation of the specialist jurisdiction for child sexual assault matters, the researchers concluded that there was little evidence of any real change and that there was little to distinguish the specialist jurisdiction from the comparison registry apart from the establishment of the remote witness suite at one of the courts studied. This remote witness suite separated child witnesses from the courtroom and the defendant, placing the child in a more comfortable and child-friendly environment. In this regard, the researchers recommend a possible extension of such services in other courts. Overall, however, their conclusions were quite negative.

> In fact, there is little evidence that the specialist jurisdiction was implemented as proposed or that the courts . . . actually constituted a specialist jurisdiction in any real sense. While the remote witness suite was well received and benefited those children who were able to use it, in practice there were few other real changes. The concerns about delays, problems with the technology and the way children are treated in court, especially during cross-examination, remain valid.[63]

In the evaluation of the Koori Court Division, the author poses a number of questions arising from a consideration that:

> [t]he Division is intended to be a response to the subjection, alienation and exclusion of Aboriginal people which has traditionally been perpetrated by the justice system, the assessment of the development process, which has the potential to provide some remedy to this legacy, is extremely important in assessing the Division. It involves asking questions such as how were the aims formulated? Who were they formulated for? Have the prescribed aims avoided the danger of paternalism that has marked previous attempts to give control over community problems back to the Aboriginal community? Is the Division an example of what Deborah Bird Rose refers to as 'colonising practices . . . still deeply embedded within decolonising institutions'? Can or should the aims of the Division be more culturally relative?[64]

What is initially evident is the author's bias in terms of what the division is intended to be a response to: that is, 'the subjection, alienation and exclusion of Aboriginal people which has traditionally been perpetrated by the justice system'. This is not to suggest that Aboriginal people have not been mistreated and discriminated against by Australia's justice system; rather, it is that such evident bias detracts from the importance of the research. In addition to this, the limitations arising from the small number of court observations and interviews should have led to a much more cautious approach to any so-called findings.

Research questions must be objective and avoid bias. As noted above, the research questions posed in the Koori Court evaluation were inherently biased. This inevitably has a negative impact on the conclusions drawn and their validity and value. This is compared to the child sexual assault evaluation where the research questions demonstrate a much more objective approach.

CONCLUSION

Graduate law students have undertaken, and continue to undertake, a diverse range of research. Historically, this has been largely doctrinal, predominantly concerned with the analysis of legal principle and how it has been developed and applied.

Whether or not there has been a major change in direction in legal research is debatable. As noted earlier, however, Manderson and Mohr in their analysis of Australian law schools found that only 20 per cent of all doctoral research projects were doctrinal, 20 per cent were law reform, 17 per cent were 'theoretical', 17 per cent were interdisciplinary, and the remaining 26 per cent were international or comparative.[65]

Based on these findings, it is evident that many graduate law students are undertaking quantitative or qualitative research or a combination of the two. This chapter is concerned with qualitative research. Doctrinal or theoretical research can be seen as non-empirical simply because it does not use empirical method. In this sense it is neither quantitative nor qualitative. It is argued in this chapter, however, that doctrinal research is qualitative on the basis that such research is a process of selecting and weighing materials taking into account hierarchy and authority as well as understanding social context and interpretation. In guiding the graduate student undertaking doctrinal research, we have argued that social science can be referred to so as to get a sense of the objectives of a research methodology. In this regard, the identification of relevant legislation, cases and secondary materials in law can be seen as analogous to a social science literature review.

Other legal research can be quite specifically defined as qualitative. We have categorised such research under three headings: problems, policy and law reform. There may well be others but we contend that these categories describe the majority of qualitative research undertaken. We also acknowledge that such research can be legal or socio-legal or a combination of the two.

The principal aim of this chapter was to assist the graduate law student, as well as his or her academic supervisor, as to how best to undertake qualitative legal research, that is doctrinal, theoretical, problem, policy and law reform research. The common factor across all these types of legal research is the need to carefully and specifically determine the research questions. In addition, the researcher must consider any resource implications involved. This is not a problem in terms of doctrinal research where the only real concern is time, but undertaking interviews or court observations, for example, has major resource implications where the graduate student is working alone and has no or very limited financial support for the research project.

This in turn impacts on the methodology adopted. For doctrinal and theoretical research we have suggested a methodology along the lines of a social science literature review. For problem, policy and law reform research, there are a variety of methodologies, such as a literature review, but they also may involve interviews, questionnaires and observations. Social science and socio-legal methodological rules or guidelines are useful benchmarks. They include the need to define and justify the target population; collect valid data; use appropriate analytic methods; and base interpretations on the data.

In addition, the researcher should collect as much data as is feasible; record the process by which data is collected; and collect data in a manner that avoids bias. A number of randomly selected research projects in the form of published articles and reports were selected in order to demonstrate these rules and guidelines. These examples have been grouped for comparative purposes. Where shortfalls have been identified, it is not to suggest that the research is of no value. The shortfalls or criticisms are identified in order to alert the graduate student to them, and by reference to other research suggest how such problems can be avoided.

FURTHER READING

R. C. Bering, 'Legal Research and Legal Concepts: Where Form Molds Substance' (1987) 75 *California Law Review* 15.

R. C. Bering, 'Collapse of the Structure of the Legal Research Universe: The Imperative of Digital Information' (1994) 69 *Washington Law Review* 9.

R. C. Bering, 'On Not Throwing Out the Baby: Planning the Future of Legal Information' (1995) 83 *California Law Review* 615.

M. Duggan and D. Isenbergh, 'Commentary: Poststructuralism and the Brave New World of Legal Research' (1994) 86 *Law Library Journal* 829.

C. N. Edwards, 'In Search of Legal Scholarship: Strategies for the Integration of Science into the Practice of Law' (1998) 8 *Southern California Interdisciplinary Law Journal* 1.

J. A. Farmer, 'A Poststructuralist Analysis of the Legal Research Process' (1993) 85 *Law Library Journal* 391.

T. Hutchinson, *Researching and Writing in Law* (2nd edn) (Pyrmont, NSW: Lawbook Co., 2006).

K. L. Koch, 'A Multidisciplinary Comparison of Rules-Driven Writing: Similarities in Legal Writing, Biology Research Articles, and Computer Programming' (2005) 55 *Journal of Legal Education* 234.

M. Leiboff and M. Thomas, *Legal Theories in Principle* (Pyrmont, NSW: Lawbook Co., 2004).

G. Mitchell, 'Empirical Legal Scholarship as Scientific Dialogue' (2004) 83 *North Carolina Law Review* 167.

L. Noaks and E. Wincup, *Criminological Research: Understanding Qualitative Methods* (London: Sage, 2004).

N. Pantaloni, 'Legal Databases, Legal Epistemology, and the Legal Order' (1994) 86 *Law Library Journal* 679.

NOTES

1. L. Epstein and G. King, 'Empirical Research and the Goals of Legal Scholarship: The Rules of Inference' (2002) 69 *University of Chicago Law Review*, 1.
2. R. L. Revesz, 'Empirical Research and the Goals of Legal Scholarship: A Defense of Empirical Legal Scholarship' (2002) 69 *University of Chicago Law Review* 169.
3. Epstein and King, see note 1 above, 1.
4. Ibid. 115–16.
5. Revesz, see note 2 above, 171.
6. D. Manderson and R. Mohr, 'From Oxymoron to Intersection: An Epidemiology of Legal Research' (2002) 6 *Law/Text/Culture* 159.
7. Epstein and King, see note 1 above.
8. It is noted that such categories are not mutually exclusive and that a single research project could encompass a number of legal research areas.
9. Note, for example, the British Home Office and Australian Law Reform Commission.
10. Epstein and King, see note 1 above, 2–3.
11. Manderson and Mohr, see note 6 above, 164.
12. Epstein and King, see note 1 above, 3. The authors qualify this, however. 'But even many articles whose main purpose is normative often invoke empirical arguments to shore up their normative points.'
13. G. Williams, *Learning the Law* (12th edn) (London: Sweet & Maxwell, 2002).
14. Ibid. 206–7.
15. Note the vast body of literature (social science) on research methodology.

From a qualitative perspective, this includes literature on sampling, questionnaire design and interviewing.

16. Epstein and King, see note 1 above.
17. T. Hutchinson, *Researching and Writing in Law* (2nd edn) (Pyrmont, NSW: Lawbook Co., 2006) 31–42.
18. Ibid. 85.
19. Ibid. 87.
20. K. M. Hansen, 'The US Legal System: Common Values, Uncommon Procedures' (2004) 69 *Brooklyn Law Review* 702.
21. D. Ezzy, *Qualitative Analysis: Practice and Innovation* (Crows Nest, NSW: Allen & Unwin, 2002) 5.
22. Manderson and Mohr, see note 6 above, 162.
23. Epstein and King, see note 1 above, 9.
24. J. O. Davidson and D. Layder, *Methods, Sex and Madness* (London: Routledge, 1994) 35.
25. A. Fink, *Conducting Research Literature Reviews: From the Internet to Paper* (2nd edn) (Thousand Oaks, CA: Sage) 3.
26. Ibid. 3–5.
27. Manderson and Mohr, see note 6 above, 159.
28. www.sweetandmaxwell.co.uk/online/cli/index.html#about
29. Acts Interpretation Act 1901 (Cth) s 15AA. See also Australian state equivalents. In the UK the Interpretation Act 1978 (UK) does not allow for extrinsic materials but see *Pepper (Inspector of Taxes) v Hart* [1993] 1 All ER 42, [1993] AC 593 (reference to Parliamentary material where wording ambiguous, obscure or leads to obscurity). A classic compilation of US statutory interpretation rules can be found in K. Llewellyn, 'Remarks on Theory of Appellate Decisions and the Rules or Cannons About How Statutes are to be Construed' (1950) 3 *Vanderbilt Law Review* 395.
30. For an example of the importance of key legal texts, see F. R. Shapiro, 'The Most-Cited Legal Books Published since 1978' (2000) 29 *Journal of Legal Studies* 397. The works cited are listed at http://lib.law.washington.edu/ref/mostcited.html. This is a US analysis.
31. R. C. Bering, 'Symposium on Law in the Twentieth Century: Legal Information and the Search for Cognitive Authority' (2000) 88 *California Law Review* 1688, 1690. See also M. E. Katsh, *Law in a Digital World* (New York: Oxford University Press, 1995).
32. For an overview of the impact on Boolean searching on legal research, see C. M. Bast and R. C. Pyle, 'Legal Research in the Computer Age: A Paradigm Shift?' (2001) 93 *Law Library Journal* 285.
33. Manderson and Mohr, see note 6 above.
34. Hansen, see note 20 above, 689.
35. See, for example, R. Mersky, and D. Dunn, *Fundamentals of Legal Research*

(University Textbook Series) (8th edn) (New York: West Group, 2002); Hutchinson, see note 17 above; P. A. Thomas and J. Knowles, *Knowles & Thomas: Effective Legal Research* (London: Sweet & Maxwell, 2006).

36. Fink, see note 25 above, 138.
37. Epstein and King, see note 1 above, 99.
38. A. Schloenhardt, 'The Business of Migration: Organised Crime and Illegal Migration in Australia and the Asia-Pacific Region' (1999) 21 *Adelaide Law Review* 81. It is unclear from the article whether this is part of the author's PhD research.
39. Ibid. 81–2.
40. A. Grant, F. David and P. Grabosky, 'The Commercial Sexual Exploitation of Children' (2001) 12 *Current Issues in Criminal Justice* 269. It should be noted that this research was undertaken by researchers employed by a leading Australian research institute (The Australian Institute of Criminology).
41. Ibid.
42. Ibid.
43. J. Roebuck, 'Delivery of Legal Services: Should Legal Services for Women be Provided by Women' (2000) 7 *James Cook University Law Review* 214.
44. Ibid. 215.
45. Ibid. 218.
46. C. J. Corley, T. S. Bynum and M. Wordes, 'Conceptions of Family and Juvenile Court Processes: A Qualitative Assessment' (1995) 18 *The Justice System Journal* 157.
47. Epstein and King, see note 1 above, 99.
48. Corley, Bynum and Wordes, see note 46 above.
49. Ibid.
50. J. Cashmore and L. Trimboli, *An Evaluation of the NSW Child Sexual Assault Specialist Jurisdiction Pilot* (Sydney: NSW Bureau of Crime Statistics and Research, Attorney General's Department, 2005). Available at: http://www.lawlink.nsw.gov.au/lawlink/bocsar/ll_bocsar.nsf/pages/bo csar_mr_r57
51. B. McAsey, 'A Critical Evaluation of the Koori Court Division of the Victorian Magistrates' Court' (2005) 10 *Deakin Law Review* 654.
52. Cashmore and Trimboli, see note 50 above, ix.
53. Ibid. 3.
54. Ibid. 5.
55. McAsey, see note 51 above, 658.
56. Ibid. 658.
57. Epstein and King, see note 1 above.
58. Schloenhardt, see note 38 above, 114.

59. Roebuck, see note 43 above, 219.
60. Corley, Bynum and Wordes, see note 46 above, 162.
61. Ibid. 167.
62. Ibid. 168.
63. Cashmore and Trimboli, see note 50 above, 64.
64. McAsey, see note 51 above, 656.
65. Manderson and Mohr, see note 6 above.

CHAPTER 2

Quantitative Legal Research

Wing Hong Chui

INTRODUCTION

This chapter is about the collection and analysis of quantitative data. It aims to introduce the rationales and benefits of using quantitative approaches in socio-legal research[1] and to demonstrate how these approaches are relevant to socio-legal topics. It is an introductory chapter designed to answer several questions surrounding the use of quantitative research methodology. For instance, what is the main purpose of this methodology? What are the specific stages in the general research process? In what ways can quantitative researchers obtain data that form the raw material of any investigation? How can the researchers collect reliable and valid data? What are the common methods of quantitative data analysis? By answering these questions systematically, it is hoped that students and university academics are better able to place quantitative research within the context of a pursuit of knowledge, and to see its wider application in the field of law and justice.

Some law students, practising lawyers and legal academics question the relevance of using social research methods in examining various aspects of law and the operation of legal systems. For instance, Lloyd E. Ohlin shared his observation that,

> Law students are most interested in discussions relating to solution of social problems and the grounds for choosing among public policy alternatives. They tend to be impatient with the theorising interests of social scientists, the complications of research design and the detailed development of proof for different hypothetical propositions.[2]

In a similar vein, Julius G. Getman recognised that,

The amount of time one needs to invest to do [empirical] research is enormous compared to the amount of time one invests in writing traditional law review articles . . . Many of my jurisprudentially minded colleagues think of it as rather low level. They do not believe that empirical research requires the type of intellect necessary, for example to develop a model of human rights or a new theory of the First Amendment.[3]

In contrast to empirical research, doctrinal research which 'is library-based, focusing on a reading and analysis of the primary [such as the legislation and case law] and secondary materials [such as legal dictionaries, textbooks, journal articles, case digests and legal encyclopaedias]'[4] is regarded as the most accepted research paradigm.[5] When reviewing a number of textbooks on legal research the bulk of their contents are concerned with identifying and analysing factual material and legal issues. Amongst these texts, none of them discusses the contribution of empirical research to legal studies.[6] Despite this, several legal scholars have urged lawyers to make more effective use of the insights and research tools of the social sciences. They acknowledge the fact that a partnership between law and the social sciences aims at improving the legal system and its administration; and guiding law reform.[7] For instance, Lee E. Teitelbaum explicitly recommends the greater use of empirical research in general to advance our understanding of law and the workings of the legal system:

If laws are intended to produce certain results, questions about whether they *do* produce the *expected* results, whether they produce *other* results, and whether the identifiable results are as consistent with the reason for law as one might have anticipated, are all important to examine. [Italics original][8]

Broadly speaking, social science methodologies can be classified in two: quantitative and qualitative methodologies. In this chapter, the quantitative research method as one particular non-doctrinal methodology will be introduced. At the outset it should be emphasised that this quantitative research method is a supplement to traditional legal research in order to investigate complexities of law, legal actors and legal activities. In particular, the tradition of quantitative research is strong in the field of criminal law and criminology[9], corporate law,[10] and family law.[11] In many respects, a sound understanding of this methodology provides us with guideposts regarding how to gather information and analyse data in a scientific and systemic manner.[12]

The remaining part of the chapter is divided into five parts. Part I begins with an overview of the core features and purposes of quantitative methods, whilst contrasting these with qualitative methods. Various phases of quantitative research design will be examined in part II. Illustrated with examples of classic and contemporary quantitative legal studies, part III focuses on main data collection techniques such as experiments, surveys and secondary data analysis. Particular emphasis will be placed on unpacking the rationales, strengths and weaknesses of each technique. In part IV, the methods of quantitative data analysis will also be discussed. The chapter will end with a review of the key ethical issues in quantitative research.

WHY STUDY QUANTITATIVE RESEARCH

Features of quantitative research

The quantitative method is one of the social sciences' frameworks or approaches for research, and has been widely used in different academic disciplines such as psychology, sociology, political science and legal studies.[13] A clear definition of the quantitative approach provided by Martyn Hammersley is:

> The term 'quantitative method' refers in large part to the adoption of
> the natural science experiment as the model of scientific research, its
> key features being quantitative measurement of the phenomena studied
> and systematic control of the theoretical variables influencing those
> phenomena.[14]

In a number of important respects, quantitative approaches are different from qualitative approaches, as indicated in Table 2.1. In contrast to qualitative research, quantitative research is used to test or verify the appropriateness of existing theories to explain the behaviour or phenomenon one is interested in as opposed to developing new insights or constructing new theories in order to understand the social phenomenon or behaviour.[15] Quantitative research deals with numbers, statistics or hard data whereas qualitative data are mostly in the form of words. Qualitative researchers tend to be more flexible than their quantitative counterparts in terms of the structure to research. A set of rules or procedures should be followed when conducting quantitative research. The rules will be examined in detail in the next part of the chapter. While qualitative research is influenced by the researcher's personal values and bias,[16] quantitative research seeks to report the findings objectively and the role of researcher is neutral.[17] Objectivity is commonly ascribed to quantitative studies, and to achieve this the researcher attempts to rule out bias through random assignment of subjects, the use of a control group in experiments and statistical manipulation.

Table 2.1 Core features of qualitative and quantitative methods

Quantitative	Qualitative
Hypothesis testing	Speculative
Hard	Soft
Fixed	Flexible
Objective	Subjective
Value-free	Political
Positivism	Constructivism / Interpretivism

Adapted from P. Halfpenny, 'The Analysis of Qualitative Data' (1979) 27 Sociological Review 799, also cited in D. Silverman, Doing Qualitative Research: A Practical Handbook (London: Sage, 2000) table 1.1, 2.

The positivistic paradigm

Quantitative research is often perceived as the most 'scientific' way of doing research, and it is sometimes called positivist research, empirical observation and measurement, and the theory-then-research method. The reason for calling it 'positivist' research is simply because of its great emphasis on the importance of examining the cause-and-effect relationship in experiments. It is about quantifying relationships between variables. In one way or another, it reflects a deterministic philosophy in which events or occurrences bring about certain outcomes or consequences, thereby suggesting the existence of laws and theories to govern the world.[18] Pure reality or natural laws can be studied and discovered by objective research. The historical roots of positivism can be traced back to the Enlightenment period of the eighteenth century when the emergence of science challenged the theological and metaphysical notions of explanation.[19] Since then, the positivist holds the view that the natural or social world should be understood by careful observation and the measurement of objective facts or behaviours. From these empirical observations, theories are developed and should be verified continuously by research so that, eventually they will become laws that can be applied to explain similar phenomena.[20] Robson gives a succinct account of the assumptions of positivism:

- Objective knowledge (facts) can be gained from direct experience or observation, and is the only knowledge available to science.
- Science is value-free.
- Science is largely based on quantitative data, derived from the use of strict rules and procedures, fundamentally different from common sense.
- All scientific propositions are founded on facts. Hypotheses are tested against these facts.
- The purpose of science is to develop universal causal laws.
- Explaining an event is simply relating to a general law.[21]

Main purposes of quantitative designs

Based upon these assumptions, three types of quantitative research design[22] have been identified. They are *exploratory, descriptive and explanatory* (or *causal*) designs.[23]

Much legal research is conducted to explore a specific problem or issue. The researcher may be interested in legal behaviour, rules, processes or problems about which little is known or understood. For instance, recent concern with access to justice might encourage efforts to estimate the extent of self-representation in civil and matrimonial proceedings. How many people choose to represent themselves in these proceedings each year? How many self-represented litigants would prefer to be represented by a lawyer? These are examples of research questions aimed at exploring the issues related to the self-representation of plaintiffs or defendants in the courtroom.[24] In brief, the primary aims of *exploratory* studies are to gain initial insights and ideas about research problems, and to identify variables associated with those problems. This quantitative design is often employed as a 'pilot study' or the first phase of a larger research project.[25]

A major aim of *descriptive* studies is to describe and document a phenomenon of interest. They can define the scope and nature of a research problem by describing the characteristics of persons, organisations, settings, phenomena and events. Typical research questions of descriptive research designs are: What is happening? How is something happening? What has happened? Descriptive studies can be either cross-sectional or longitudinal. The former provides a snapshot of the variables included in the study and collects these data at a given time whereas the latter measures each of the variables with the same sample or different sample population over two or more time periods. The reason for repeated measurement of the same variables from the same people or subjects in a descriptive longitudinal study is to measure any change in variables over time. For instance, in order to measure the changing attitudes and confidence levels of the public towards the criminal justice system, opinion or community surveys may be conducted once every five years.

A third general purpose of quantitative research design is to explain things and identify how one or more variables are related to one another.[26] Causation is the focus of *explanatory* research. These studies are often concerned with the question of why something happens (for example, why X leads to Y), and they may be either correlational or experimental research designs. There are studies to explain why some people obey the law and others do not.[27] Is it because of people's fear of punishment? Or is it due to people's belief in the legitimacy of legal authorities? Through the use of correlational statistics, correlational studies are able to measure the degree and direction of the relationships between or among two or more variables. Only if the statistics in the form of correlational coefficients show a strong relationship between two variables, can the cause-and-effect relationship be tested by using an experimental design. The general notion of causality appears to be simple and straightforward but indeed is more complicated than one may expect. As described by Thomas Cook and Donald Campbell, there are three major criteria for causality, namely, the cause (or independent variable) precedes the effect (or dependent variable) in time; there is empirical association between two variables; and there is no plausible alternative explanation on the covariation of the independent and dependent variables.[28] In this respect, any relationship that fails to satisfy the three criteria is not causal.

One of the questions frequently asked by research students and new researchers is whether one particular type of research design is superior to others. It is indeed difficult to answer this question because the selection of the research design depends very much on the questions the researchers would like to answer in the first place. For example, if the research question is to identify factors associated with sentencing decisions, or to understand the best predictors of juvenile offending, then an explanatory research design is the best. If the research question is to understand the problems encountered by unrepresented litigants in the court proceedings, a descriptive or exploratory study seems appropriate. Despite different emphases in each research design, it is important to bear in mind that the three research designs are not mutually exclusive. In addition to the research aims and objectives, there are other factors to be considered in developing a quantitative study, and these factors include critical analysis and synthesis of prior studies in the area, feasibility, setting for the study and access to potential subjects, the study team, and ethics of the study.[29] If numerous studies have already shown that the majority of unrepresented litigants lack faith in the legal profession, another descriptive study in this field may not be needed. Instead the next logical step in this example is to explore the relationship between people's decisions to represent themselves and their level of trust in the legal professions such as lawyers and judicial officers. Several questions should be asked regarding the feasibility of the study: Can the proposed study be completed within a realistic timeframe? Will there be a sufficient number of potential research respondents to be recruited? Are there adequate resources such as manpower and funding available to conduct the research? Do the investigators have expertise and skills to manage and implement the research project? Does the experiment pose dangers to the research subjects? The following section of the chapter will address some of these questions systematically by outlining the steps in the quantitative research process.

II PHASES OF QUANTITATIVE RESEARCH DESIGN[30]

Quantitative research adopts a highly structured approach and usually takes place in a clear and logical sequence of events, phases or stages. Broadly

Figure 2.1 Stages of planning and executing a study

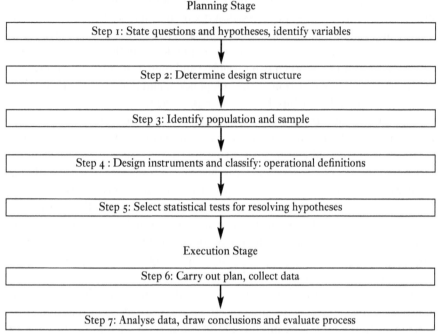

Planning Stage

Step 1: State questions and hypotheses, identify variables

Step 2: Determine design structure

Step 3: Identify population and sample

Step 4 : Design instruments and classify: operational definitions

Step 5: Select statistical tests for resolving hypotheses

Execution Stage

Step 6: Carry out plan, collect data

Step 7: Analyse data, draw conclusions and evaluate process

Modified and adapted from T. R. Black, *Doing Quantitative Research in the Social Sciences: An Integrated Approach to Research Design, Measurement and Statistics* (London: Sage, 1999) figure 2.1, 27. The linear sequence of stages of designing and carrying out a study is presented in the figure and readers are reminded that in an actual research process, these steps do not work in a sequential fashion, and at times the research process may be chaotic.

speaking, the approach has been divided into two stages: planning and execution. Figure 2.1 describes a set of procedures for conducting specific quantitative research. The seven-step process begins with the identification of research questions and setting out hypotheses, then goes on to include the selection of design structure, identification of population and sample, instrument design and the operationalisation of abstract concepts and variables in the study, selection of statistical tests for testing hypotheses, implementation of the research plan and data collection, and data analysis, generalisation of the findings, and evaluation of the research process. The end of one research cycle is the start of another, thereby reflecting the progress of scientific knowledge.[31]

Step 1: Identifying research questions, hypotheses and variables

The first step in the design of a quantitative study is to identify the research problems in the form of specific research questions and research objectives.

Figure 2.2 Use of theories in quantitative research

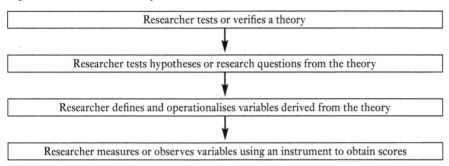

Adapted from J. Creswell, *Research Design: Qualitative, Quantitative, and Mixed Methods Approaches* (2nd edn) (Thousand Oaks, CA: Sage 2003) figure 7.4, 125.

Social researchers have used the acronym FINER (feasible, interesting, novel, ethical, relevant) to assess the quality of the research question.[32] Words such as 'what', 'when', 'who', 'where', 'which', and 'how' are often used when formulating research questions. 'What', 'when', 'who' and 'where' questions seek descriptive answers; 'why' questions seek understanding and explanation; and 'how' questions seek appropriate interventions to bring about change.[33] If research questions are not specific and answerable, it is very likely that the remaining research activities will be fruitless and meaningless. The transition from a general to specific question sometimes consumes a considerable amount of time, nonetheless it is a necessary task to be completed before proceeding to the next stage of research process.

One may ask how a researcher can define or delimit the research problem or question. A crucial part of the early development of a quantitative study is carrying out an extensive review of the published literature or theories.[34] Selecting a theory or set of theories most appropriate to the topic under research is paramount. A theory usually consists of a set of propositions and definitions, and each of these has predictive qualities in a way to explain the inter-relationship between variables or concepts.[35] As discussed earlier, quantitative studies collect data to test or verify a theory and their results will confirm or deny what has been discovered, thereby advancing a theory or knowledge. As shown in Figure 2.2, the choice of the theoretical framework of a quantitative study will guide researchers to formulate research questions or hypotheses, and inform the data collection procedure.

Without a sound theoretical or conceptual framework, the quantitative researcher will be unable to produce a series of hypotheses, concepts or variables to be tested and measured.[36] As suggested by Chava Frankfort-Nachmias and David Nachmias,

A hypothesis is a tentative answer to a research problem, expressed in the form of a clearly stated relation between the independent and the dependent variables. Hypotheses are tentative answers because they can be verified only after they have been tested empirically.[37]

As an example, a study proposes to explain why courts often ignore the legal relevance of social science research.[38] Several theories were first reviewed by the researchers, and some of the examples are the 'judges are conservative while social scientists are liberal' theory, 'judges do not believe they need help from social science' theory, and 'it is the human nature to think unscientifically' theory. These theories were derived from both formal large-scale studies on the topic and informal hunches or speculations from laypersons or participants in the previous research.[39] Based upon these theories, one hypothesis used in the study is: judges' and law students' socio-political attitudes affect their judgments about the legal relevance and admissibility of social science research evidence. It is apparent that the independent variable[40] of the study is the 'judges' and law students' socio-political attitudes' and the dependent variable is 'judgments about the legal relevance and admissibility of social science research evidence'. However, these variables are still abstract and broad, and need further clarification (see Step 4 below).

Step 2: Determining design structure

Having defined the research problem and questions and identified the theoretical framework, the next step is to determine the overall research design. As discussed, a quantitative study can adopt an exploratory, descriptive or explanatory design in the light of the overall aim of the study. The design not only indicates how data will be collected and analysed, but it is also a plan of action which directs the researcher to answer the research questions in a systematic manner. Numerous research designs, including experimental research design, cross-sectional or survey design, secondary analysis, case study design, prospective research design and comparative design, are open to researchers, and some of these designs will be discussed in detail in Part III of this chapter.

Step 3: Identifying population and sample

The researcher is often posed with the question of obtaining credible conclusions from quantitative study. In other words, how would the researcher select and recruit samples from the sampling frame;[41] and ensure the conclusion drawn from the findings is generalised.[42] Quantitative researchers employ probability sampling where each sample unit such as people, interest groups, suburbs and companies of the population has an equal chance of being selected for study. For example, if a researcher wants to study the population of all law students on a campus, he or she must decide which parameters are used to define the type and current status of the students, as they could, for example, be: undergraduate and postgraduate students; full-time and part-time students; local and international students; visiting students; mature or school-leavers; or students who have deferred their studies, but remain officially registered. Once the actual population under study or sampling frame has been determined, the next task is to obtain a full list of students who meet the sampling criteria, and then identify a method to select students who will be invited to participate.

Three types of probability sampling, such as simple random sampling, systematic sampling, and stratified sampling are often favoured because of their high degree of representativeness, and therefore results can be generalised.[43] The most commonly used is simple random sampling because its selection procedure is the best way to avoid sample bias. From the previous example on defining students' type and status, assume that there are 1,000 law students in the sampling frame and the researcher decides to choose to sample 200 of them. An efficient method is to assign a unique number to each student on the list from one to 1,000, and 200 numbers can be randomly generated either by a computer, or from a predetermined set of random numbers available in most textbooks on research methods. Unlike simple random sampling, systematic sampling involves choosing samples in a systematic pattern by taking every nth element in the sampling frame until the total is reached. If 1,000 law students are divided by 200, the sampling interval is five. So the researcher can choose any number as a starting point and conveniently pick every fifth name thereafter to create a sample of 200 law students. While the process involved in random sampling and systematic sampling is random, there is a chance, though improbable, that the sample drawn will contain males only. Also, it may be possible that smaller sub-groups such as international students are under-represented or excluded. Therefore, stratified sampling procedure is recommended to avoid these statistical issues.

Stratification intends to divide the sampling frame into various sub-groups, sub-populations or strata before selecting the sample. Each stratum should be mutually exclusive, and also exhaustive in order not to exclude potential research participants. A typical example of the stratified sampling is to divide the population (of 1,000 students) by gender and then select 100 from each group. Characteristics other than gender, age, and ethnicity can be used to divide the sampling frame into strata, if well justified; otherwise a proportionate sample[44] is expected. One advantage of this sampling is that it ensures better coverage of the population than random and systematic sampling. However, this procedure requires greater effort in defining strata and identifying the characteristics of each stratum.[45]

Table 2.2 A summary of common non-probability sampling

	Description
Purposive	Hand-pick subjects on the basis of specific characteristics
Quota	Select individuals as they come to fill a quota by characteristics proportional to populations
Snowball	Subjects with desired traits or characteristics give names of further appropriate subjects
Convenience (or accidental)	Subjects are convenient or available to the researcher or the sample the researcher chances upon by accident

Modified and adapted from T. R. Black, *Doing Quantitative Research in the Social Sciences: An Integrated Approach to Research Design, Measurement and Statistics* (London: Sage, 1999) table 5.1, 118.

Admittedly in real life, the use of probability sampling which employs ran-domisation is not always possible for various reasons such as limited resources and sampling frame unknown to the researcher. Under these circumstances, non-probability sampling, such as purposive sampling, quota sampling, snow-ball sampling, convenience (or accidental) sampling, is an alternative. Non-probability sampling has been commonly used in exploratory and descriptive studies. Table 2.2 gives a brief account of these four types of non-probability sampling.

Step 4: Designing research instruments and operationalising variables

After the sampling procedure, the next step is to determine which research instruments should be used and which concepts or variables should be counted or measured. Quantitative researchers have to decide what is to be measured or evaluated in a research instrument such as a questionnaire. For example, if gender is an important focus in the study, categorical or discrete variables with just two categories should be used: male or female. If examining the public's atti-tude towards the criminal justice system and criminal victimisation is the main purpose of a study, attitude scales (see, for example, the Revised Legal Attitude Questionnaire,[46] Attitudes towards the Criminal Legal System Questionnaire,[47] and Victim—blaming and Society—blaming Scale)[48] that provide continuous data should be used. These scales usually consist of a number of positive and negative statements from which respondents can choose by ticking one of five possible responses: 'strongly agree', 'agree', 'undecided', 'disagree' and 'strongly disagree'. For instance, the scale to measure the attitudes towards the criminal legal system contains a list of thirty-eight statements that deal with judges, juries, defence counsel, prosecutors, the law and punishment of offenders. These thirty-eight statements measure attitudes towards integrity, competence and fairness within the criminal justice system. However, measuring instruments for attitudes, opinions and views may take the researchers several years to be validated before it can be relied upon.[49]

Step 5: Selecting statistical tests for resolving hypotheses

In order to test the hypotheses with one or more samples, a body of statistical tests or techniques may be selected by researchers before and after data are collected. For instance, a proposed study intends to explore the gender differences in terms of the views on the criminal justice system. In addition to using simple statistics such as the average of a distribution of value, the study looks for differences between males and females that are statistically significant. To measure whether these differences did not occur through chance alone, a predetermined acceptable level of confidence (or sometimes called significance level) such as 90 (or $p < 0.10$), 95 (or $p < 0.05$) or 99 (or $p < 0.01$) per cent should be used to reject or accept a hypothesis or hypotheses about a difference. The most common level of confidence is 95 per cent which means the finding has a 95 per cent chance of being true and at the same time a 5 per cent chance of not being true. The levels of significance use probability theory and are mostly used to measure the association between variables and a difference between two means in a study which employs probability sampling. More descriptive statistical methods (for descriptive and exploratory studies) and inferential ones (for exploratory and explanatory studies) will be introduced in Part IV of the chapter.

III MAIN TECHNIQUES OF DATA COLLECTION

Referring to Figure 2.1, Step 6 is concerned with data collection. In a quantitative study, data are categorised into two main types: primary and secondary. Primary data refer to those 'new' data generated by the researcher via a number of techniques such as conducting surveys, experiments and interviews. Secondary data refer to the statistical material and information originally obtained for other purposes and by other researchers.[50] Negotiating and accessing primary and secondary data is often very time-consuming and in most circumstances administrative approval should be obtained prior to the commencement of the study. Gatekeepers may deny the researcher access to the target group, data sets or research site that are of interest. In this respect, compromises in terms of the scale of research, research aims, research design and sampling methods are sometimes necessary.

As suggested by Alan Bryman,[51] there are five main methods of quantitative social science research (see Table 2.3). Each of these methods has its own

Table 2.3 Five major methods of quantitative research

Method	Features	Advantages
Social survey	Random samples	Representative
	Measured variables	Tests hypotheses
Experiment	Experiment stimulus	Precise measurement
	'Control group' not exposed to stimulus	
Official statistics	Analysis of previously collected data	Large datasets
'Structured'	Observations recorded on	Reliability of
observation	pre-determined 'schedule'	observations
Content analysis	Pre-determined categories used to	Reliability of measures
	count content of mass media products	

D. Silverman, *Doing Qualitative Research: A Practical Handbook* (London: Sage, 2000) table 1.2, 3.

special features and advantages. Illustrated with examples of quantitative research, three of them including experiment research, survey research and secondary analysis will be introduced to demonstrate their wide application in social science and legal research.

Experiment

Experimental research builds on the principles of positivism or natural science more than any other quantitative methods. It is often carried out in the field or in a laboratory, where the researcher attempts to manipulate certain controlled conditions into a controlled environment, in order to examine the relationship between two or more variables. The reason for manipulating variables is to eliminate all possible alternate explanations of the relationship. A recent study of such randomised experiment is the Natalie Taylor and Jacqueline Joudo study of the impact of pre-recorded video and closed circuit television testimony by adult sexual assault complainants on jury decision-making.[52] Its aim is to investigate whether the mode of testimony (that is, face-to-face, CCTV or video) and degree of emotionality of testimony (that is, neutral or emotional) have a differential impact on jurors' perceptions of the adult sexual assault complainant and defendant. Here, the experiment was based on comparisons between the groups, and was commissioned by the New South Wales Attorney General's Department in Australia. A total of 210 people were recruited from the public to participate in eighteen mock trials, and they were randomly allocated to one of the three particular modes of victim testimony and two styles of victim presentation.[53] Different groups in the sample were exposed to the same information and certain controlled conditions (as the independent variable); they were tested for differences between each other in the dependent variable. One key finding in this experimental research showed that the mode

Table 2.4 Continuum of quantitative research designs

Experiment	Quasi-experiment	Non-experiment (Correlational survey)
• Manipulation of independent variable(s) • Random allocation of treatment groups	• Naturally occurring treatment groups • Statistical control of co-variate(s)	• Naturally occurring variation in independent variables • Statistical control of co-variate(s)

K. F. Punch, *Introduction to Social Research: Quantitative and Qualitative Approaches* (Thousand Oaks, CA: Sage, 2005) figure 5.2, 7.3.

of testimony and victim's presentation had no significant effect on the jury outcomes. However, the juror's personal belief, the requirement to convict beyond reasonable doubt, and the difficulty in understanding what 'consent' meant were important factors that had an impact on the deliberations in determining a guilty verdict. To summarise, a true experiment manipulates one or more independent variables for the purposes of research, and involves the random allocation of subjects to experimental or control groups.[54]

While an experimental research design is considered the best method of establishing causality between variables, it is not practical to be used in the real-life situation or natural setting. If a research project intends to measure the impact of a prison sentence on the offender, random allocation of convicted criminals is unfeasible and undesirable. It is also unethical to allocate those criminals who were originally given a custodial sentence to receive other forms of punishment such as community or non-supervised sentences for the sake of conducting experimental research. Instead, quasi-experimental and non-experimental designs can be used as a substitute to a true experimental design. Table 2.4 shows the continuum of these three quantitative research designs.

While a quasi-experimental research design is about as near as the researcher can get to an experimental design, it does not involve random allocation of subjects in treatment and comparison groups. Rather researchers use statistical control of the independent variable exposed to both groups such as matching the characteristics of the sample, and then inferences between variables are drawn. In contrast to experimental and quasi-experimental research, a non-experiment does not aim at establishing causality but instead investigates whether relationships or associations can be found between and among variables. It is sometimes called a correlational survey.

Surveys

Surveys are usually carried out as part of a non-experimental design and are ideal methods of understanding people's attitudes, beliefs, views and opinions on different aspects of social life. Many surveys provide a detailed description of a population on a number of variables, and look for correlations or associations between variables. For instance, a recent study endeavoured to understand the perceptions of law students from six different countries, and to highlight some correlations between the student background and perceptions of law and lawyers.[55] This survey was conducted using a questionnaire that consists primarily of closed questions. According to each closed question, a set of pre-designed replies such as multiple-choice responses and 'Yes or No' was offered to the research participant to choose. While answers to the closed question are very easy to code and analyse, it is indeed very difficult for the researcher to exhaust all possible responses to the question.

There are two main types of data collection methods for the survey questionnaire: self-administered and interviewer-administered.[56] The self-administered questionnaires include postal questionnaires, delivery and collection questionnaires, and online questionnaires, whereas examples of the interviewer-administered questionnaires are structured, face-to-face interviews and telephone surveys. The advantages and disadvantages of these types of survey methods are summarised in Table 2.5.

Secondary analysis

Another common method of quantitative research is secondary analysis. It uses 'old' data for 'new' ideas and researchers are usually unfamiliar with how these data were collected. Generally speaking, there are three major sources of secondary data: surveys, official statistics and official records. Some of the secondary data or databases on both civil and criminal aspects of the legal system are now made accessible to the public online. Some of them are even available for users to download for further analysis. A classic example of the database is *Access to Justice in Ontario, 1985–1988*, which was compiled by the Civil Litigation Research Project at the University of Wisconsin.[57] Other databases include: *Alaska Plea Bargaining Study, 1974–1976* and *Survey of Tort Litigants in Three State Courts, 1989-1990: United States*.[58] There are advantages to using secondary analysis, including time saved for data collection, cost saved for carrying out large-scale surveys, high quality data bank readily available, and making difficult populations accessible. However, using other people's data sets to answer research questions poses challenges to researchers who may interpret the raw data from a very different theoretical and methodological orientation.[59]

Table 2.5 Advantages and disadvantages of survey methods

Types of survey methods	Advantages	Disadvantages
General to all surveys using respondents	• A relatively simple and straightforward approach to the study of attitudes, values, beliefs and motives • High amounts of data standardisation	• Data are affected by the characteristics of the respondents such as their memory and motivation • Respondents will not necessarily report their beliefs and values accurately, and would respond in a way that shows them in good light
Self-administered surveys	• Less costly to reach larger sample • Less labour-intensive to collect or train researchers • Allow anonymity	• Response rate may be low, thus limiting generalisability • Easy to misunderstand or skip around survey questions • Cannot guarantee whether the person intended completes the questionnaire
Interviewer-administered surveys	• Can clarify the meaning of questions • Can tell whether the respondents treat the exercise seriously	• Limited to smaller samples • Interviewer characteristics such as gender and age could bias responses • Anonymity not guaranteed

Adapted from C. Robson, Real World Research (2nd end) (Oxford: Blackwell, 2002) Box 8.2, 233–4; P. M. Nardi, *Doing Survey Research: A Guide to Quantitative Methods* (Boston, MA: Pearson, 2006) Box 1.4, 17–19.

IV METHODS OF DATA ANALYSIS

The final phase of quantitative research design is the analysis and interpretation of data (see Figure 2.1). Quantitative data analysis can be divided into three major types, namely univariate descriptive, bivariate descriptive, and explanatory.[60] They are used for various purposes, which include describing the characteristics of social phenomena, and to understand, predict, explore, and explain the relationship between and among a number of variables measured in the research. Univariate descriptive analysis is to give a snapshot of the data by providing a basic summary of each variable in the study. This is commonly represented in a frequency distribution, or with some descriptive statistics such as the mean, mode and median which are measures of central tendency (see Table 2.6).

Table 2.6 Measures of central tendency / Basic descriptive statistics

Measure	Brief description
Mean	The 'mathematical average': the sum of values for all cases divided by the total number of cases
Mode	Category with the highest percentage in a frequency distribution
Median	The mid-point along a ranked frequency distribution

Adapted from M. Henn, M. Weinstein and N. Foard, *A Short Introduction to Social Research* (London: Sage, 2006) table 8.2, 207.

In contrast to univariate analysis, bivariate analysis refers to the attempt to look at the variables together. Bivariate descriptive analysis has two main aims: to explore the similarities and differences between scores for two variables; and to identify the association between two variables. To achieve the first aim, scores in terms of averages or means are compared (for example, differences between the mean scores of female or male respondents regarding their attitudes towards the criminal justice system). To establish the strength of the relationship between two variables, statistical tests such as the correlational coefficient will be used, for example, measuring the correlation or association between age and law-breaking behaviour.

Explanatory analysis goes beyond describing characteristics and establishing relationships, and answer the 'why' questions instead of 'what' questions.[61] It also attempts to look for one or more causes for the patterns and sequences in social life. In other words, explanations are sought to investigate why certain factors lead to the outcome. Various methods of multivariate analysis such as logistic regression, factorial analysis, discriminant analysis and structural equation modelling can be used to explore the effect of two or more dependent variables on one or more independent variables.[62] Various computer software packages such as the Statistical Package for the Social Sciences (SPSS)[63] and Stata[64] are able to provide researchers with a vast number of statistical and mathematical functions in order to analyse a massive amount of data systematically.

V ETHICAL ISSUES ASSOCIATED WITH QUANTITATIVE RESEARCH

To conclude this chapter, some basic principles of ethical social or socio-legal research are discussed. While it is important to advance knowledge on different aspects of the social world, researchers are expected to conduct their empirical studies in an ethical manner. Learning from previous experience, there are a number of questionable or unethical practices in research, and examples include: involving people in a study without their consent or knowledge, deceiving the participant intentionally, withholding information about the aim and nature of the experiment, or causing participants physical, emotional and psychological harm.[65] For instance, the Stanford Prison Experiment is a classic example to illustrate how a true experiment that aimed to study the psychological effects of imprisonment on inmates and prison officers caused harm to the research participants. The experiment was terminated six days after the experiment began.[66] Professional social science, socio-legal studies and criminology associations have codes of ethics which state what constitutes acceptable and unacceptable behaviour. The codes are concerned with the issues of informed consent, privacy, confidentiality, anonymity, harm and consequentiality.[67] In summary, researchers are encouraged to uphold professional integrity by explaining their research to participants, funding bodies and gatekeepers as clearly as possible; and to protect the interests of participants by guaranteeing confidentiality and anonymity while obtaining both oral and written consent.

In addition, quantitative researchers are required to use high methodological standards and to strive for accuracy as suggested earlier in the chapter. Novice researchers are worried when their statistical analysis does not support the hypotheses or does not find the relationships between variables. The ultimate goal of quantitative research is to expand knowledge that truly reflects the social reality – not to defend a particular body of knowledge or theory blindly. Also a sound knowledge of both elementary and advanced statistics is a prerequisite for researchers to analyse and interpret quantitative findings, and to be able to present the findings in a precise manner. In this respect, the best protection against being misled by statistics is to not ignore the numbers.

FURTHER READING

N. Blaikie, *Analyzing Quantitative Data* (London: Sage, 2003).

A. Bryman and D. Cramer, *Quantitative Data Analysis for Social Scientists* (revised edn) (London: Routledge, 1994).

R. H. Carver and J. G. Nash, *Doing Data Analysis with SPSS Version 14* (Belmont, CA: Thomson-Brooks / Cole, 2006).

D. E. Gray, *Doing Research in the Real World* (London: Sage, 2004).

M. Henn, M. Weinstein and N. Foard, *A Short Introduction to Social Research* (London: Sage, 2006).

P. M. Nardi, *Doing Survey Research: A Guide to Quantitative Methods* (Boston, MA: Pearson, 2006).

C. Robson, *Real World Research* (2nd edn) (Oxford: Blackwell, 2000).

N. Salkind, *Statistics for People Who (Think They) Hate Statistics* (London: Sage, 2003).

L. S. Wrightsman, A. L. Batson and V. A. Edkins (eds), *Measures of Legal Attitudes* (Belmont, CA: Wadsworth / Thomson Learning, 2004).

NOTES

1. Socio-legal research, mostly conducted by academic staff based in law schools or independent research institutions, 'claims or aspires to be an interdisciplinary subject with particular ties with sociology'. See R. Banakar and M. Travers, 'Law, Sociology and Method' in R. Banakar and M. Travers (ed.), *Theory and Method, in Socio-legal Research* (Oxford: Hart Publishing, 2005) 1.
2. L. E. Ohlin, 'Partnership with Social Sciences' (1970–71) 23 *Journal of Legal Education* 206.
3. J. G. Getman, 'Contributions of Empirical Data to Legal Research' (1985) 35 *Journal of Legal Education* 493.
4. T. Hutchinson, *Researching and Writing in Law* (2nd edn) (Pyrmont, NSW: Lawbook Co., 2006) 7.
5. Ibid. 7–8, 19. According to Hutchinson, doctrinal research is defined as 'Research which provides a systematic exposition of the rules governing a particular legal category, analyses the relationship between rules, explains areas of difficulty and, perhaps, predicts future development' (p. 7).
6. Several textbooks on legal research have been consulted when preparing for this chapter. See, for example, S. Barber and M. A. McCormick, *Legal Research* (New York: Delmar Publishers, 1996); D. Stott, *Legal Research* (2nd edn) (London: Cavendish, 1999); S. Elias and S. Levinkind, *Legal Research: How to Find and Understand the Law* (8th edn) (Berkeley, CA: Nolo, 2000); I. Nemes and G. Coss, *Effective Legal Research* (2nd edn) (Chatswood, NSW: Butterworths, 2001); R. Watt, *Concise Legal Research* (5th edn) (Sydney: The Federation Press, 2004).
7. W. B. Lockhart, 'Social Research and the Law' (1970) 23 *Journal of Legal Education* 1; H. Zeisel, 'Of Social Science Research Methods and Competency for Lawyers Therein' (1970–1971) 23 *Journal of Legal Education* 240; D. Bok, 'A Flawed System of Law Practice and Training' (1983) 33 *Journal of Legal* Education 570; P. E. Leighton, 'The Case for Empirical Research' (1984) 18 *The Law Teacher* 13; R. Tomasic, 'Using Social Science Research Methods in the Study of Corporate Law' (1996) 3 *Canberra Law Review* 24–5; T. S. Ulen, 'A Nobel Prize in Legal Science: Theory, Empirical Work, and the Scientific Method in the Study of Law' (2002) 4 *University of Illinois Law Review* 875; T. E. George, 'An Empirical Study of Empirical Legal Scholarship: The Top Law Schools' (2006) 81 *Indiana Law Journal* 141.

8. L. E. Teitelbaum, 'An Overview of Law and Social Research' (1985) 35 *Journal of Legal Education* 466.

9. See, for example, R. D. King and E. Wincup (eds) *Doing Research on Crime and Justice* (Oxford: Oxford University Press, 2000); V. Jupp, P. Davies and P. Francis (eds) *Doing Criminological Research* (London: Sage, 2000); H. Douglas and L. Godden, *The Decriminalisation of Domestic Violence* (Nathan, QLD: Griffith University, 2002); S. Bushway and D. Weisburd (eds), *Quantitative Methods in Criminology* (Aldershot: Ashgate, 2005).

10. See, for example, P. Grabosky and J. Braithwaite, *Of Manners Gentle: Enforcement Strategies of Australian Business Regulatory Agencies* (Melbourne: Oxford University Press, 1986); M. I. Weinstein, 'Share Price Changes and the Arrival of Limited Liability in California' (2003) 32 *Journal of Legal Studies* 1.

11. See, for example, G. R. Mullane, 'Evidence of Social Science Research: Law, Practice, and Options in the Family Court of Australia' (1998) 72 *Australian Law Journal* 434; S. Mechoulan, 'Divorce Laws and the Structure of the American Family' (2006) 35 *Journal of Legal Studies* 143.

12. J. Monahan and L. Walker, 'Teaching Social Science in Law: An Alternative to "Law and Society"' (1985) 35 *Journal of Legal Education* 480. They both recognised that a basic understanding of methodology and statistics is essential for law students to comprehend the applications of social science knowledge and theory to the law. See also D. Kaye, 'Thinking Like a Statistician' (1984) 34 *Journal of Legal Education* 97; D. L. Faigman, 'To Have and Have Not: Assessing the Value of Social Science to the Law as Science and Policy' (1989) 38 *Emory Law Journal* 1004.

13. According to John W. Creswell, the three approaches are quantitative, qualitative (discussed in Chapter 1 of this volume) and mixed methods, and each of them 'brings together claims being made about what constitutes knowledge, a strategy of inquiry, and specific methods'. See J. W. Creswell, *Research Design: Qualitative, Quantitative, and Mixed Methods Approaches* (2nd edn) (Thousand Oaks, CA: Sage, 2003) xxii.

14. M. Hammersley, 'What is Social Research?' in M. Hammersley (ed.), *Principles of Social and Educational Research: Block 1* (Milton Keynes: Open University Press, 1993) 39.

15. M. Henn, M. Weinstein and N. Foard, *A Short Introduction to Social Research* (London: Sage, 2006) 1. Of course, quantitative research can also give rise to new theoretical insights and can overturn existing qualitative-based paradigms: see, for example, M. McConville and C. Mirsky, *Jury Trials and Plea Bargaining* (Oxford: Hart Publishing, 2005).

16. N. Denzin and Y. Lincoln (eds), *Handbook of Qualitative Research* (Thousand Oaks, CA: Sage, 1994) 4.

17. This is at least how it is depicted; but the very selection of data to be collected and its interpretation involve subjectivity.

18. Creswell, see note 13 above, 7.

19. Henn, Weinstein and Foard, see note 15 above, 11. A fuller account of the positivist approach can be found in the work of Auguste Comte's *The Positive Philosophy* (New York: AMS Press, 1974).

20. Henn, Western and Foard, see note 15 above, 12. See also D. E. Gray, *Doing Research in the Real World* (London: Sage, 2004) 18.

21. These assumptions are adapted and extracted from C. Robson's *Real World Research* (2nd edn) (Oxford: Blackwell, 2002), Box 2.1, 20.

22. Research design is defined as 'all the issues involved in planning and executing a research project – from identifying the problem through to reporting and publishing the results'. See K. F. Punch, *Introduction to Social Research: Quantitative and Qualitative Approaches* (Thousand Oaks, CA: Sage, 2005) 62.

23. D. E. McNabb, *Research Methods for Political Science: Quantitative and Qualitative Research* (New York: M. E. Sharpe, 2004) 100–3.

24. See, for example, L. Mather, 'Changing Patterns of Legal Representation in Divorce: From Lawyers to *Pro Se*' (2003) 30 *Journal of Law and Society* 137; P. Pleasence, H. Genn, N. J. Balmer, A. Buck, and A. O'Grady, 'Causes of Action: First Findings of the LSRC Periodic Survey' (2003) 30 *Journal of Law and Society* 11; R. Moorhead and M. Sefton, *Litigants in Person: Unrepresented Litigants in First Instance Proceedings* (London: Department of Constitutional Affairs, 2005).

25. McNabb, see note 23 above, 101.

26. M. G. Maxfield and E. Babbie, *Research Methods for Criminal Justice and Criminology* (4th edn) (Belmont, CA: Wadsworth, 2005) 20.

27. See, for example, T. Tyler, *Why People Obey Law* (Princeton, NJ: Princeton University Press, 2006).

28. T. Cook and D. Campbell, *Quasi-experimentation: Design and Analysis Issues for Field Settings* (Boston, MA: Houghton Mifflin, 1979).

29. B. M. Melnyk and R. Cole, 'Generating Evidence through Quantitative Research', in B. M. Melnyk and E. Fineout-Overholt (eds), *Evidence-based Practice in Nursing and Healthcare: A Guide to Best Practice* (Philadelphia: Lippincott Williams and Wilkins) 242–50.

30. In this part, the discussion is concerned with those steps involved in the planning stage. Parts IV and V of the chapter deal with steps 6 and 7 respectively.

31. Henn, Weinstein and Foard, see note 15 above, 48.

32. S. R. Cummings, W. S. Browner and S. B. Hulley, 'Conceiving the Research Question' in S. B. Hulley, S. R. Cummings and W. S. Browner, D. Grady, N. Hearst and T. B. Newman (eds), *Designing Clinical Research* (2nd edn) (Philadelphia: Lippincott, Williams and Wilkins, 2001) 17–23.

33. N. Blaikie, *Analyzing Quantitative Data* (London: Sage, 2003) 13.
34. D. E. McNabb, see note 23 above, 70.
35. Gray, see note 20 above, 5.
36. Research hypotheses are usually required to answer 'why' questions which seek explanations. In contrast, 'what' questions look for description of a particular issue, and research questions should be developed instead of hypotheses.
37. C. Frankfort-Nachmias and D. Nachmias, *Research Methods in the Social Sciences* (5th edn) (New York: St Martin's Press, 1996) 62.
38. R. E. Redding and N. D. Reppucci, 'Effects of Lawyers' Socio-political Attitudes on Their Judgments of Social Science in Legal Decision Making' (1999) 23 *Law and Human Behavior* 31–2.
39. Robson, see note 21 above, 61–2.
40. Independent variable is the first part of a causal hypothesis, and it may cause a positive or negative change in a dependent variable.
41. The sampling frame is the source of the eligible population from which the sample is drawn. See Robson, note 21 above, 240.
42. Generalisability (sometimes called external validity) refers to the degree to which the conclusions we learn from one study sample would hold for the larger group or population from which the sample was drawn.
43. For a more detailed discussion of different probability sampling methods, please consult Ch. 8 of W. L. Neuman, *Social Research Methods: Qualitative and Quantitative Methods* (6th edn) (Boston: Allyn and Bacon, 2006).
44. A proportionate sample implies that the number of sample according to each stratum is proportional to their numbers in total sampling frame.
45. T. R. Black, *Doing Quantitative Research in the Social Sciences: An Integrated Approach to Research Design, Measurement and Statistics* (London: Sage, 1999) 121.
46. D. A. Kravitz, B. L. Cytler and P. Brock, 'Reliability and Validity of the Original and Revised Legal Attitudes Questionnaire' (1993) 17 *Law and Human Behavior* 661–77.
47. T. A. Martin and E. S. Cohn, 'Attitudes Toward the Criminal Legal System: Scale Development and Predictors' (2004) 10 *Psychology, Crime and Law* 367–91.
48. C. L. Mulford, M. Y. Lee and S. C. Sapp, 'Victim-blaming and Society-blaming Scales for Social Problems' (1996) 26 *Journal of Applied Social Psychology* 1324–36.
49. See A. Bryman and D. Cramer, *Quantitative Data Analysis for Social Scientists* (revised edn) (London: Routledge, 1994) 70–4. The reliability of a measure refers to its consistency whereas a valid measure is one which is measuring what it purports to measure.
50. M. Riedel, *Research Strategies for Secondary Data: A Perspective for*

Criminology and Criminal Justice (Thousand Oaks, CA: Sage) 1. Secondary data such as the National Crime Victimization Survey and Uniform Crime Reporting Programme have been used by criminal researchers in the United States.

51. A. Bryman, *Quantity and Quality in Social Research* (London: Unwin Hyman, 1988) 11–12.

52. N. Taylor and J. Joudo, *The Impact of Pre-recorded Video and Closed Circuit Television Testimony by Adult Sexual Assault Complainants on Jury Decision-making: An Experimental Study* (Research and Public Policy Series no. 68) (Canberra, ACT: Australian Institute of Criminology, 2005).

53. Ibid. iii.

54. Punch, see note 22 above, 69.

55. M. Asimow, S. Greenfield, G. Jorge, S. Machura, G. Osborn, P. Robson, C. Sharp and R. Sockloskie, 'Perceptions of Lawyers – A Transnational Study of Student Views on the Image of Law and Lawyers' (2005) 12 *International Journal of the Legal Profession* 409.

56. Gray, see note 20 above, 108–12.

57. W. A. Bogart and N. Vidmar, *Access to Justice in Ontario, 1985–1988* (Ann Arbor, MI: Inter-university Consortium for Political and Social Research, 1999). Available at: http://webapp.icpsr.umich.edu/cocoon/NACJD-STUDY/09729.xml

58. Riedel, see note 50 above, 32.

59. D. Burton, 'Secondary Data Analysis', in D. Burton (ed.), *Research Training for Social Scientists* (London: Sage, 2000) 348–51; S. Arber, 'Secondary Analysis of Survey Data', in N. Gilbert (ed.), *Researching Social Life* (2nd edn) (London: Sage, 2001) 269–86; Punch, see note 22 above, 103.

60. Blaikie, see note 33 above, 29.

61. Ibid. 30.

62. For further details on the use of multivariate analysis, please consult a textbook on statistics. See, for example, N. Salkind, *Statistics for People Who (Think They) Hate Statistics* (London: Sage, 2003).

63. R. H. Carver and J. G. Nash, *Doing Data Analysis with SPSS Version 14* (Belmont, CA: Thomson- Brooks/Cole, 2006).

64. S. Rabe-Hesketh and B. Everitt, *A Handbook of Statistical Analyses Using Stata* (3rd edn) (Boca Raton, FL: Chapman & Hall/CRC, 2004).

65. Robson, see note 21 above, 69.

66. C. Haney, C. Banks and P. Zimbardo, 'A Study of Prisoners and Guards in a Simulated Prison', in E. Aronson (ed.), *Readings about the Social Animal* (7th edn) (New York: W. H. Freeman and Company, 1995) 52–67.

67. M. Israel, 'Strictly Confidential? Integrity and the Disclosure of Criminological and Socio-legal Research' (2004) 44.

Doing Ethnographic Research: Lessons from a Case Study

Satnam Choongh

INTRODUCTION

The politics of police research and its funding have changed considerably over the last couple of decades. One author has noted the tendency since the late 1980s for research to focus increasingly on 'the search for good practice rather than issues of police discretion, deviance, and accountability',[1] research which he describes as 'pragmatic' and 'governed by the overriding goal of crime reduction.'[2] This is no doubt partly due to the fact that since the 1980s successive governments have become increasingly concerned with 'value for money' when it comes to research funding, and accordingly much of the recent research into criminal justice has focused on whether or not the latest government crime reduction initiative has worked. In this political climate, there is unlikely to be any meaningful funding for studies which focus on the behaviour of actors within the criminal process in order to discover and explain low-visibility practices.

Against this backdrop, PhD and Masters students have become critical (at least in the short-term) to the survival of a fine tradition in criminology, namely the detailed study of the day-to-day world of police officers, lawyers, social workers, probation officers, suspects, offenders, prisoners or prison officers which sets out to discover how they make sense of the world within which they operate, and how their views influence behaviour and the operation of the criminal process. In the jargon of the academy, this is often referred to as 'ethnographic' research, the salient qualities of which have been helpfully summarised in the following way:

> First and most obviously, its preference is for carefully-nuanced reportage, based on deep immersion in the life-worlds of the subjects being studied; hence ethnography has a preference (usually a strong

preference) for qualitative rather than quantitative data. Secondly and relatedly, ethnography places much more emphasis than does positivism on the meaning of social actions to actors, and on their detailed understandings of particular social contexts. Thirdly, therefore, the ethnographic approach emphatically rejects the view that social science can be studied in the same way as natural science, for the phenomena studied in natural science do not attribute meaning to their life-worlds as human beings do. These three attributes . . . lead, collectively, to a particular strength of the ethnographic tradition, . . . namely, its ability to uncover some of the deep cultural meanings and normative bonds which are often so important in everyday social life.[3]

Almost by its very nature, ethnographic research is exploratory: it does not begin with a firm hypothesis which is to be tested, and neither does it set out to confirm or dismantle some general over-arching theory. The student whose interest lies in qualitative research will for the most part want to look at a particular social context, and reach a deep understanding of how the players within it structure their interaction with each other and the outside world. This understanding may prove useful in furthering a policy-oriented debate, or it may make a useful contribution to theory. However, such outcomes are neither sought nor guaranteed, and the success of the project is not to be judged by their delivery. And this is the reason that the PhD or Masters student can reach parts the established researcher increasingly cannot – the long hours and consequent expense involved in ethnographic research can rarely be justified to sceptical funding bodies, which for the most part crave quantitative data which can be easily reduced to statistics and pressed into immediate service. Doctoral and Masters students need not concern themselves with overheads, or the expectations of a funding body, and, if prepared to work hard, they possess the flexibility to put in the long hours that are needed to produce the data required for a good monograph.

However, time and resources, whilst necessary for a successful project, are not sufficient. It is also important to know how to prepare for the fieldwork, gain access with the minimum of compromise, gather as much data as possible, ensure that the data is preserved and understood properly, and ensure that the research project is written up in a way which exploits the data to its maximum. No research project is going to run exactly to plan, and there are probably very few researchers who can honestly say of projects in which they have been involved that every angle was covered. There will always be regrets about questions that were not asked, moments that were missed and words uttered that would have been best saved for another occasion. The purpose of this chapter is to provide some pointers which will hopefully minimise the need for such regrets.

The way in which I hope to do this is by describing some of the practical difficulties I encountered in the course of conducting fieldwork for my DPhil, and setting out some of the lessons learnt which others can take forward when planning and carrying out their own fieldwork. It was the first time that I had conducted any empirical work, and I went into the field without any training in research methodologies, and without having read a single word on the subject. Although some may say I 'got away with it' (the research was subsequently published as a monograph),[4] with the benefit of hindsight (and a little maturity) I can admit that it was neither big nor clever to proceed in this way. Had I not been so ignorant, I would undoubtedly have saved myself a great deal of time, avoided much despair and confusion, and emerged from the field with a much richer and more detailed set of data.

BACKGROUND TO THE RESEARCH

My interest lay in pre-trial criminal procedure, and I knew from the outset that my focus was going to be on what I had come to view as the pivotal role of the police within the criminal process. In brief, I was interested in police powers and suspects' rights, and how the interaction between the two impacted upon the formal rules of criminal evidence. Although I commenced my DPhil with the firm intention of conducting empirical research, I was wholly unclear as to what form this would take. The reason for this was that I had not as yet formulated any clear-cut hypotheses or theories that could be tested through empiricism. It is important, by way of contextualisation, to explain my confusion by reference to the debate that was taking place in the late 1980s about police powers and the rules of evidence.

My starting point was Packer's 'Crime Control' and 'Due Process' models of the criminal process,[5] which had influenced a great deal of the writing on the operation of the English criminal justice system. These two models of the process identified with remarkable clarity the broad and conflicting concerns which underlay the controversy which had surrounded the matter of police powers and practices since at least the early 1970s. The debate over what powers the police ought to possess, and what rights ought to be accorded to suspects, was for the main part conducted between those who believed that extensive police powers were necessary in order to apprehend and convict criminals quickly and efficiently, and those who contended that powers already possessed by the police were so wide and unchecked that they facilitated unfair and oppressive treatment of suspects, and possibly contributed to miscarriages of justice.

This debate was re-ignited following the publication of the report of the Philips Commission in 1981.[6] In their report the Commissioners had stated that in putting forward their recommendations, they had sought to strike 'an appropriate balance between the individual's rights and the community's interest'. Not surprisingly, perhaps, this led to a spate of articles and books in which academics and commentators pored over the report and promptly disagreed with each other as to whether an appropriate balance had indeed been struck. What made the whole affair interesting, at least for me, was that the Philips Commission had as part of its deliberations commissioned a series of empirically based studies looking at various aspects of the criminal process in operation. This empirical data provided an opportunity to test whether the assumptions upon which the Commissioners based their recommendations were supported by what was actually known about the operation of police powers and the exercise by suspects of their rights. I was fascinated by what these studies revealed, and became convinced that the best way to move the debate forward was by finding out more about what actually took place within the confines of police stations.

The recommendations of the Philips Commission were more or less reflected in the provisions of the Police and Criminal Evidence Act 1984 (PACE). Proponents of the Act argued that although it conferred greater powers of arrest, search, seizure, detention and interrogation, its provisions nonetheless represented a net gain for suspects because they were granted a comprehensive set of rights and protections (the right to legal advice; tape-recording of police interrogations; protection through the creation of an independent custody officer; regular reviews of detention by senior officers). As I was beginning my DPhil in 1990–91, the results of a number of empirical studies into the operation of PACE were beginning to emerge. For the most part, these studies were concerned with ascertaining whether suspects were being informed of their rights; whether they were being allowed to exercise their rights; whether the right to legal advice had resulted in suspects having access to meaningful, professional legal advice; and whether the police were obeying the rules in respect of tape-recording interrogations.

FORMULATING THE QUESTION

Although keen to carry out empirical work of my own, I began initially with the view that what was really needed was a theory of the criminal process that would go beyond Packer's 'Crime Control' and 'Due Process' models. I found the Philips Commission approach of 'balancing' suspects' rights against the rights of the 'community' unsatisfactory and sterile, and became convinced that the debate raging between the proponents of PACE and those critical of it could not meaningfully proceed further without a new theory of the role of the suspect within the criminal process. I was unsure of what this new theory would be, but I became persuaded of two things: (1) that I could not possibly commence any form of fieldwork without having some over-arching theory about the role of the police and suspect in the adversarial system of justice, and (2) that the key to building this theory lay in understanding something about the historical development of pre-trial procedure that had hitherto been overlooked by those who had studied the history of English criminal justice.

To this end I spent the first eighteen months burrowing extensively into the history of English criminal procedure, as well as reading anything I could find of a theoretical nature on the subject of 'fairness' in general, and procedural fairness in particular. This extensive reading (interspersed with writing draft papers on the nature of procedural fairness and the Marian preliminary inquiry of the mid-sixteenth century) was by no means wasted, and was to provide an invaluable part of the thesis that eventually emerged. Unsurprisingly, however, the 'grand theory' I had been seeking did not materialise.

This provided the first lesson of conducting empirical research, a lesson which is of particular relevance to those who wish to conduct qualitative research. The lesson is that empirical research, whilst it can and should take cognisance of general theories which have the potential to provide a framework within which the empirical work can be conceived, has to be grounded in the practicalities of that which is being studied. If my main interest was how criminal process was functioning at the police station, the key was to concentrate on the actors (police and suspects) within that location, and devise a project which would allow me to speak with and observe these actors. I could have avoided a great deal of the angst I endured before reaching this conclusion had I read Bottoms' observation that

> writers in the ethnographic tradition are generally speaking rather
> suspicious of theoretical generalizations. For them, the particular
> contexts of specific social situations are all-important, and they
> therefore tend sometimes to have difficulty in generalizing from these
> particulars. In so far as they do generalize, they have a strong preference
> for the inductive rather than the deductive approach to theory
> construction: that is to say, they prefer to build theory 'upwards' from
> an understanding of specific social situations, rather than formally
> testing hypotheses.[7]

Having said that, I could not simply walk into the police station and stand around without a fairly firm idea of what it was that I had come to observe and why. What was needed in terms of an empirical project was something that was practicable and deliverable within the time and resources at my disposal, but which would also make a contribution to the important debate about police powers. Having read the literature on procedural fairness, most of which had been North American in origin, I decided that there was a gap in the British writings on the criminal process in that, unlike their counterparts in the United States, British criminologists had paid little regard to whether suspects viewed police procedures as fair and just, and next to nothing was known about the criteria or framework utilised by suspects in making such evaluations. Accordingly, I decided that there was merit in carrying out an empirical study which would look at the suspect's perspective on police station procedures.

I wanted to find out how suspects evaluated the fairness of their treatment, and whether such evaluations of fairness were affected by the offence category, outcome of the case, the grant or withholding of police bail, and the type of police officers (uniformed or specialist) who were in charge of the case. In addition, and equally as important, I wanted to discover how suspects evaluated the fairness or otherwise of specific aspects of the process (arrest, confinement, interrogation and general interaction with the police whilst at the police station), and what impact these specific evaluations had on overall evaluations of fairness. Finally, I set myself the more difficult task of seeing if I could discover whether, and the extent to which, evaluations of fairness were influenced by ethnicity, previous experiences of policing, and general attitudes towards policing.

In broad terms, I wanted the outcome of the research to be that of giving a 'voice' to suspects. I appreciated that this was only going to work if I won over the trust of the interviewees, and persuaded them to speak to me openly and in detail. Accordingly, formulating the questions and deciding how and where suspects were going to be interviewed was of critical importance. In terms of formulating the questions, good qualitative research requires the use of a semi-structured interview format. An experienced criminologist has written that 'the success of this kind of research hinges on the personal qualities of the researcher, whose key tool is his or her imaginative insight'.[8] Whilst this is undoubtedly true, there are some fairly basic points which, if adhered to, will maximise the prospects of emerging from the interview with good results.

DECIDING WHEN AND WHERE TO INTERVIEW

Although much has been written about gaining access in order to carry out research, one of the matters that I would emphasise is that gaining access is not a one-off event. Although I had been given access to the police station, this was of little help to me when I approached individuals to ask whether they would be willing to participate in my research. Indeed, the fact that I was based at the police station, and that many of the suspects had seen me in the custody block (sometimes conversing with police officers in the custody block), was a positive hindrance to persuading suspects to talk to me. The researcher has to be prepared to negotiate access on a case-by-case basis, weighing up each individual, and judging what is and is not likely to persuade him or her to co-operate.

I had based myself at the police station, and approached suspects as soon as the police had made a decision on disposal (that is, when they had been charged, refused charge or bailed for further inquiries). Getting interviewees relaxed is obviously very important if they are going to talk in detail and at length about themselves to someone who is a complete stranger. Accordingly, I gave great care to choosing the venue for holding the interviews. I wanted to get interviewees out of the pressured atmosphere of the custody block, wanted them to appreciate that their detention was over, and wanted them to know that they were free to leave at any time. I had persuaded the police at both research sites to provide me with a small interview room, and had worked hard to ensure that this room was not one of the rooms used to interrogate suspects. The room I chose was based fairly close to the exit of the police station and was one used to take witness statements from members of the public. This meant that when I began the interview by informing them that it was totally up to them whether they wished to spend time talking to me, and that they were free to get up and leave any time they chose, it was an assurance and a promise that received credibility from the physical surroundings.

Clearly, this approach was not possible with those suspects who were remanded in custody, and they were interviewed in the police cells. However, I soon learnt that those remanded in custody relished the opportunity to talk to someone, for the simple reason that it provided a means of passing the time. Indeed, the research taught me two related lessons: firstly, the probability of persuading someone to participate in the research decreases as the event or events in question recede in time and, secondly, if given the chance to interview someone on the spot, it is best to grab the opportunity with both hands. I had originally planned to persuade the police to provide me with the names and addresses of those who had been processed at the police station, so that I could write to them to ask whether they would participate in the research. The police were unable to provide such information for fear of breaching data protection legislation, and this was probably just as well because the chances of people responding favourably to a letter and then being available were slim.

This was brought home to me by the fact that not one of those who said that they could not stay behind to be interviewed at the police station but promised to contact me to be interviewed later in fact did so. Although I managed to persuade some to give me their name and contact details, I found that trying to locate them to arrange an interview was extremely time-consuming. Many of them showed little interest when I did manage to contact them, others arranged a time and place but failed to show up, and some of the home visits I carried out were unproductive as the interviews were constantly interrupted by dreary domesticity in the form of telephone calls, people at the door, crying children and over-enthusiastic dogs.

QUALITATIVE INTERVIEWING

The key to ethnographic research is a desire to understand the referential framework used by those being studied. Accordingly, the questions must allow the interviewee to talk about himself (or herself) in his own words, and at his own speed. Although I had an organised list of issues that I wanted to cover, I learnt early on that the best way to get detailed responses was to be flexible with the order of questions, and not to rush the pace of the interview.

Every effort was made to establish an informal, relaxed and conversational atmosphere. The one matter which initially detracted from this more than any other was the production of the tape recorder. This was probably because the tape-recorded police interrogation was the centre-piece, and probably the most stressful part, of the entire ordeal for those who had been detained at the police station, and the last thing they wanted was to face another tape recorder. I learnt early on that the threat posed by the tape-recorder was neutralised if I kept it in my pocket or briefcase until the individual had agreed to take part in the interview. It is much more difficult to withdraw consent than to withhold it. Also, having produced the tape recorder I always took care to explain that tape recording was of benefit to the interviewee because it ensured that his story was recorded accurately in his words. Finally, suspects were told that recording the interview was optional – if they felt uncomfortable with the tape recorder they could always turn it off, and I would accompany this with the gesture of pushing the tape recorder across the table and explaining to the interviewee that the machine was theirs for so long as the interview lasted and they could turn it off at any point.

The interview format was designed so that suspects were given the opportunity to talk about specific matters before they were questioned about general matters. So, for example, I wanted to discover individuals' attitudes towards the police, and about policing and the law in general. This was because I wanted to know whether evaluations of fairness were conditioned by previous dealings, and whether those previous dealings had forged a mind-set towards the police (positive or negative). However, I left these general questions towards the end, because they required a discursive approach and this was more likely to develop as the interview progressed and the interviewee became accustomed both to me and the process of being interviewed. Initial questions are best restricted to those which are unimportant but sociable ('So how long have you been here?'; 'What time did they bring you in?'; 'How're you going to get home?'; 'So are you from Grimeston?').

Suspects were asked about all aspects of their experience, from arrest until charge, and were encouraged to talk in detail. I always adopted a supportive attitude when suspects recounted incidents in which they thought they had been unfairly treated, because I did not want to give the impression that they were not being believed. Any such impression would have been fatal to establishing a rapport: my aim throughout was to provide a supportive, easy-conversational atmosphere but without in any way seeking to lead or prompt individuals. Suspects were promised anonymity, and were told in clear terms that what they told me could not affect the way in which their case would subsequently be handled. I explained that I had no influence over the police, and that my only connection with the police was that they had agreed to allow me to position myself in the police station. I also emphasised that I was not a lawyer, and could not help them by offering legal advice.

The overall aim was to make myself anonymous – I wanted to bring out the suspect's voice, and this was best done by ensuring that interviewees feared no harm from me, but neither did they expect any assistance. Questions were asked in an open way, providing a platform for interviewees to talk about their experiences. The role of the researcher is to listen and observe, or, even better, that of 'forcing yourself to be tuned into something that you then pick up as a witness – not as an interviewer, not as a listener, but as a witness to how they respond to what gets done to and around them'.[9]

NEGOTIATING ACCESS

It had been noted by a number of those who had conducted research into the police that the police station is closed, police territory, and that the secrecy of that which takes place inside the station is closely guarded by the police because it helps them achieve many of their objectives. My presence in the custody block of the police station occasioned surprise, and sometimes unease, on the part of police officers. Although most officers were quite friendly, the following comment from one of the custody sergeants made me ponder the extent to which I was really being accepted:

> Listen. As far as I'm concerned you're just another problem in my custody area. You're pretty privileged to be in here, looking at what's going on. I mean it's not many people who can just walk into a police station and look.

This underlines the point made above with regard to negotiating access on an individual basis in respect of each of the suspects who eventually formed part of the sample. Although the chief superintendents of both police stations had sanctioned my presence in the custody block, custody sergeants were no doubt simply informed of this decision rather than having an input into it, and I have no doubt that uniformed and Crime Investigation Department (CID) officers at the stations had no idea who I was until I introduced myself or they asked the custody sergeant who I was and what I was doing there. Having got myself through the front door, I still had the task of creating a comfortable relationship with the police ahead of me. As Reiner has noted, '[i]n general the very fact of having official approval for the research can be a difficulty when it comes to being trusted by the research subjects themselves, who may regard the researcher with suspicion as a tool of management'.[10]

Given the difficulties others have described in gaining formal access to the police station, one of the most surprising aspects of my research was that my decision to position myself in the police station was taken almost casually, and came about at the suggestion of the police themselves. It has been observed that 'No matter how carefully one plans in advance, the research is designed in the course of its execution. The finished monograph is the result of hundreds of decisions, large and small, made whilst the research is underway.'[11] This decision to position myself at the police station was a 'large' one, which, as I shall go onto explain, had a profound impact on the nature of the thesis that emerged as the final product of the research.

I had no previous relationships with or contacts within the police force, the study was not officially backed (that is, it was not a government sponsored study) and I had no track record as a researcher. Luckily, my supervisor was a renowned criminologist, had contacts within the police force, and had previously carried out Home Office funded research. He organised and accompanied me to a meeting with the Assistant Chief Constable, where it was explained that my interest lay in how suspects viewed the fairness of their treatment. The police were rather bemused by this as a research concept, arguing that anyone arrested and taken to the police station is unlikely to have anything good to say about the police. We explained that they may be pleasantly surprised, and, furthermore, the research may identify causes of perceived unfairness together with easy and practicable methods by which those causes could be addressed. I have no idea whether they were persuaded by this argument, but the fact that my focus was not on the police themselves probably meant that I was not seen as a threat.

This meeting was a critical part of the research process, but as a young, inexperienced and somewhat over-enthusiastic student I completely failed to appreciate its importance at the time. I simply assumed that the police would assist me. The whole episode demonstrates the importance of having the backing and know-how of someone experienced in the matter of negotiating access. My supervisor ensured that the research was packaged and sold as a project which posed no threat to the police and could in fact be of benefit to them.

The initial conception of the project was to restrict myself to carrying out a semi-structured interview with those who had been arrested and detained at the police station. Accordingly, the only assistance I wanted from the police was to allow me to look through their custody logs so that I could identify the names and addresses of a representative sample of suspects who had gone through the police station process over the last six months. The plan was to then write to these individuals, and arrange to interview them outside the police station (either at their homes, in prison, or at my college). However, as already explained, the police were concerned that this could put them in breach of the data protection legislation, and they suggested that the easiest way to pick up a sample of suspects was for me to come to the police station, position myself in the custody block, and approach suspects once the police had concluded their interrogation and made a decision with regard to outcome.

Given that I had been allowed access to the police station on the basis that I was not there to study the police, but merely to approach suspects as they were being released from the station or as they were waiting in the police cells having been remanded in custody, the issue of protecting the confidentiality of the police force or individual officers was not, as far as I can recall, discussed at all. However, disguising the name of the force and ensuring that no police officers are individually identified is not going to compromise research output, and is done as a matter of course. More important, however, is the issue of editorial control. This was not discussed with the police, and, with the benefit of hindsight, I wish it had been. This would have avoided a rather unpleasant spat with the police when the monograph came to be published. As a matter of courtesy, I supplied the police with a draft so that they would have the opportunity to comment, and so that I could correct any obvious errors or legitimate concerns they may have had. I received a letter from the police, in which they criticised what they saw as a lack of balance in the reporting, and refused permission for the book to be published. I wrote a reply in which I politely pointed out that a right to veto publication had not been agreed as the price for access.

THE DYNAMIC NATURE OF RESEARCH

Before embarking on the task of interviewing suspects, I arranged to visit both police stations in order to familiarise myself with their layout and to observe the procedures utilised by the police to process suspects. The police had not laid down any time limits on my stay at the police stations, and accordingly I decided that I would take matters at a fairly leisurely pace and try and see as much as possible about how the procedure worked before I began approaching suspects. Once I began to approach suspects for the purpose of administering the semi-structured interview I had devised, it dawned on me that compiling a reasonable sample was going to take a lot longer than I had envisaged. The fact was that since I had no idea as to when someone would be arrested or released, and no idea as to whether they would agree to be interviewed, I had to spend very long hours, during both day and night, simply waiting in custody areas and station canteens. In total, I observed in excess of 144 eight-hour shifts.

Despite my distinct lack of interest in fieldwork manuals, I was aware from reading the criminological literature that one of the concerns that fieldworkers have is that their presence may affect the behaviour of those who are being observed (the so-called 'researcher effect'). Accordingly, I decided that I would try to blend into the background, being as unobtrusive as possible, so that with a bit of luck the police would forget that I was actually there. The difficulty with this strategy was that I quickly became bored: my natural tendency was to socialise, chat and pass the time of day with anyone that was available (the custody sergeant; his assistants who had the task of taking and fetching 'prisoners' from the cells; investigating officers who came into the custody block; social workers; solicitors; doctors, even (or especially) the canteen staff who brought down refreshments).

My overall assessment is that this certainly did no harm, and probably worked to ensure that the police became comfortable in my presence, viewing me as a 'friendly sort'. However, I suspect that I was assisted in this regard by the fact that I took every opportunity to explain to anyone that asked (and even those who did not) that I was there merely to talk to suspects. In fact, in the eyes of the police the very nature of my interest (attempting to find out whether suspects viewed the procedures as fair) confirmed my rather naïve and other-worldly student status, and this also contributed to my not being seen as a threat. After some time, I decided that there was no harm in talking to officers about matters that were 'controversial', provided I did so in a manner that showed I was not dogmatic, but someone who was genuinely interested in how the police went about doing their job, the difficulties they encountered and what their views were about the criminal justice system in general. The aim was to always ask questions, rather than proffer strong opinions of my own. If I voiced disagreement (a pathological trait that I find difficult to repress), I did so in a mild way, stressing uncertainty and surprise ('Well, I'm not so sure about that'; 'Really? I am surprised by that'; 'Come on, that can't always be the case, can it?') So, for example, although I was beginning to form my own views about the reasons why virtually all suspects were interrogated, I would probe the matter in the following way:

Tell me, why is it that you interview, even when, on your admission,
there is enough evidence to get a conviction? I mean sometimes the case
is clear cut, like a shop-lifting case where you've more or less got the man
doing it on video, and you still interview. Why is that? And what do you
look for in an interview? How do you go about structuring the interview?

As the research progressed, I became increasingly interested in every aspect of what was taking place before me in the custody block. It was a unique opportunity to view in detail (and spend many hours thinking about) the nature of interaction between police and suspects. I became interested in the routines of the custody block, how police and suspects spoke to each other, their body language relative to each other, the terminology used by the police to describe suspects and their own practices, what was expected of suspects and how this was communicated to them, and what the police said to me about suspects and about the nature of policing in general, and I began to draw connections between what suspects were telling me in the semi-structured interviews and what I was observing in the custody block.

Initially, I did not realise the sociological importance of what I was observing. I failed to keep a log-book, and did not note down what I saw or my thoughts on it. Many of the interesting conversations that I had with solicitors, doctors and social workers simply did not get recorded. There were many more conversations with police officers that I could and should have recorded. However, fortunately, a few weeks into the research I decided that I would, during the quieter moments, sit and write down, as fully as possible, what people were saying to me and what I was seeing. Sometimes the importance of it would emerge only once I had gone back from the station and was reading back over my notes, and in other cases I only saw the significance when I came to think about the fieldwork as a whole at the writing-up stage.

In some situations ethical issues may arise about whether what one has been told in confidence ought to form part of the data that is eventually recorded and reported. In my study, for example, the police were clearly under the impression that it was not they but suspects who were the focus of the study. I had not been given access on the understanding that I was there to observe and report what I saw in the custody block, and those officers who engaged in conversation with me probably assumed that what they were saying would not be recorded or used as part of the research study. However, I had no qualms about using the data in the manner that I did. As with suspects, I had made no promises other than that of respecting anonymity. What assumptions others made was a matter for them, and I did not consider it part of my role as researcher to correct assumptions which other people may or may not have made. It is, however, advisable to give careful thought to what assurances and promises are going to be provided at the outset. In common with most, if not all, other social contexts, if promises are made or assurances given, the researcher will be under an ethical (and in some cases legal) obligation to respect them.

Researchers have in the past often noted the tension that fieldworkers experience between doing 'closeness' and 'distance', between immersing themselves amongst those who are being studied and remaining sufficiently detached to be able to analyse and explain that which is being observed and heard.[12] This for me did not pose as much of a difficulty as it may have done had I been studying only suspects or only the police: my long periods of interaction with the police in the custody block, and hearing their views of what was happening, were counterbalanced by regularly spending thirty to forty-five minutes with one or more suspects in any given shift who had their own perspective on what the police and police station procedures were about. Nonetheless, the astute fieldworker is well advised to constantly remind him- or herself never to take anything at face value, to suspend judgment rather than to abandon it, and to reflect, more than once, on everything seen and heard. I found that reading through my field notes and thinking about them at the end of each shift was a good way of piecing together an overall picture of what I was observing and hearing. It would have been all too easy to view police station procedures as 'unproblematic'; to form the view, as I wrote in the study,

> that interaction at the station is no different from that which takes place between citizens and state officials in any other type of state building, such as the local council offices or the out-patient department of a hospital. There is no apparent antagonism between suspects and the police: the police are polite even if somewhat formal and stern, and suspects do not appear to resist the routine.

However, a close, critical and lengthy period of observation revealed a very different perspective on the action. In my view, the project succeeded in unearthing something of interest because I was interested in recording the minutiae of everything that took place, and seeing whether everyday occurrences, phrases and views, when looked at as a whole, revealed something that was worthy of sociological note. The overall picture that I saw (and heard about) persuaded me that much of what took place both on the streets and inside the police station was not explicable by reference to Packer's 'Crime Control' or 'Due Process' models, but was an integral and essential aspect of a social disciplinary model of control.[13] As I wrote in the final study,

> The majority of suspects, when brought to the police station, surrender control over their actions to the police. They are told where to sit, when to stand and precisely where to stand, when to talk and when to remain silent . . . It is common knowledge amongst the policed that to resist police control entails the risk of being physically assaulted, threatened, insulted, refused bail, charged with a more serious offence or refused blankets, water, exercise or cigarettes. Not surprisingly, very few suspects seek to challenge the way in which the police treat them . . .

The power to arrest individuals and put them through the processes described above gives the police the weapon they require to exercise authority over the policed. Those who challenge the 'right' of the police to stop, search, question, threaten or be abusive can be carted off to the 'punishment block' and subjected to summary imprisonment. Regardless of what happens in court, the police will have shown the suspect what happens to those who do not accord them the deference which they expect. Indeed, in some cases the police have no intention of charging whatsoever, and in these cases detention at the station is the end of the sanctioning process.

The irony was that it was the unintended aspect of my research that yielded the most interesting data and probably made the most original contribution to the literature. My experience attests to the correctness of Bottoms's observation, set out above, that ethnographic research is about studying the particularities of social situations, and it is only once these are understood that the researcher ought to try and see whether that understanding can help formulate a general theory that can explain a larger process. So although I was keen to formulate a theory or model of the criminal process that would open up a fresh perspective on this area of study, taking it outside the tried and tested 'Crime Control' vs 'Due Process' analysis, the mistake I made was to assume that this new model or analytical framework was buried somewhere in the Bodleian. The reality was that the insight I sought was ingrained into the fine-texture of everyday happenings in the custody blocks of two provincial police stations.

OPTIMISING THE DATA

I have already noted that doing qualitative research is time-consuming and labour-intensive. Although its output (if done well) is held in high regard for its richness of detail, 'the price of its arguably greater validity is that it is usually based on only a limited number of sites and times, and the representativeness of these will always be problematic.'[14] My research had a number of limitations: it looked at only two police stations in one police force; I interviewed only eighty suspects; I was unable to interview women or juveniles; and the number of ethnic-minority suspects in my sample was too low to draw any meaningful conclusions about the impact of this characteristic on overall views and attitudes. Although I wanted to examine the extent to which suspects were being permitted to exercise the rights and protection granted by PACE, my ability to do so was hampered by the fact that I had no access to police custody records, no access to police interrogations, and had not been given permission to formally interview police officers.

However, in writing up the fieldwork it is possible (and I would say necessary) to place the findings in the context of all the available literature. So although I did not observe any interrogations, the final study included an extensive chapter on police interrogation in which I set out suspects' views and experiences of interrogation, but did so in the context of what other studies, drawn from the fields of sociology, psychology and law, had discovered about the subject, using a variety of research methodologies. This not only enriched the final report, but provided a means by which my conclusions could be tested. Similarly, although I spent the entirety of my time within the police station itself, the monograph includes an important chapter dealing with how policing takes place out on the streets. Once again, what suspects told me about their experiences of arrest and their dealings with the police in general was placed within the context of the wealth of data and writings on the subject of who gets policed and how.

CONCLUSION

It is probably true of most research methodologies that there will be slippage between the project as originally conceived and as finally executed and written up. Questionnaires frequently do not work as envisaged and have to be re-written; statistics that one thought would be readily available prove to be elusive or inconclusive; those who said they would co-operate fail to do so; and even books which promise one thing on the cover frequently contain something very different inside. Imagination and a willingness to adapt must be the stock in trade of all researchers.

The tendency for slippage, and the requirement for imagination and flexibility, is particularly marked in qualitative research. This is because qualitative research, or certainly ethnographic research, is inherently exploratory. Those who go out to explore should be prepared to cope with the unexpected when they find it, and, even more importantly, have the ability to recognise it. More than any other type of research, ethnography is heavily dependent on the social skills of the individual researcher. There must be a willingness, an ability and an interest in observing and listening, or as Goffman put it, the capability to transcend to the role of a witness to how others interpret, mould themselves to deal with, and influence their world.[15] That which may appear mundane, and that which those who are being studied view as normal, needs to carefully unpacked in order to gain sociological insight. Despite my best efforts to arm myself with a grand theory before entering the field, I was fortunate in that I ultimately approached the fieldwork with a narrowly conceived project, the essence of which forced me to listen to what suspects had to say.

FURTHER READING

A. Bottoms, 'The Relationship Between Theory and Research in Criminology' in R. D. King and E. Wincup (eds), *Doing Research on Crime and Justice* (Oxford: Oxford University Press, 2003).

R. M. Emerson and M. Pollner, 'Constructing Participant/Observation Relations', in M. R. Pogrebin (ed.), *Qualitative Approaches to Criminal Justice: Perspectives From the Field* (Thousand Oaks, CA: Sage, 2003).

J. Flood, 'Researching Barristers' Clerks', in R. Luckham (ed.), *Law and Social Enquiry: Case Studies of Research* (Uppsala: International Centre for Law in Development, 1981).

J. Foster, 'Two Stations: An Ethnographic Study of Policing in the Inner City', in D. Downes (ed.), *Crime and the City: Essays in Memory of John Barron Mays* (Hampshire: Macmillan, 1989).

R. Gold, 'Roles in Sociological Field Investigation', in G. McCall and J. Simmons (eds), *Issues in Participant Observation* (Reading, MA: Addison-Wesley, 1969).

P. Hillyard and J. Sim, 'The Political Economy of Socio-legal Research' in P. A. Thomas (ed.), *Socio-legal Studies* (Aldershot: Dartmouth, 1997).

D. Hobbs and T. May (eds), *Interpreting the Field: Accounts of Ethnography* (Oxford: Clarendon, 1993).

T. Jefferson and J. Shapland, 'Criminal Justice and the Production of Order and Control: Criminological Research in the UK in the 1980s', (1994) 34 *British Journal of Criminology* 265.

J. V. Maanen, 'Notes on the Production of Ethnographic Data in an American Police Agency', in R. Luckham (ed.), *Law and Social Enquiry: Case Studies of Research* (Uppsala: International Centre for Law in Development, 1981).

R. Wright and T. Bennett, 'Exploring the Offender's Perspective: Observing and Interviewing Criminals', in K. Kemp (ed.), *Measurement Issues in Criminology* (New York: Springer, 1990).

NOTES

1. R. Reiner, 'Police Research', in R. D. King and E. Wincup (eds), *Doing Research on Crime and Justice* (Oxford: Oxford University Press, 2000) 215.
2. Ibid. 225.
3. A. Bottoms, 'The Relationship Between Theory and Research in Criminology', in R. D. King and E. Wincup (eds), *Doing Research on Crime and Justice* (Oxford: Oxford University Press, 2000) 30.
4. S. Choongh, *Policing As Social Discipline* (Oxford: Oxford University Press, 1997).

5. H. Packer, *The Limits of the Criminal Sanction* (Stanford: Stanford University Press, 1968).
6. *Report of the Royal Commission on Criminal Procedure* (Cmnd. 8092) (London: HMSO, 1981).
7. Bottoms, see note 3 above, 30.
8. M. Maguire, 'Researching 'Street Criminals': A Neglected Art', in R. D. King and E. Wincup (eds), *Doing Research on Criminal Justice* (Oxford: Oxford University Press, 2000) 127.
9. E. Goffman, 'On Fieldwork' (1989) 18 *Journal of Contemporary Ethnography* 125.
10. Reiner, see note 1 above, 220–1.
11. H. Becker, 'Review of "Sociologists at Work: Essays on the Craft of Social Research"' (1965) 30 *American Sociological Review* 602–3.
12. See R. M. Emerson and M. Pollner, 'Constructing Participant/ Observation Relations', in M. R. Pogrebin (ed.), *Qualitative Approaches to Criminal Justice: Perspectives from the Field* (Thousand Oaks, CA: Sage, 2003) 28.
13. M. McConville and C. Mirsky 'Guilty plea courts: A social disciplinary model of criminal justice' , *Social Problems* (1995) (no. 2) 42: 216.
14. Reiner, see note 1 above, 219.
15. Goffman, see note 9 above.

CHAPTER 4

Comparative Legal Scholarship

Geoffrey Wilson

INTRODUCTION

One of the most remarkable features about the study of law, whether in the course of legal education or by way of legal scholarship, has been its intensely national orientation. Even comparative law has, more often than not, been seen as an extension of the study of national law. By looking overseas, by looking at other legal systems, it has been hoped to benefit the national legal system of the observer, offering suggestions for future developments, providing warnings of possible difficulties, giving an opportunity to stand back from one's own national system and look at it more critically, but not to remove it from first place on the agenda. Comparative studies have been largely justified in terms of the benefit they bring to the national legal system. In some areas it is easy to see why. In countries that have adopted codes or constitutions which originated in another system, it has been natural for legal scholars to look at the way that system has developed and has been developed in its original habitat. This applies particularly to those systems in which legal scholarship has a major part to play in the practical working of the system, where the courts pay great attention to doctrine and where it is legal scholars who are mainly responsible for the analysis and development of doctrine. And where doctrine plays a major role, the incentive to see the way it has developed elsewhere is reinforced by the notion that the development of doctrine is in some way scientific – that is, it does not depend on the accidents of time and place, though it is often not scientific in another equally important sense that doctrine is tested empirically to see what impact it has had in practice, how effective the law and the legal system have been in dealing with the problems facing it, not simply the technical doctrinal problems but the social and economic problems that lie behind them, or to see what other factors have played a part in deciding outcomes.

But this looking at other systems for the benefit of one's own is not confined to doctrinal systems. It is something which happens even among common law countries, where one finds cases being cited in courts from other common law jurisdictions and where legal scholars show a natural interest in developments in their areas of expertise in other common law jurisdictions. And it has been a particular feature of law reform bodies such as the Law Commission in the United Kingdom that they have been ready to look at the work done by their counterparts in other common law countries.

In this respect the study of comparative law has been both national and practical. Its purpose has been to make a practical contribution to the local national system. In other areas the comparative study of law has had a more international dimension. This has occurred whenever groups of scholars and practitioners from different systems have come together to try to work out a common solution to a common problem. And here the scope has often been wider because representatives from different families of legal systems have been involved. The facilitation of international trade has been a major stimulus for this kind of comparison and co-operation together with the desire to reduce the problems of jurisdiction and choice of law which result from transactions or events that have features which link them to more than one legal system, that is, problems of conflict of laws. The harmonisation of the laws of member states of the European Community (now the European Union) has been a conspicuous example of a regional enterprise of a similar kind. It has involved lawyers from different legal systems and different legal traditions coming together to design a common Community law which can be applied directly in the courts of member states. This has led in some cases to a more general interest in the legal systems of other member states even in areas not directly affected by membership of the Community, such as criminal procedure, and the role of the police and the prosecutor and the judges in the process, and the relative advantages and disadvantages of the adversarial and the inquisitorial systems. However, in general, it has to be admitted that the willingness of scholars to cross over the boundaries between the civil law systems and the common law has not been particularly large. Civil law scholars find it difficult to look beyond the structures of their conceptual schemes. Common law scholars are still often deterred by an inadequate knowledge of the relevant language. All suffer from pressures which arise from the shortage of time and the need to fulfil what are seen as more urgent and immediate goals and functions. And under schemes like the Erasmus and the Socrates programme run by the European Union more students have crossed the physical boundaries between systems than scholars.

However, even where comparative study has had this more international character, it is still largely justified by the direct practical effect it is intended to have. It is international because some areas of the practice of law are international, because some areas of law in practice have an international character. But there is another tradition which does not have its roots in the practice of law nor have as its main purpose a direct practical impact on the law of any particular legal system. It has its roots instead in legal scholarship. Of course, to say that something is rooted in legal scholarship does not necessarily change its character, scope or direction if the legal scholarship is itself only concerned with the practical aspects of a national legal system. This applies in particular to systems in which legal scholars play an important and direct role in the working of the system itself. But this is not the only form of scholarship. In the UK where there is no code to identify the appropriate subject-matter or boundaries of private law and no constitution to identify the appropriate foundations and limits of the study of public law, where it is the legislature and the judges rather than legal scholars who carry the main burden of clarifying and developing the law, where only part of the university degree counts towards a professional qualification and where it is the universities that set and mark their own examinations, there is a greater degree of freedom as to what may be included as the subject matter of legal study and how it should be organised. However, it has to be admitted that not all law schools take full advantage of this freedom and that students themselves often take a narrower view of what is relevant than their teachers might like. Even where the students are given a choice, they often feel a pressure to take what they think are practice-oriented subjects or, what is perhaps worse, to take an even shorter-term view and choose subjects which they think may help them get through their next series of professional examinations or which they think might appeal to future employers when they apply for their first jobs or for places in firms in which they can complete their required period of apprenticeship. It is often quite difficult to persuade them in the face of such pressures that the foundations they are laying for themselves at law school and the skills and perspectives and attitudes they are acquiring may in some respects have to last them a lifetime. These same skills, perspectives and attitudes many also have to contribute to the whole of their lives and not just the career part of them, at least under present conditions in which the opportunity for university study tends to occur only once in a lifetime, at the beginning of a student's career. Even where provision is made for refresher courses at later stages in a career, these tend to be updating on new technical aspects of the law and its practice, and not the kind of refreshment and reorientation that a university is there to provide at the beginning of their careers.

THE COLUMBIA EXPERIMENT: A COMPARATIVIST APPROACH

It remains one of the advantages of the non-doctrinal, more pragmatic common law legal scholarship that even where the emphasis continues to be put on those aspects of legal study which are seen to be related to legal practice, there may be more opportunity for changing its scope and orientation, for redrawing its internal boundaries, for injecting a greater sense of social and economic reality into it. A good example is the so-called Columbia experiment that took place at the Law School of Columbia University in New York in the 1920s. It was centred on a revision of the curriculum. It had for some time been a criticism of the teaching of law in the United States that, in keeping with the Langdell method of teaching law, too much emphasis had been placed on the analysis of the judgments of appeal courts as the hard core of a lawyer's education. One of the aims of the new proposals at Columbia was to emphasise the importance of other legal materials such as statutes. More important, however, was the attempt to reorganise the curriculum on what might be called functional lines and to add non-legal materials which were seen as relevant to the study of the problems with which law and the legal system had to deal and to give the problems themselves greater prominence.

The whole experiment is well described by Currie in an article in the *Journal of Legal Education*.[1] 'The first difference . . . consisted in the organisation of materials in terms of social and economic problems rather than legal doctrine'. Dean Stone in his report on the programme in 1923 spoke of so 'rearranging and organising the subjects of law school study as to make more apparent the relationship of the various technical devices of the law to the particular social and economic function with which they were concerned.' Secondly, the proposals 'proceeded on the assumption that certain non-legal materials were directly and pointedly relevant'. Thirdly, 'courses utilised statutory materials to an extent which was unusual'. Each of these features, he added, 'emphasised the role of creative reason, as opposed to deduction from a priori principles in the solution of social and legal problems'.

It could be said that in many respects the actual experiment was a failure. The group of scholars who had initiated it moved on to other institutions. And there were flaws in the programme which not only caused difficulties at the time but also continued to cause difficulties when similar experiments were undertaken in the 1960s. The most important of these was the emphasis when looking at non-legal materials on the social sciences. This emphasis proved misplaced for a number of reasons. In the first place it underestimated the degree of expertise needed to take full advantage of their insights, let alone to enable lawyers to undertake social scientific work themselves. Secondly, it exaggerated what they could deliver in terms of useful insights. This was particularly true of empirical research which for many law professors proved a distraction from their main interests and also often trivial or of temporary importance in its results. Thirdly, for many it was the social theory that proved more attractive and then often to the point where it became itself an autonomous subject of study which they and others found it difficult to link back to the mainstream studies of law which it was intended to illuminate. Instead of contributing to a reorientation of legal studies as a whole, it tended to become in its turn the province of specialists. And finally the identification of the social sciences as the appropriate other disciplines to look at had the effect of downplaying the contributions that other disciplines, in particular in the fields of the arts and humanities, could play in any revision of the scope and orientation of legal education and legal scholarship.

Whatever one's final judgment of the experiment as a whole or of the whole Legal Realist movement in the United States, of which it was a small and early part, it can still stand as an inspiration for those who are willing to be inspired by it and it still has lessons for the comparative study of law. There is much to be said even at the national level for a functional study of law that places the emphasis not on doctrine and the methods of elaborating and applying it, but on the purposes which the law and the legal system are designed to serve. There is a strong argument to be made for the study of law not as an abstract phenomenon or as an unreflective method of training for obtaining a living but as a means of dealing with major problems facing individuals and society and making plain the links between law and real life. But putting the major social and economic problems facing individuals and society as the principal concerns, with law being seen as one of the instruments designed for their solution or amelioration, involves a number of changes of attitude. Not only may the legal means of dealing with them cut across the traditional internal classifications of the law such as public and private, civil, criminal and administrative, but the scope of legal study will be expanded in a number of directions. It will include, for example, a closer attention to the nature of these problems – not in the first place other disciplines, which is one of the mistakes made by those who call for an interdisciplinary approach to the study of law, but the problems themselves, and the issues they raise as a matter of fact. For lawyers to be interested, concerned and knowledgeable about social, economic and political matters does not mean that they must become experts in other disciplines but, at least in the first instance, that they should develop a broader notion of what is relevant to their own. Taking the problems as the main focus of interest means that it is not the law of housing or the environment or family life that is the starting point, but it is the problems associated with the provision of housing in general and obtaining a roof over one's head in a particular case, the problems of the protection of the environment or the consumer or the employee, the problems of family life, that are seen as central, with the role of the law in dealing with them in general as well as in particular cases following on. In this way law students and legal scholars are being invited to become more learned and to acquire a greater expertise about these problems in a systematic and structured way. They are, to put it another way, being invited to pay more attention to the variety of contexts in which the law is used and which may affect its effectiveness. This is in contrast to traditional approaches to the study of law which concentrate on the current legal answers to problems that are often presented as purely legal problems with no clear or systematic connection with the larger problems in society with which they are intended to deal. A functional approach will include reference not only to the legal means of dealing with problems and the question of which of those legal means and in what combination will be the most effective, but it will also raise the question of what non-legal means may also be helpful and how best they can be combined with or be supplemented by or supplement any legal means adopted. It will also clearly take the study of law beyond the formal substantive and procedural law to consider other aspects of the legal system as a whole which may affect outcomes in particular cases and its general impact on the life of the community. This includes the institutional structures, the recruitment; training, conditions of work, monitoring, promotion and disciplining of judges and members of the other legal professions; the accessibility – physical, financial and psychological – and quality of legal advice and representation; public attitudes to the law; and the use of law, and the effectiveness of different legal and alternative means in achieving desired results.

Illuminating as this approach to the study of law may be even at the national level, it is probably even more useful when it comes to the comparative study of law because it provides a far more general basis for comparative study than any comparative study which begins with a comparison of doctrine. Many of the basic problems with which different countries and different legal systems have to deal are the same or similar, and often more similar than the relevant legal doctrines. The problems therefore provide a common basis of comparison. And in any event the differences between the law and legal systems of different countries are not simply a question of differences of doctrine. They are often far more fundamental and complicated and may have their roots deep in the legal system as a whole and indeed in the society as a whole. Looking, for example, at the English law of negligence, would give a very incomplete view of the ways in which personal injuries at work are dealt with in the UK, just as looking at the law of contract would give only a partial view of consumer protection. Looking at the ways different systems deal with similar social and economic problems is much more likely to expose their basic characteristics and the real similarities and differences between them. Accounting for those differences and trying to understand what makes one or another means more or less effective in particular contexts is one of the more interesting and rewarding aspects of the comparative study of law – it is interesting and rewarding for its own sake and not for the immediate impact it may have on one's own legal system, though it remains an important aim of the study of other systems to add to the understanding of one's own. Anyone who has studied another legal system is immediately aware that both in principle and practice it is deeply affected, and rightly affected, by non-legal factors, and this is true of both private and public law. In fact, it is even more obvious in relation to public law where the same formal structures can work in very different ways in very different circumstances.

Although modern scholars have been critical of what has often been regarded as the excessively romantic and nationalistic concept of the Volksgeist, put forward by Savigny as part of his resistance to what he argued was a premature codification of German law, it contains, if not a grain of truth, a word of warning. Not only are legal systems affected by the context in which they work; they probably have to be if they are to be successful and if they are to be properly integrated into other patterns of social behaviour and to win the support and commitment that all systems of law need if they are to be effective. One sometimes forgets that lawyers looking at their own systems can often rely on a general knowledge both of what the general problems facing it are and the way in which non-legal factors may affect any attempt to use law to deal with them, simply from being familiar with the social and economic context in which they have been brought up. Foreign legal scholars looking at the same legal system and society will usually not have this advantage and must be prepared to undertake a more systematic study of these factors which may seem so obvious to a local lawyer that he may – mistakenly from a comparative lawyer's point of view – take them for granted. And it is important when doing so that he keeps an open mind as to what may be relevant.

There may be different ways of identifying the problems which will provide a foundation of comparisons of this kind. One relatively simple way is to start with the problems that face every individual in society and then generalise them so that they are seen as problems facing societies as a whole. One should not be afraid, on the grounds that it may appear too unscientific, of addressing directly the subjects which self-evidently can be seen to be of major concern to individuals, such as how to get a roof over one's head, conditions at work, protection from unscrupulous producers, employers, neighbours and public bodies, and asking what contribution the law makes to their solution. In this way topics emerge such as education, the family, employment, housing, town planning and the environment, healthcare, consumer protection, and the organisation of business and commercial activity which includes the forms of business organisation and the methods by which they conduct their business, as well as problems relating to security and credit, which leads on to problems of monopoly and competition and world trade. Public law concerns would be represented by the whole question of constitutionalism, and would include political organisation and political rights. The maintenance of law and order will include questions about the role, recruitment, training, management and discipline as well as the formal powers of the police and the armed forces. Understanding doctrine for its own sake – and this includes what is called black-letter law in common law systems as well as the conceptual forms of other systems – without regard to the problems of individuals and society to whose solution it is intended to make a contribution, may on the face of it appear more scholarly and scientific and can certainly be expressed in a more scholarly and scientific form. However, but it may be achieved at too heavy a price if it either makes too many assumptions about the effectiveness of the translation of doctrine into practice or leaves the major responsibility of dealing with these problems to non-lawyers.

Not everyone, and indeed not every tradition of legal scholarship, will find it easy to look at things in this way. Those legal scholars who work in systems rooted in doctrine, in particular scholarly doctrine, will not find it as easy to approach the study of law in this way as those who work in more pragmatic and less highly structured systems like those of the common law. Someone, for example, who believed that the traditional classifications and divisions of the law were in some way fundamental to the scientific study of law or that the existing specialisations among legal scholars were something more than the product of history or convenience, might find it difficult to accept proposals of the kind put forward in the Columbia experiment or anything resembling them. Because of the strength of the divisions within the law with which they are familiar, they might be tempted to banish more general approaches of this kind to a separate heading: legal theory, sociology of law, even legal history. There may, too, be some traditions of legal scholarship in which the study of law is seen as a discipline – not in the relaxed sense that it is the study of one of the subject matters into which the world of knowledge and understanding has been divided as a matter of tradition and convenience and which may vary from culture to culture, but as a discipline in the much more rigorous sense that it has a particular subject matter and methodology which enables a sharp line to be drawn between what is relevant and what is irrelevant to it and what is a legitimate and what is an illegitimate method of study within it. This rigour may be reinforced by the view that the study of law is a science which in some sense has a universal validity and of course it is particularly strong in countries in which there is such a close association between legal scholarship and the practice of law that the legal scholars feel the need to operate under the same constraints as lawyers and judges working in the legal system, both as regards subject-matter and methodology. Where views such as these are held, whatever scientific or scholarly value they may have, they can easily be reinforced in practice by pressures such as decisions as to what kind of work will count for promotion or what kind of work will be published in the learned journals, a phenomenon which itself is important in any comparative study of other legal systems.

But there is no reason why self-imposed inhibitions of this sort should prevail generally. From a common law perspective the preoccupation with doctrine is not the product of scientific necessity. It is a product of national culture and tradition and it cannot and should not survive the exposure to genuine comparative study. Doctrine, far from being autonomous, is a means to an end, and the differing emphasis on doctrine from one system and culture to another is a reflection of national difference and not scientific sophistication.

The generally more pragmatic approach of common law systems, for example, takes a far more relaxed view about the subdivisions of the law and the specialisations in them. New specialisations and combinations of specialisations constantly arise as circumstances change, and even vary according to individual preference. And of course, common law scholars are not tied to the texts or conceptual structures of particular documents, codes or constitutions, or the jurisdictions of particular courts or, because they play a subordinate role to the judges when it comes to the development of the law, to the subject-matter and methods of courts and legal practice. The absence of rigorous specialisation has an advantage when considering re-ordering the study of law on functional lines. It has another incidental advantage, again of particular importance when it comes to comparative study: It makes it easier to look at legal systems as a whole. Specialisation stands in the way of this attempt to get an overall view without prejudging the different roles that different parts play in different legal systems.

There may, too, be further advantages for a legal scholar from the common law tradition which are not simply a result of characteristic features of common law scholarship but which are rooted in characteristics of the common law approach itself. One is the emphasis it places on facts rather than concepts. Although common lawyers use concepts and categories as a necessary part of using rules, the concepts and categories have never been developed beyond what has been regarded as necessary to dispose of a particular case or class of case. English law in particular still bears the imprint of the fact that its original development was by way of separate writs and forms of action, often, as in the case of law and equity, in different courts. Even when the major differences between different procedures and different courts were removed in the nineteenth century, no attempt was made to conceptualise the whole system in the way that the draftsmen of the German Civil Code did for German private law, and implicitly for German law in general. At best it provided the opportunity for developing more general principles than had existed before but without doing away with a traditional reluctance to develop them beyond what was strictly necessary to deal with particular facts or sets of facts. English law is still much more fragmented into generalised factual situations and has never had the ambition to be comprehensive or complete. It does not treat its rules of law as part of an overall comprehensive conceptual scheme.

This emphasis on facts is reinforced by the heavy reliance of English law on precedents since precedent works by comparing the facts of cases. If the facts of cases are comparable, the same rules apply. And the facts are not merely the starting point. It is clear that they continue to exercise an influence right down to the final judgment. And one can see this if one looks at the importance English judges attach to the facts of a case in their judgments.[2] It is certainly arguable that the common lawyer's traditional concern with facts makes the transition from the facts of particular cases to the factual position of whole societies much less difficult than it would be to move from a concern with abstract concepts to general problems of a social or economic kind.

And there is another feature of the English legal system that may make the transition easier. In the absence of a written constitution and a constitutional court, the British constitution relies heavily on what are known as constitutional conventions, that is, political practices which have come to be recognised as constitutionally binding on the participants. It follows that public lawyers in the UK are bound to have regard to non-legal means of achieving goals if they are to make sense of the British constitution. In fact, they have to make the subject of their study constitutionalism and the ways in which it is achieved, which, once again, provides a more convenient basis of comparison world-wide than the text of any particular constitution or the legal doctrines associated with it, which are the normal subject-matter of a public lawyer's concerns in other systems. It also makes the transition from strictly legal means to non-legal means of dealing with problems less stressful than for scholars whose constitutional law is related to the jurisdiction of a particular court and the law applied in it.

Those engaged in the Columbia experiment, though imaginative, still had a practical aim: to increase and deepen the understanding of American law and its functions. Forty years earlier, in 1885, another American, Oliver Wendell Holmes, later a judge of the Supreme Court of the US, in a rhetorical passage in an address to lawyers took a quite different approach. His was not a practical proposal for increasing and deepening the understanding of law and the problems facing it. His purpose was to inspire in his audience a sense of excitement, intellectual excitement, and to present legal scholarship as part of wider network of scholarly activities. Extravagant as it may sound, this way of looking at things, too, still has a contribution to make when one is thinking about the comparative study of law since it presents legal scholarship not simply as the scholarly dimension of the practice of law but as part of the world of scholarship itself.

> 'All that life offers any man from which to start his thinking . . . is a fact.
> And if this universe is one universe, if it is so far thinkable that you can
> pass in reason from one part to another, it does not matter very much
> what that fact is. For every fact leads to every other . . . Only men do
> not yet see how, always. And your business as thinkers is to make

plainer the way from some thing to the whole of things; to show the rational connection between your fact and the frame of the universe. If your subject is law, the roads are plain to anthropology, the science of man, to political economy, the theory of legislation, ethics and thus by several paths to your final view of life. It would equally be true of any subject. To be master of any branch of knowledge, you must master those which lie next to it, and thus to know anything you must know all.'[3]

Two things stand out in this short passage. The first is the notion that all facts are in some way connected. The second, even more important, is that these connections are not always self-evident. They have to be sought out and thought out. Holmes speaks of the lawyer as a thinker and of the activity he is describing as thinking. But it is a special kind of thinking. It is not logical thinking. It is not even disciplined thinking. It is, in the first instance, imaginative thinking, inventing and formulating connections rather than discovering them and justifying them, not by the use of logic – either the deduction of particulars from first or basic concepts or the formulation of basic principles or concepts from a number of particulars in the way that scientists are often represented as doing – but by an appeal to something far more open-ended and even speculative: the freedom to make one's own way through the intellectual universe.

IMAGINATIVE COMPARATIVE LAW

Imagination is not a word that is commonly used in relation to legal studies. Traditionally more emphasis is placed on knowledge and understanding. And even when imagination is seen as a virtue of legal scholarship, it is far more likely to be the disciplined imagination that enables legal scholars to formulate new legal concepts and principles within the constraints of the local legal and scholarly tradition than an open-ended imagination that in principle knows no bounds.

Here, once again, the common law scholar may have some advantages. The quality of common law reasoning depends much more on its general persuasiveness than its ability to use and manipulate a limited number of concepts as logical stepping stones to a final conclusion. This is true even of the legal reasoning used by a judge to justify his judgment. It is even more true of legal argument by an advocate. Common lawyers arguing a case in court will often allow themselves even more freedom in trying to persuade the judge to accept and adopt their version of the facts and the law than judges allow themselves. In fact, leaving aside legislation, it is probably the stimulus to be inventive on behalf of their clients, especially at the appeal stage, which is one of the major motivating forces for change in the English legal system, rather than the scholarly article in a journal or the semi-authoritative statement of a legal scholar in a commentary. It is one of the advantages of the adversarial system that the whole legal system is constantly being presented not only with new factual situations, but also with suggestions of new ways of looking at things by lawyers keen to get their views across. These suggestions are then tested by lawyers on the opposing side, and finally are filtered through the judge's view as to what he or she can legitimately adopt as decisive within the framework of the law and legal system as a whole, and the present state of development of the relevant of law, taking particular account of existing precedents and the doctrine of precedent itself. And this dynamic in the system is fed by imagination. It is not of course an open-ended imagination but it would probably be more accurate to call it an informed imagination than one which is strictly disciplined.

This means that even a common law scholarship or a common law legal education tied to legal practice ought to find scope for encouraging the use of, and using, the imagination. For a common law education or scholarship that is not so tied, there is even more scope, for it does not even have to observe the limits of relevance and the methodology of the courts. Its scope for imagination knows no bounds.

Once again, however useful imagination may be at the national level, where the scope for it may vary from legal system to legal system and from one tradition of legal education and scholarship to another, the need for a wide-ranging imagination of this kind is even more relevant when it comes to comparative study and when one is searching for the keys that will unlock the secrets of the character and working of other legal systems for a particular audience.

There was a time when the energies of comparative legal scholars were appropriately taken up in the search for information. And this was slow and difficult work. But it is here that the information revolution will make a major difference. Much of the information, won with such difficulty in the past, will soon be available at the touch of a button, and the availability of aids to understanding will soon follow. The old problem will soon be reversed. Instead of a shortage of information, there will be a surfeit of information. And it is here that imagination will be needed to select from the mass of what is available that which is truly illuminating. Up until now the recording of information about other legal systems has been worthy of praise because of the difficulties associated with its acquisition. In the future it is the selection and use of the information that will become far more important, and this applies to the comparative lawyer attempting to explain his own system to others as well as to the foreign scholar seeking to understand another system. Individuals, groups, institutions and cultures will be judged not for their assiduity in collecting information but for the creative use that they make of it.

Whereas the disciplined imagination may be fed on strictly legal materials, especially those which embody the highest legal doctrinal scholarship or the highest quality judgments of the best judges in the land, the open-ended imagination knows no limits as to what will nourish it, and it is certainly not limited to what is formally designated as legal. Of course, in countries where law students and legal scholars are by tradition reconciled to a study of law and a legal scholarship which do not purport to offer the same kind of wide-ranging excitement that scholarship generally offers and which restrict the use of imagination to the imaginative subjects – literature, art and mathematics or the theoretical sciences – or in countries where scholarship itself is lost in a tradition of meticulous footnotes and a conceptual framework, there will be not so much scope for this unlimited range. But, once one accepts that the development of the imagination should be an important feature of legal education and legal scholarship alongside the acquisition of knowledge and the increase of understanding, the means of stimulating it can, in principle, be as wide-ranging as possible.

It is of course difficult to generalise about what will contribute to a more imaginative comparative law since the sources of imagination are both open-ended and unpredictable. But the gap between existing tradition and practice and a wider use of the imagination is easily illustrated. Anyone who has attended a law lecture or picked up a legal textbook must be struck by one distinguishing feature: the absence of the use of visual images. This must at least raise a question, since of all the innovations that have taken place over the past few decades the use of the visual image as a means of communication, as an aid to understanding and as a stimulus to the imagination has been one of the most spectacular. We are surrounded, and have in fact always been targeted to some extent, by images aimed at us by people who regard the visual image as an important way of influencing us either in the benign way of increasing our understanding or in the less benign way of attempting to influence us for their own purposes. Legal writing and legal communication have by contrast generally remained in a pre-visual stage. In the whole literature of the law it is still Wigmore's *A Panorama of the World's Legal Systems*[4] that stands out as one of the few comparative law books, indeed one of the few law books altogether, to emphasise the need for pictures.

Wigmore, who said he had come under the spell of comparative law while living in Japan, published his *A Panorama of the World's Legal Systems* in 1928. He claimed that it was 'perhaps the first attempt to apply in the field of comparative law the . . . pictorial method.' But his purpose was limited. In the first place his subject-matter was mostly historical. Secondly, his pictures were limited in scope. They were, he said, pictures of 'the edifices in which law and justice were dispensed (whether temples, palaces, tents, courthouses or city gates); the principal men of law (whether kings, priests, legislators, judges, jurists or advocates); and the chief types of legal record (whether codes, statutes, deeds, contracts, treatises or judicial decisions).' And he included not only photographs of records (those in the section on Japanese law include early deeds from the Imperial Museum at Nara) but paintings such as that by Titian of the Council of Trent, Benjamin Constant's painting of Justinian presiding over the compilation of the Digest, and Serra's fresco of Irnerius at Bologna, which as illustrations of the past probably did little to add to historical accuracy. But this was probably not his goal which was much more simply to see 'the dry history of law' being 'enlivened with pictures'. At the end of the day the book remains a curiosity. More striking than the pictures are some of the revelations of how ancient are some of the basic principles of modern legal systems. For example, Wigmore cites the edict of Harmhab:

> 'I have sailed and travelled throughout the entire land. I have sought out
> two judges perfect in speech, excellent in character, skilled in
> penetrating the innermost thoughts of men, and acquainted with the
> procedure of the palace and the laws of the court . . . I have furnished
> them with the official records and ordinances. I have instructed them in
> the ways of justice. I have said to them "You shall not take money from
> one party and decide without hearing the other . . . And I . . . have
> decreed . . . that the laws of Egypt may be bettered, and that suitors
> may not be oppressed."'[5]

There are already signs of a change in the relevance of the visual image and it is also a change from the Columbia experiment's preoccupation with the economic and the social. The topic of the cultural heritage and its preservation and the question of the right to retain or the duty to restore cultural artefacts or treasures which have a particular association with or special significance for a particular country have now appeared on the legal agenda. A reference to the cultural heritage is included in the European Union's Treaty of Maastricht. It is typical of the way in which both legal education and legal scholarship have developed in the past that once a subject gets on to the legal agenda and becomes the subject-matter of law and jurisdiction, it is not long before it gets on the agenda of legal education and scholarship. One will expect therefore to see an increase in pictorial representations at least in those books and articles which deal specifically with visual images, though whether this in turn may do something to legitimise the use of and concern about the visual image generally has yet to be seen.

This distinction between what is seen as a specialism and what is seen as something more generally important is, of course, a challenge that still faces the comparative study of law. Looking at law from a comparative point of view has made major strides since the beginning of the century. But in many places it still remains a specialism. It cannot yet be said that it has become part and parcel of the basic orientation of law students or legal scholars, let alone legal practitioners. National systems still dominate the agenda of most legal scholars and the curricula of most students of law not simply for practical reasons but as much because this remains for most people the definition of what legal education and legal scholarship are about. But law students and legal scholars deserve something better, and it remains a major task for comparative lawyers to show them the ways to get it. But it may need some imagination.

FURTHER READING

J. Bell, *Judiciaries within Europe: A Comparative Review* (Cambridge: Cambridge University Press, 2006).

D. Bradley, 'A Note on Comparative Family Law: Problems, Perspectives, Issues and Politics'(2005) *Oxford University Comparative Law Forum* 4 (available at: http://ouclf.iuscomp.org/articles/bradley2.shtml).

R. David and J. E. C. Brierley, *Major Legal Systems of the World Today: An Introduction to the Comparative Study of Law* (3rd edn) (London: Stevens, 1985).

P. de Cruz, *A Modern Approach to Comparative Law* (Deventer: Kluwer, 1993).

H. P. Glenn, *Legal Traditions of the World: Sustainable Diversity in Law* (2nd edn) (Oxford: Oxford University Press, 2004).

J. Gordley and A. T. von Mehren, *An Introduction to the Comparative Study of Private Law: Readings, Cases, Materials* (Cambridge: Cambridge University Press, 2006).

J. Hill, 'Comparative Law Reform and Legal Theory' (1999) 9 *Oxford Journal of Legal Studies* 101.

W. Kamba, 'Comparative Law: A Theoretical Framework' (1974) 23 *International and Comparative Law Quarterly* 485.

O. Kahn-Freund, 'On the Uses and Misuses of Comparative Law' (1974) 37 *Modern Law Review* 1.

C. van Laer, 'The Applicability of Comparative Concepts' (2002) 2 *The Electronic Journal of Comparative Law* 2.

B. S. Markesinis, *Foreign and Comparative Methodology: A Subject and A Thesis* (Oxford: Hart Publishing, 1997).

B. Markesinis, 'Comparative Law: A Subject in Search of an Audience' (1990) 53 *Modern Law Review* 1.

W. Menski, *Comparative Law in a Global Context: The Legal Systems of Asia and Africa* (2nd edn) (Cambridge: Cambridge University Press, 2006).

E. Orucu, *The Enigma of Comparative Law: Variations on a Theme for the Twenty-First Century* (Leiden: Martinus Nijhoff, 2004).

J. Reitz, 'How to Do Comparative Law?' (1998) 4 *American Journal of Comparative Law* 617.

A. Riles, 'Wigmore's Treasure Box: Comparative Law in the Era of Information' (1999) 40 *Harvard International Law Journal* 221.

G. Samuel, 'Comparative Law and Jurisprudence' (1998) 47 *International and Comparative Law Quarterly* 817.

I. Stewart, 'Critical Approaches in Comparative Law' (2002) *Oxford University Comparative Law Forum* 4 (available at: http://ouclf.iuscomp.org/articles/stewart.shtml).

J. Stone, 'The End to Be Served by Comparative Law' (1951) 25 *Tulane Law Review* 325.

S. C. Thaman, *Comparative Criminal Procedure: A Casebook Approach* (Durham, NC: Carolina Academic Press, 2002).

N. Witzleb, D. Martiny, U. Thoelke and T. Frericks, 'Comparative Law and the Internet' (1999) 3 *The Electronic Journal of Comparative Law* 2 (available at: http://www.ejcl.org/32/abs32-1.html).

K. Zweigert and H. Kotz, *An Introduction to Comparative Law* (3rd rev. edn) (Oxford: Clarendon Press, 1998).

NOTES

1. B. Currie, 'The Materials of Legal Education' (1955–56) 8 *Journal of Legal Education* 1.

2. Although it is perhaps an exceptional example from a not absolutely typical English judge, the following extract from a judgment of Lord Denning illustrates this in a striking way. 'It happened on April 19, 1964. It was bluebell time in Kent. Mr and Mrs Hinz had been married some ten years, and they had four children, all aged nine and under. The youngest was one. Mrs Hinz was a remarkable woman. In addition to her own four, she was foster-mother to four other children. To add to it, she was two months pregnant with her fifth child. On this day they drove out in a Bedford Dormobile van from Tonbridge to Canvey Island. They took all eight children with them. As they were coming back they turned into a lay-by at Thurnham to have a picnic tea. The husband, Mr Hinz, was at the back of the Dormobile making the tea. Mrs Hinz had taken Stephanie, her third child, aged three, across the road to pick bluebells on the opposite side. There came along a Jaguar car driven by Mr Berry, out of control. A tyre had burst. The Jaguar rushed into this lay-by and crashed into Mr Hinz and the children. Mr Hinz was frightfully injured and died a little later. Nearly all the children were hurt. Blood was streaming from their heads. Mrs Hinz, hearing the crash, turned round and saw the disaster. She ran

across the road and did all she could. Her husband was beyond recall. But the children recovered.' (*Hinz v Berry* [1970] 2 QB 40)

3. Oliver Wendell Holmes, *The Law* (1885), quoted by M. Lerner, *The Mind and Faith of Justice Holmes: His Speeches, Essays, Letters and Judicial Opinions* (New York: Modern Library, 1943).

4. J. H. Wigmore, *A Panorama of the World's Legal Systems, 3 Vols* (Washington, DC: Washington Law Book Company, 1928).

5. Ibid. 15, cp. his citation from the Jo-Yei Shikimoku of 1232 which sets out the oath to be taken by the members of the Supreme Council. 'In general . . . whenever questions of right or wrong are concerned, there shall be no regard for ties of relationship; there shall be no giving-in to likes or dislikes; but in whatever direction reason pushes and as the inmost thought of the mind leads, without regard for companions or fear of powerful houses, we shall speak out.' And the observance of the articles is reinforced by an oath, 'If even in a single instance we swerve from them either to bend or break them, may the gods Bonten, Taishaku, the four great Kings of the Sky, and all the gods great and little, celestial and terrestrial, of the sixty odd provinces of Nippon, and especially the two Gongen of Idzu and Hakone, Mishima, Daimyojin, Hachiman, Daibosatsu and Temman Dai Jizai Tenjin, punish us and all our tribe, connexions and belongings with the punishments of the gods and the punishment of the Buddhas' (Wigmore, 4 79). For more on the subject of the comparative study of past legal systems, see G. Wilson, 'Comparative Law and the Past' in T. Gross (ed.), *Legal Scholarship in International and Comparative Law* (New York: Peter Lang, 2003).

CHAPTER 5

Integrating Theory and Method in the Comparative Contextual Analysis of Trial Process

Mark Findlay and Ralph Henham

INTRODUCTION

In this chapter we employ comparative contextual analysis of the trial process[1] in order to reveal the crucial importance of theoretical foundations for socio-legal research. Comparative contextual analysis[2] is the methodology selected to contrast trial traditions, and in so doing translates compatible theoretical frameworks into research outcomes.

The paper begins by summarising some of the major theoretical challenges faced by comparative research into the criminal process and their influence on the theoretical framework chosen for analysis. Within this conceptualisation we then describe our approach to contextual modelling and explain how this may be utilised in comparative settings through the adoption of inductive and deductive methodologies. The chapter concludes with an illustration of the potential for comparative contextual analysis, suggesting how it can provide a unique and valuable approach to the integration of theory and method in socio-legal research.

THEORETICAL CHALLENGES

The fact that comparative contextual analysis requires an appreciation of the social reality of historical, social, political and economic variables impacting on the trial process means that it becomes necessary to deconstruct the ways in which criminal justice processes are conceptualised in respective jurisdictions. This involves a recognition that the normative significance of process may represent different philosophical interpretations of what constitutes epistemologically accepted empirical 'truths'. It also means that the moral validity of principles about punishment is seen as relatively contingent, as are the symbols and structures which manifest these.[3] As a consequence, the theoretical framework we advocate must be capable of elucidating both objective and subjective conceptions of process.[4] As Norrie suggests, this kind of theorising should emphasise the dialectic form of justice within different cultures by recognising that external or purely historical and structural accounts of process fail to account for human subjectivity and ambivalence about justice.[5]

Recognising the moral relativity of concepts such as 'justice' and 'fairness' requires a contextual appreciation of the subjectivity of trial participants'[6] experiences in terms of these measures. Such terms may, nevertheless, be justifiable according to particular 'objective' criteria. The deconstruction of participant experience so contextualised provides a phenomenological account of process and its ideological significance. It also enables us to identify the major dimensions of what might constitute comparable justice referents across jurisdictional boundaries, and provides linkage to process.[7]

There must, therefore, be a recognition that social theory is generally capable of conceptualising the socio-historical context and consequences but not the human subjectivity of moral action. This is highly significant in terms of its methodological implications for any analysis of the criminal trial process which should ideally be capable of providing mechanisms of 'description and explanation' of social phenomena that reflect internal/external (objective/subjective) experiences of social reality for trial participants and hence the basis for comparison.

We have argued[8] that Giddens's structuration theory[9] provides a reflexive theoretical conception that recognises the structural, organisational and interactional levels of process analysis as interconnected aspects of the same social practice, offering three levels of understanding depending on context (see Figure 5.1). Rather than drawing a conceptual distinction, these analytical levels are designed to reveal the multi-faceted context of social interaction as it is practised and sustained. They are, therefore, essential preconditions to understanding which necessarily precede the comparative analysis of social interaction in international sentencing. The key factor is the recognition that structuration theory provides a set of organising or interpretative constructs which allow us to identify elements and processes concerned in the recursive nature of the application of rules and resources by social actors.[10] Whilst our development of structuration theory implicitly recognises that structure is recursively reproduced through human agency, it does not preclude, as Vaughan suggests,[11] the objective existence of structure. We use structuration merely as an abstract theoretical framework which allows us to conceptualise how the criminal trial process is created recursively over time and space. The theory therefore suggests different levels or layers of meaning for understanding legal contexts comparatively which can be modelled at different levels of abstraction (from macro to micro).

Figure 5.1 Conceptualising the structuration of trial process

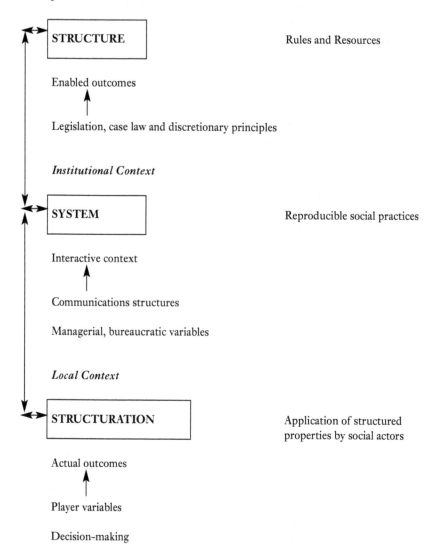

Jurisdictional Context

STRUCTURE   Rules and Resources

Enabled outcomes

Legislation, case law and discretionary principles

Institutional Context

SYSTEM   Reproducible social practices

Interactive context

Communications structures

Managerial, bureaucratic variables

Local Context

STRUCTURATION   Application of structured
                                         properties by social actors

Actual outcomes

Player variables

Decision-making

In utilising structuration as a sensitising perspective we acknowledge the possibility of objectivism in social relations by drawing an analytical distinction between the context and the situational circumstances of interaction. This makes it possible to understand the way in which different structures of trial process exist and are recursively created and patterned over time whilst also appreciating the ways in which their instantiation is actually determined in institutional practice through human agency. Consequently, for example, the patterning of sentencing principles and their existence as formal rules provides the structural context in which the situational reality of discretionary decision-making determines sentence outcomes. Further, the modelling and methodological dimensions of our analysis are sensitive to the different levels of meaning and understanding attributed to action and process by trial participants.

Consistent with Giddens's advice regarding the selective application of structuration theory as a sensitising device,[12] this interpretation does not try to account for the 'meaning' of action; rather, it postulates its use as a processual paradigm or sensitising construct[13] designed to elucidate the major dimensions of decision-making. In this connection processes of decision-making may be seen in context as a series of frames of action. As such, the context of trial process may be envisaged in terms of series of pathways of decision-making wherein each outcome depends upon understanding how and why relationships between trial participants are resolved at crucial sites for decision-making within the trial. Each such frame of action contributes to mould the trial process since each pathway is dependent upon influences that shape, drive and emanate from these relationships. Socio-historic accounts of the manufacture and development of process are dependent on the constituents of previous frames of action in as much as instantiation recursively contributes to our understanding of contextualised social action.

Thus, context[14] is three-dimensional and *dynamic* across time and space, whilst the relationship between structure and agency depends for its relative existence upon context from which it is never separate or autonomous. As such, the relativity of each frame of action is established through our ability to consider interaction within the context of the frame against past and present action outcomes. Hence, our analysis envisages that the various dimensions of decision-making, their contextualisation and comparison, in terms of a series of frames which comprise a moving picture: contextualised social action. Taking the example of rights, therefore, the reality of rights can be seen as dependent on their engagement with or translation into (or out of) social action. They can be envisaged as principles that require reflection against (and cannot be autonomous from) structure and action within context, and context in transition.

Particularly important in the present context is Giddens's[15] assertion that sociological descriptions are implicated in the task of mediating the frames of meaning within which actors orient their conduct. Structuration theory facilitates the adoption of methodologies which allow us to signify the objective/ subjective meaning of social action by conflating the theoretical and empirical imperatives dictated by epistemological controversies. In so doing the contextuality of *process* in terms of its objectivity (both conceptual and concrete) and the subjective account of that objectivity (in terms of its phenomenological content) are revealed.[16] The crucial point is that the relative realities of fact and value are merged in process.[17] Consequently, where the fact/value distinction is drawn in this research, we do so as Tamanaha suggests 'standing on the ground', in context and not proposing a perspective-free versus a perspective-bound contrast. It is argued that one cannot view the world beyond context (perspective), and that a fact/value distinction only has relevance within the researcher's actions in a real world, where values and facts are naturalistically conceived as functionally distinct aspects of experience. The distinction, therefore, is drawn in common-sense terms, within the action of the trial.

The criminal trial process is conceptualised within the theoretical framework provided by the theory of structuration at three interrelated levels of social reality: legal, organisational and interactive. As described, these levels constitute the components of a process model that envisages human agency as the *dynamic* variable which reproduces the social reality of trial process through structuration. This is a social reality that is shaped by the dimensions of fact/value dependent upon context. At the macro-level, structuration theory provides a higher-level theoretical formulation for understanding how process is created through human agency and the way in which the different levels of analysis are implicated in this dynamic. At the micro-level, such as the comparative victim participation study by Henham and Mannozzi[18] described later, these levels are examined in comparative context in relation to particular aspects of the trial process (in this case sentencing). This is achieved by focusing on specific decision sites which have relevance for the issue under investigation, looking at them as if they were literally a micro representation of structuration and examining those crucial aspects of human agency which operate within that particular context to produce sentence outcomes. For victim participation we are therefore looking for those factors that are relevant to understanding the way in which the three levels we have identified are actually implicated through the human decision-making that is structuration in creating the conditions that determine inclusivity or exclusivity for victims within the trial. This decision-making is discretionary, and influenced by contextual factors within and beyond the trial itself that will determine the direction and outcome of the process. Our analysis seeks to determine the meaning of what is happening in context:

- what are these different pathways of influence that feed into the decisions relating to victim inclusivity?
- how are they constituted and what is their significance for outcome?
- how are the three levels of analysis implicated in our understanding of this process?

In broader terms, we examine how and why value is added to fact and what this means for outcome in a micro-representation of structuration in action. Figure 5.2 purports to show how the three analytical levels of this model relate to one

Figure 5.2 Modelling the relationship between structuration and sentencing decisions

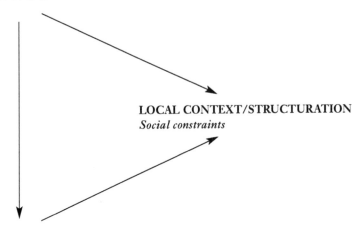

JURISDICTIONAL CONTEXT/STRUCTURE
Legal constraints

LOCAL CONTEXT/STRUCTURATION
Social constraints

INSTITUTIONAL CONTEXT/SYSTEM
Situational constraints

Notes: this sentencing model is a micro-representation of structuration adapted to show the predominant influences on sentence decisions within the framework for action suggested by structuration theory.

another by providing an overview of the sentence decision-making process as structuration.

There follows a more detailed description of the three interrelated aspects which comprise the social reality of trial process as conceptualised within the terms of structuration theory:

- Legal/Jurisdictional – the nature, function and discretionary choices presented by legal rules and principles. Substantive legal rights accorded to trial participants, legal procedure and relationships between legal form, policy and social control variables may be regarded as aspects of structural properties (rules and resources). Rules also include conventions, presumptions and discretion. 'Allocative resources' include material resources enabling an organisation and/or its human participants to function effectively, whilst 'authoritative resources' might include the status and hierarchical position of trial participants. Resources are linked to power by focusing on a person's transformative capacity, that is, their ability to effect change.

- Organisational/institutional – strategic rationales for the operation and function of the trial process may be envisaged as part of systems existing as regular reproducible social practices, namely as modes of social interaction where structural properties are implemented. This analytical level, therefore, encompasses information regarding communication structures that impact on the roles of significant players in the trial process and influence the outcome of courtroom interaction. Analytical links between symbolism, ideology and power may also be explored at this level.
- Interactive/local – the social reality of decision-making within the courtroom may be seen as forming part of the process of the application of structural properties by social actors through the mechanism of social institutions. This level is, therefore, concerned with *actual* decision-making processes in the courtroom and would reflect the fact that discretionary choices (the capability of social actors to act otherwise) determines the conditions of structuration, that is, the continuity or transformation of structures (rules and resources) and, therefore, the reproduction of systems. It is also important to note that discretionary power and the *locus* (jurisdictional setting) which determines the conditions of its exercise is patterned through the activities of trial participants who recursively create the meaning and social reality of discretion as both action and structure. It is the need to explain process involving different levels of analysis that demands a theoretical account of process capable of accommodating conceptual diversity. Thus, at the empirical level, the limiting factor which circumscribes our theoretical mission concerns the nature of trial decision-making. The interaction of these levels of analysis produced in our pilot methodology the particular understanding of pathways of influence. Jurisdictional constructs lead on to organisational process opportunities creating contexts for interaction through decision-making. The requirement to decide legal questions is followed by a means for decisions within comparative institutional frameworks which are contextualised by specific factors of decision-making and discretionary mechanisms. In this respect, the analysis (as with the decision-making being analysed) proceeds down identifiable decision pathways, formulated through pressures from players and institutional patterns, formulating a process with features and functions of influence.

To summarise, we use structuration theory as a sensitising perspective from which to view relationships between structure and agency which are relative depending on context. By envisaging 'action in context' in this way structuration enables fact and value to be observed as part of the same dynamic so that there is no need to maintain a sharp distinction between observations in context and normative judgments. In this way it is easy to 'add value' and meaning to observations in context. The application of context within structuration therefore becomes crucial to the reconciliation of the subjective and the objective, since values and facts are naturalistically conceived as distinct features of the research and the trial experience.

We argue that the concept of 'context' has a broader significance than 'culture' in comparative analysis. Context suggests a universal and unifying construct for conceptualising the wider social, cultural, political and economic determinants of trial process. Within context, legal culture constitutes a crucial component of trial praxis.[19] Our theoretical interpretation and methodology are grounded firmly in a belief that it is necessary to become familiar with the different cultures nominated for comparison in a contextual sense which identifies themes for comparison on the basis of similarity and difference *prior* to any comparative endeavour. In this respect we develop a platform for cultural comparison that recognises cultural integrity at the same time as allowing for comparison which entertains similarity and difference.

CONTEXTUAL MODELLING

Within this conceptual framework we elaborate the need for a contextual model as a heuristic device. This postulates specific ways in which we may proceed in order to comprehend the nature of process within different contexts by suggesting contrasting (yet complementary) ways of conceptualising trial decision-making. These paradigms may be based on existing theoretical positions which deal with different levels of abstraction implicit in process interaction. However, the model is neither theoretically, nor methodologically prescriptive. The testing of theoretical propositions and data generated from grounded theory methodologies collectively inform the refinement and development of the macro-theoretical position. Different methodologies required to fulfil the demands imposed by modelling reflect different ways of conceiving of the relationship between theory and the production of 'new' knowledge about the trial process. These methodologies are driven by the need to understand comparative context.[20] A contextual model is, therefore, in reality a *locus* for testing various (possibly competing) versions of what constitutes the process of trial decision-making.

In later writings[21] we have developed such a *contextual model* for the comparative contextual analysis of trial process which allows for consideration of particular aspects of different (possibly conflicting) theoretical positions to be identified within the explanatory framework provided by structuration theory. In particular, we have argued that the contextual model facilitates the integration of theoretical and methodological propositions derived from positivist, ethnographic and grounded theory approaches. The model focuses on the context of trial decision-making as a micro- representation of penality[22] (with its specific audiences, players, processes, institutions, power relations and symbolic structures), and lends itself to reconstruction at various analytical levels which are relevant from culture to culture, vertically or horizontally (from local to global), and holds good for analysis of the temporal contexts of discretionary decision-making.

In common with others,[23] we recognise that the reality of practice (or process) is central in shaping context; the meaning of facts is determined by an account of their significance for local actors; a common language and identity shape collective reality. However, whilst indicative of the reflexive nature of the relationship between ideology and praxis within specific local contexts, Bell's model for deconstructing legal culture[24] falls short of providing a heuristic tool for comparative purposes: a tool that would enable us to test the degree of congruence between the meanings attributed to criminal process by human agents across contexts at the global and local level (both horizontally and vertically). Our model of trial decision-making enables a comparison of 'meanings' (through narrative) as well as competing (and contrasting) processes of meaning creation (by looking at common pathways of influence).

Sentencing (as a consequence of trial decision-making) provides a focus for how these various trial 'pathways' converge to confirm or deny justice as measured against particular rights paradigms. Whilst the comparative contextual analysis of trial narrative is sufficient to provide speculations about the relationship between policy and legal process, broader interrogation of the social and cultural factors that influence discretionary decision-making is necessary to suggest its significance for process outcomes. For example, an important dimension of the rights paradigm for victim participation is concerned with the determinants of inclusivity/exclusivity within the trial context. Comparative contextual analysis enables us to focus on the form and reasons for influence depending on judge and court level; it facilitates our understanding of the forces that are at work in the relationship and how they relate (or work against) each other. In this way we can identify how different pathways of influence produce different configurations of fact/value whose practical effects are manifested in greater or lesser participation for victims in those aspects of the trial process that are relevant for victims and sentence.

The comparative contextual model proposes a conceptual distinction between the notion of *evaluators of context* and *evaluation in context* that is dependent on the nature of the theoretical (evaluative) paradigm chosen to explore the different contexts of discretionary decision-making. In short, the role of the contextual model is to ensure that possible sentencing outcomes are evaluated *in context and across contexts* in ways which remain sensitive to the social reality of process within and across different legal cultures.[25]

Figure 5.3 Inductive and deductive parallels

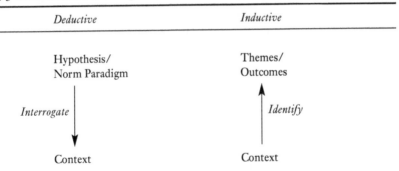

The twin components of the contextual modelling approach can be sum-marised as follows:

- *Evaluators of context* – these are theoretical propositions selected on the basis that they are likely to provide some conceptual insights that will contribute to our understanding of the particular social phenomenon chosen for analysis. The focus is on *process*, or, more particularly, the construction of process in comparative context.
- *Evaluation in context* – this refers to the *practice* of comparative contextual analysis, utilising those interpretative methodologies which have been dictated by the theoretical positions chosen on the basis of the problem posed.

Hence, *evaluators of context* may be regarded as consisting of 'accepted knowledge' which is tested against 'reality' and becomes modified by the 'emerging knowledge' produced through the recursive process of *evaluation in context*. The latter gradually allows us to modify (and/or confirm) accepted knowledge through theory verification, whilst the process of theory generation may suggest confirmation, integration and postulate new evaluators. Essentially, the model, initially at least (or at the formulation stage), must follow on from a deconstruction of context(s).[26]

Consequently, this notion of modelling and comparativism proposes that the incorporation of particular evaluators (that is, evaluation in context) should follow on from an examination of context and speculation as to which particular evaluative paradigms are relevant for understanding specific social interactions. The model is designed to facilitate the adoption of methodologies derived from paradigms based on theory verification (deductive) or developed through theory generation (inductive) processes (see Figure 5.3).[27]

The methodological imperatives modelled in Figure 5.3 suggest a pragmatic (yet principled) approach which permits the penetration of the internal aspects of fact/value within trial decision-making. For instance, by reducing decisions on penalty down to a consideration of the manner in which the judge's discretion is influenced by the harm to the victim and the mitigation of the accused's liability, what lies behind the negotiation of justice through sentencing should be more apparent. At the same time, the decision site model will show how these understandings enable us to appreciate the meaning of process in all its complexity.

In summary, the initial formulation of the model we propose for comparative contextual analysis derives from a deconstruction of context(s) against an application of insights from existing theory which are thought likely to have the potential to infuse the analysis with meaningful comparative conclusions.[28] Although the selection of theoretical postulates for modelling is necessarily predetermined, their subsequent verification and modification, and the ultimate content of the model, are, therefore, dependent on contextual analysis.

METHODOLOGY

The primary methodology for our comparative trial research involves the identification, description and analysis of communication structures and interactive process as revealed through the comparative contextual analysis of trial narrative.[29] Where necessary, narrative is supplemented by various ethnographic approaches, including direct observation (participant or otherwise), interviewing and expert contextual commentary.

Although narrative itself records dimensions of formal process, it does not permit us to understand how each player in the trial process subjectively interprets any aspect of that process. A narrative simply records the ways in which formal requirements are interpreted (acted upon) as external processes. We also acknowledge that the meaning or value of the trial narrative, as a record of what is said and done, may be distorted by researchers through interpretative methodologies.[30] This is not essential, however, if contextual analysis of trial narrative takes place prior to any comparative analysis. It may be argued, nevertheless, that the observer sees what the participants may take for granted, and may not question. The narrator's questions are also different so that, despite the reservations made below, it remains valid to present something *as an outsider to an outsider*. For instance, in discussing narrative as a source for analysis, Twining[31] highlights the fact that there is an absence of a definite and uniform legal vocabulary. There is also a 'fringe of vagueness' or 'open texture' within legal methodology[32] that is compounded where the analysis of difference and synthesis is applied across different procedural traditions. As such, different meaning may be given to the same text. We would say, however, that rather than a limitation of the methodology, this value-adding potential enhances the meaning produced through comparative analysis. Meaning is not, in social science, a process of distilling one truth. The aggregation of participants' meaning is a positive process which is necessary to fully describe and understand the social reality of human interaction (as in trial decision-making).

Comparative contextual analysis, therefore, facilitates culturally sympathetic understanding where rules are applied to contexts and situations previously unforeseen by the original inventor of the phrase, word or meaning. Similarly, contextual analysis recognises and addresses Parker's[33] point that 'narrative' is a notion which is frequently culturally bound and, therefore, other jurisdictions may place greater importance on other forms of expression to record their trials. Comparative contextual analysis is about adding value to methodology, as well as simply discovering contextually embedded meanings. In this respect the comparative exercise is geared to 'opening up new levels of understanding' for those working within any particular legal cultural context.

Another methodological contradiction concerns the interpretation of trial records. This issue has been raised by Bennett and Feldman[34] who suggest that 'both the teller and the interpreter of a story always have some margin of control over the definition of certain key symbols.'[35] Physical gestures may not be recorded in some trial records despite their obvious impact upon an account, and translations may lose the symbolic nature of the original text, or may reflect the (or a) dominant cultural stance (without regard for other minority influences), once again relating back to the problem of cultural bias in interpretation. Jackson[36] further suggests that those rules which embody the legal institution form a negative structure; therefore, the order of the rules is not accidental. One must identify those rules within a given legal context in order to maintain their narrative structure and coherence. Consequently, trials may be conceived as the site of a set of discourses, each with its own set of codes and participants. The introduction of modelling into narrative analysis, and the elaboration of the narrative through selective observation and expert commentary as part of comparative contextual analysis in its initial phase are designed to counter these tendencies towards methodological distortion.

As described, our narrative method is sensitive to phenomenological description, in providing accounts of the subjective reality of process at the symbolic and ideological level.[37] It also aims to counter the problem of cultural bias implicit in conventional comparative method through the ongoing critical evaluation of contextual analysis provided by expert commentators and subsequent interpretations of their accounts. In specific terms, contextual analysis helps us to understand the context and significance of the story, the storytellers and the interpretation of stories regarding events within the courtroom. We maintain that our methodology is capable of responding to the objective/subjective dimensions of narrative interpretation and is sensitive to different levels of meaning and understanding attributed to action and process by trial participants in different legal cultures.

However, we reach beyond conventional interpretations of culture; our interest is in 'culture construction', hence we focus on process more than normative frameworks or outputs. For example, the instrumentality of discretionary decision-making in the English sentencing process exists in the capacity of the judiciary to reproduce particularised justifications for sentencing. This instrumentality has been integral to maintaining the pre-eminence of the judiciary as lawmakers and *de facto* determiners of sentencing policy for many years, and proved a significant means for frustrating executive attempts to control judicial discretion. Thus, the instrumentality of that discretion exists and is re-enforced through the recursive process of sentencing in the higher courts. Comparative contextual analysis provides the means for interrogating the cultural determinants of its motivation and intent and its processual significance.

In our comparative contextual analysis of trial process in England and Italy, we have found narrative analysis enough, in combination with a normative framework of understanding, to allow for some unique insights into both the applicability of trial modelling, and the critical evaluation of trial practice.[38] The utility of narrative analysis for exploring trial decision-making in particular is ensured through its compatibility as reflective of official normative requirements, as an externalisation of reasons for action, and an interpretation of language contingent on decisions. Furthermore, we found that temporal and spatial sequence can be given new directions through the application of associated methodologies in order to enhance the dynamic suggestions of narrative. The fact/value distinction, grounded (as it should be) and transitional, provides a criterion for managing subjective and objective meanings in the narrative and its analysis. Such meanings emerging out of the narrative are instantaneous, yet can reflect back on rules/structures and the application of discretion in a more generalised and systematic fashion. The narrative provides a static, one-dimensional snap-shot of the transformation of rules and structures through human agency. The narrative reflects an interpretation of that process and how other interpretations might be mediated through interaction and conversation.

By concentrating on the examination of trial transcripts and the observation of trial practice with the benefit of close and expert commentary, the methodology is well placed to observe the actualities of trial process in various jurisdictional settings. As suggested, since the methodology is driven by the need to understand comparative context(s), the contextual model provides a *locus* for testing and facilitating the emergence of various (possibly competing) versions of what constitutes the process of discretionary decision-making in the criminal trial within and across jurisdictional boundaries.

To achieve this, the comparative trial research seeks to identify common themes in trial practice (which may connect with essential and universal outcomes for the trial) and make these relative to the trial settings under analysis by then identifying difference in the contextual application of these themes. We suggest that the notion of *pathways of influence* provides a conceptual and practical tool for interrogating universal themes whether they emerge from jurisdictional, organisational or interactive paradigms. For instance, all trials are directed towards the verdict. This decision will arise out of an eventual site for decision-making (be it a judge, judicial chamber, judge assisted by lay assessors, or a jury). The decision is worded in the common language of guilt or innocence but may be conditional or accompanied by reasons or questions unique to the practice of a particular trial type. The verdict will be informed by evidence which achieves particular levels of probative (factual) value. However, the sources and nature of evidence will differ across trial types.

This methodological approach fits with our observations on modelling.[39] A contextual model is constructed through the identification of core or common themes which emerge from watching different trials in context. What derives is a model of the trial (as decision-making), a model of sites for decision-making (in terms of common participants, interactions and outcomes), and a model of trial decisions, where relativity and difference is at its most apparent and interesting despite the decisions being grounded in a largely common process. This is also inductive and deductive, down and back up to the levels of analysis. The modelling process becomes part of the exercise in reconciling relativity and universalism, one in which grounding in the common contexts of process and action is crucial.

At the level of understanding trial process and sentencing in particular contextually, the pilot comparative exercise conducted by the authors provided a methodology which undoubtedly adds value and meaning to narrative accounts.[40] In general terms the analysis allowed us to explore the comparative historical contexts of two contrasting procedural styles of sentence decision-making, and facilitated an understanding of the impact of procedural norms on sentencing. It also provided insights into the respective pressures and common themes within these processes, particularly the unique problems posed by the developing hybrid jurisdiction in Italy. Finally, it enabled us to sense particular issues which have significance across the two jurisdictions. These methodological insights influenced the design of the comparative analysis described in the following section.

COMPARATIVE CONTEXTUAL ANALYSIS

In this section we utilise observations from Henham and Mannozzi's[41] comparative research on victim participation and sentencing in England and Italy to illustrate how the contextual modelling approach developed within structuration theory's reflexive framework provides an understanding of process that is *context* driven, and that deconstructing process decisions is to do with understanding comparatively the relationship between fact/value at those levels of decision-making which connect with sentencing outcomes.

This approach acknowledges the problematic nature of focusing solely on the relevance of sentencing within the 'trial' as the context for analysis, particularly the relativity of meaning and significance for the concept of 'trial' in different jurisdictional contexts. It also recognises that adequate representation of both lay and professional interests in trial decision-making is concerned with evaluating different modalities of discretionary behaviour and intervention regarding the perception, evaluation and use of information for sentencing purposes. Finally, it moves beyond the notion of decision sites and their relative significance as process variables and focuses on *context*; – and more specifically, on the cultural contexts in which significant trial relationships are created and merge to determine the exercise of discretionary power at significant decision sites for sentencing in the trial process.

The analysis also provides a significant context for exploring internationalisation. The reasons for adopting internationalisation as a context for analysis is are initially to test the adequacy of existing notions about the nature of victim participation in the criminal trial and their transferability to a variety of justice process contexts. More than this, and recognising our commitment to comparative contextual analysis as a methodology, from internationalisation comparable generalisations can be drawn out about the trial and contrasted with universal and idiosyncratic themes at regional and local/comparative levels. The analysis, therefore, explores similarity and difference and the extent (or not) that to which these are harmonised through merged trial traditions.

Comparative contextual modelling provides the basis for adopting methodologies capable of identifying and defining crucial concepts across jurisdictional boundaries. In the instant case, therefore, our contextualisation of victim participation in sentencing in England and Italy demands criteria which reveal culturally meaningful descriptions of concepts at analytical levels that relate to the contexts of structure, system and structuration and their interrelationship, as described in our earlier discussion of Figure 5.2. The relevant conceptual issues relating to victim participation concern are:

- The the notion of victim
- Participation and interaction
- Significance of process and outcome
- Ideological and socio–historic context
- Nature of relationships in the judicial decision-making process.

Ultimately, therefore, the significance of the phenomenon of victim participation in sentencing depends upon the extent to which contextual analysis is successful in exposing *comparable* descriptions and evaluations of process in terms of participant and interactive decision-making. The fundamental difference between comparative contextual analysis and previous attempts to provide theoretically grounded methodologies capable of providing giving meaningful accounts of trial practice at different levels of analysis, hinges on its methodological ability to evaluate process *within* context. Our examination of victim participation in sentencing across jurisdictions exposes the advantages of linking theory and method in this way through revealing the processual reality of decision-making at each of the three significant levels mentioned previously; namely, structure (legal); system (organisational); and structuration (interactive). For victim participation, this is achieved more specifically through a critical evaluation of relevant legal and policy contexts; procedural rules and trial practice; and, the impact of rights-based and restorative justice paradigms within and across the two historically different trial traditions of England and Italy.

For the victim participation study, no *a priori* propositions based on particular theoretical *evaluators of context* were developed for inclusion in the contextual model other than those suggested by our elaboration of how trial process is reproduced recursively by structuration theory (see Figure 5.1). The approach in terms of modelling for comparative purposes was, therefore, predominantly one of theory generation (*evaluation in context*), in that discrete accounts of the nature and extent of victim participation were evaluated against structuration theory's reflexive macro-conceptualisation of process generation. Within this conceptualisation we are able to speculate upon the principal relationships which determine the outcome of particular interactions and discretionary decisions within the course of the trial and are crucial for informing rationalisations, and determining sentence. Of these, the relationship between victims and the judiciary is pivotal in delineating the relative reality of victim integration across jurisdictions and internationally.

More specifically, we focus on how the principal aspects of this relationship can be deconstructed at the legal, organisational and interactive levels of analysis, focusing particularly on verdict and sentence delivery and the role of discretion in decision-making. Throughout, our discussion aims to explore the extent to which the nature, development and transformation of sentencing process are interrelated and influenced by normative principles relating to fair trial and access to justice.[42]

We can relate the conceptual framework of structuration to the notion of victim participation in sentencing in the following way;[43] legal/structural variables entail examination of the nature and extent of legal norms providing for victims' rights, remedies and participation in the process of sentencing, whilst organisational/system variables are concerned to describe the organisational reality of process – the administrative, bureaucratic and process-generated communication structures which sustain decision sites relating to victim participation. Finally, interactive/discretionary variables as reflective of structuration relate to the interactive reality of individual and collective processes of discretionary decision-making which concern victim participation and judicial engagement.

These interrelating levels of processual reality are conceived in theoretical terms as being simultaneously both constitutive and productive of existing process paradigms. In other words, the reality of process (be it at the local or global level) is envisaged as being created and sustained recursively. Conceptualising the particular and comparative reality of process depends, therefore, on our ability to envision ways in which issues and relationships at these interdependent (but distinct) levels of meaning are intimately connected to produce the social reality of decision-making in criminal trials.

In essence, we are concerned to discover the nature and content of the interface in the fact/value dichotomy for different trial participants as processual reality in order to comprehend how the meaning of social action is constructed within the criminal trial (for example, as between victims and judges). In the present context this means understanding the social construction of victim participation in those trial processes which determine sentencing outcome, particularly through our investigation of victim/judge relationships. The notion of pathways adds to this conceptualisation of process. If we focus on relationships (such as victim and judge), what we are adding is *context*. The context we are adding relates to the cultural origins of influence, its practical effect and significance for decision-making and its relative effects on sentencing outcomes. More specifically, we are examining the cultural context in which the influences of the judge and victim are created and merge to determine the exercise of discretionary power at significant decision sites for sentencing in the trial process.

More particularly, the legal/structural, organisational/system and interactive/discretionary levels of analysis implicit in structuration theory were examined against the theme of victim integration in the sentencing process by looking at the ways in which victim-related information is evaluated during the course of the trial and how this impacts on sentence decision-making.[44] Conceptually, it recognises that the sentencing decision should be conceived as an amalgam of process decisions, and, more generally, that the underlying theme of integration allows us to investigate connections made between penal justifications, policy and decision-making. The methodological approach was for law and policy to be *evaluated in context* through expert commentary and analysis. This included the contextual analysis of narrative sources in English and Italian, the latter being translated into English.

Since the analysis was informed by a conceptualisation of social process suggested by structuration theory, it was possible within this theoretical model to develop an integrated analysis in terms of the relationships between process and outcome, and to address the problem of conceptualising victim participation as social action against some coherent propositions that relate to the way in which process is manufactured over time and space. More specifically, whilst structuration explains how the process exists over time and space, contextual modelling is employed to describe how and why it takes the form it does in specific legal and jurisdictional contexts. An important aspect of the micro-paradigm developed for victim participation is concerned with the determinants of inclusivity/exclusivity within the trial context. In fact, the adoption of a micro-paradigm enables us to focus on the form and reasons for influence depending on judge and court level; it facilitates our understanding of the forces that are at work in the relationship and how they relate (or work against) each other. In this way we identify how different pathways of influence produce different configurations of fact/value whose practical effects are manifested in greater or lesser participation for victims in those aspects of the trial process that are relevant for victims and sentence.

Thus, the evaluation of victim participation and sentence decision-making was located within the levels of analysis suggested by structuration theory in the following way:

- legal/structural level of analysis,
- organisational/system level of analysis, and
- interactive/discretionary level of analysis.

Legal/Structural level of analysis

Sentencing models and structures

These relate to the jurisdictional justifications for sentencing values and norms.

Henham and Mannozzi argue that, in the context of sentence modelling, it is the instrumentality of judicial discretion which distinguishes the English and Italian paradigms. In Italy, the neo-classical form of retributivism embodied in the framework for decision-making has been judicially interpreted within a civil law, non-adversarial paradigm and jurisprudential tradition that regards the creativity and interpretative function of the judiciary with circumspection, whereas the opposite has been the case in England since the outset of the enlightenment project in criminal law and justice.

The significance of the comparative accounts regarding the role of judicial discretionary decision-making in sentencing relates to its instrumentality in the reproduction of particularised justifications for sentencing. In England, this instrumentality has been integral to maintaining the pre-eminence of the judiciary as lawmakers and *de facto* determiners of sentencing policy (or executive attempts to direct it). In Italy, discretion has not been instrumental in determining process since, historically, this has not been a crucial determinant in the development of the judicial role. The emphasis on procedural form and the failure of legislative or juridical attempts to rationalise contemporary punishment justifications has been countered defensively by the Italian judiciary. This phenomenon appears to have been exacerbated by the more recent adversarialisation of the Italian trial process. Henham and Mannozzi's conclusion that the concept of judicial discretion is a fundamental determinant of how fact and value are presented in sentencing is not surprising. What is significant is that our understanding of why this might be the case provides a critical perspective for evaluating the position of the victim in the criminal trial process.

Nature and role of sentencing law and policy

This is concerned with both the conventional doctrinal analysis of sentencing law, practice and procedure, and its broader sociological context.

It is the legal culture and the broader contextualisation of process that has determined the response of the Italian courts to the victim concept. It is these factors which condition the circumspection with which victim evidence is received and treated by the Italian judiciary. In legal/structural terms, Italian sentencing process appears typified by legal formalism and the restrictive judicial interpretation of particular procedural constraints as regards the appropriation of information that might be deemed relevant to victim participation in sentencing decisions. This narrow ideology consequently delimits the appropriate terrain for victim participation in sentencing in terms of due process and the potential for restorative justice themes to be developed beyond any communitarian function that might be attributed to denunciation as an aspect of retribution.[45]

By contrast, in English sentencing, the principle of judicial independence has by convention placed the judiciary in the vanguard of determining the ambit of substantive and procedural sentencing law and the parameters of policy. Furthermore, the context in which this judicial discretion has been exercised has been one which supports and sustains the concept of individualisation of sentences. Within this conceptual framework retributive considerations are balanced against utilitarian concerns such as deterrence, rehabilitation and reparation.

In both Italy and England, for what appear to be entirely different reasons, the legal and political contexts of judicial discretion have resulted in a narrow and partisan conceptualisation of the victim, and restricted the extent to which victim participation in sentencing should be promoted. Pursuing the analysis further, the following dichotomies are suggested as characterising the contexts of judicial discretionary behaviour across the two jurisdictions:

Table 5.4 Instrumental factors in judicial discretionary behaviour

England	Italy
Individualisation	Proportionality and legality
Independence	Marginalisation
Adversarial process	Hybrid process
Binary model	Unitary model
Pragmatism	Social contract theory

The distinction made between individualisation and proportionality and legality in the general approach to sentencing in Figure 5.4 is a function of distinct legal and political judicial cultures. In England, these are the contexts which sustain the principle of judicial independence, whilst, in Italy, the judiciary do not (and need not) exercise the same juridical and political power over the policy and development of sentencing. Similarly, the dichotomy of process styles and the sentencing models for sentence are reflective of movements of significant socio-historical and political importance.[46] In essence, the certainty, restraint and control of discretion demanded of neo-classicism continues to inform the culture in which Italian judicial discretion is exercised, whilst the norms governing English judicial discretionary behaviour remain rooted in the values of Victorian pragmatism.

Organisational/System level of analysis

Significance of process and procedure

There the emphasis is on sentencing as a reproducible social practice so that the focus is on the nature and reasons for the existence of structural constraints on process.

English and Italian sentencing processes exhibit important differences in the interactive structuring of decision-making. The most significant concerns the nature of the sentencing decision paradigm. Evidently, the English decision model is essentially individualistic and pragmatic, although, paradoxically, the justificatory component is articulated publicly. By contrast, the Italian decision model requires collective behaviour with justifications (presumably) argued in private. The Italian discretionary decision-making paradigm established by Articles 132 and 133 of the 1930 Criminal Code has remained an obstacle to the development of justificatory aims for sentencing, thus permitting judges to persistently avoid public articulation and accountability for sentence justifications.

In both jurisdictions the structuring and processing of information relevant to sentencing is largely completed by the sentencing stage itself. Legal constraints and protocol dictate the nature and context of information delivery.

Information is subsequently filtered, juxtaposed and utilised by legal professionals to fulfil the categorisations necessary to enable sentencing to take place. The mode in which these structures are created and sustained is, therefore, a crucial determinant of judicial discretionary decision-making in sentencing.

In terms of process integration and the potential for victims to participate in the trial, Henham and Mannozzi observe that, for different reasons, both the Italian and the English systems have failed to develop rational justifications for sentencing which address reparative or restorative justice concerns other than through reaching some accommodation with the predominant philosophy of limited retributivism and the framework of proportionality it imposes. The position of victims has therefore been weakened through the introduction of particular procedural reforms (some designed to further restorative concerns) within a penal context focused primarily on blame allocation, censure and proportionate punishment.

Interactive/Discretionary level of analysis

Relationship between process and outcome

This level analyses the nature and effects of the process of sentence decision-making on the eventual sentencing outcome. As described, it is essentially concerned with the actual application of structured properties (that is, the rules and resources analysed at the legal/structural level) by social actors which constitutes structuration – hence the focus on social interaction and the significance of relationships. Local context is, therefore, examined against variables relating to participant status, judicial style and the collective nature of decision-making.

The move towards a more adversarial trial procedure in Italy has had serious implications for trial process, and judicial culture in particular. For example, the principle of orality and the nature and order of permissible testimony resemble elements within common law trials. Yet, significantly, inquisitorial elements remain; judges may direct the further exploration of issues on their own initiative, intervene with their own questions during the examination of witnesses, subpoena experts, and require the acquisition of further evidence where absolutely necessary. The principle of immediacy also means that the judge who collects the evidence is also the one who decides on the merits of the case, further pressure coming from the fact that the trial must be held within a reasonable time to permit clear recollection of the evidence at the time of its evaluation. For these reasons, there may be even greater restraint on the part of victims to exercise their procedural rights, or expose themselves unduly to the rigours of adversarial evidential procedure and possible further questioning at the discretion of the judge.

A comparison with the English judiciary is instructive at this level. Again, for reasons relating to the judicial culture of independence and its relationship to sentencing policy referred to, the English judge appears more detached and free from processural constraint than his Italian counterpart. Consequently, judicial style is more idiosyncratic, with judicial authority and control over the sentencing phase of the trial also possibly serving wider ideological or pragmatic judicial concerns such as the principle of judicial indepenedence. Trial interaction is more judicially proactive and confrontational, and through the sentencing homily, the judge may address specific victims' concerns, or express wider communitarian justifications for sentence.

Hence, an unfettered adversarial paradigm *per se* is not the issue that distinguishes Italian and English judicial practice in the exercise of any discretion relating to the extent of victim participation in ordinary criminal trials. Generically, the crucial determinant is the context which informs the instrumentality of judicial discretion. This context reflects the legal, social and political culture of the judiciary and provides the basis for recognising the nature and extent of victim intervention in discretionary decision-making. It is a dynamic context that influences discretionary decisions and differs in its effects on the sentencing outcome according to different sites of decision-making.

EVALUATION

As indicated at the outset, the purpose of Henham and Mannozzi's contextual comparative analysis was to produce meaningful comparative evaluations of the legal and policy contexts of victim participation in Italian and English sentencing at the legal, organisational and interactive levels of analysis. This exercise was conducted within the wider aspirational context of speculating upon the potential for the exercise of judicial discretion within an integrated sentencing process. This involves acknowledging that the outcome of discretionary decisions is influenced by the nature of judge/victim relationships, and that (in turn) such decisions provide different contexts for influence which shape the pathways to particular sentence outcomes. Hence, a conceptualisation of sentencing was envisaged which acknowledged the relationship between the justifications for sentence, sentencing policy and judicial discretionary decision-making.

The furtherance of victim participation in sentencing, therefore, recognises a need for victim *integration* throughout the criminal trial process. This involves an appreciation of the relative contexts of influence on victim inclusion in discretionary decision-making. In this respect, the comparative study tends to confirm the view that the prospects for victim integration and the development of restorative justice strategies are not advanced within the constraints imposed by proportionality and deserts-based ideology. Further, the fragmentation of process through the introduction of discrete structures for dealing with particular forms of offender or offending behaviour understandably does little to advance the cause of integration, either in theory or practice. As the Italian experience suggests, changes in structure and form without a corresponding re-evaluation in the overall purposes of prosecution, trial and sentence beyond a basic need to remedy procedural deficiency produces penal structures whose philosophical justifications are impossible to reconcile within the existing stated aims of punishment and the legislative model which embodies them.

The findings of the comparative study confirm the pilot methodological exercise[47] where it was found that observing the dynamics of action *contextually* through analysis of the English and Italian sentencing transcripts revealed the instrumentality of judicial discretion as a crucial determinant of what recursively constitutes process. Similarly, the most important single outcome of the present research exercise for the comparative contextual analysis of sentencing is its validation of the overriding significance of *process* over form and structure. As we have suggested, it is through the deconstruction of the objectivity of process that degrees of subjectivity are revealed by exploring the capacity of judicial discretionary decision-making to add value to fact. As Tamanaha contends,[48] we are concerned here with the generic process of decision-making, the extent to which the *internal judicial attitude* balances the dialectical requirements of rule orientation and instrumental rationality. As such, judicial discretionary decisions are relative and pragmatic; they involve appraisal and evaluative judgements based on preferred objectives.

In observing the dynamics of action *contextually*, the English and Italian research reveals the instrumentality of judicial discretion and the manner in which it is influenced as a crucial determinant of what recursively constitutes process. In so doing, the interpretation of action is not objectified as with conventional comparative analyses. The analysis is projected beyond the *locus* of the narrow interpretative community of legal professionals to the pluralistic modern state. The contextual analysis of sentencing practice, therefore, permits us to generalise about discretionary practices which are reflective of tensions between rule-governed behaviour and norms orientated towards justice and the individualisation of sentences.

At the level of understanding sentencing process contextually, the exercise has provided a methodology which undoubtedly adds value and meaning to conventional comparative accounts. It has identified and elaborated crucial aspects of sentencing as a site of decision-making, such as:

- the role of judicial discretion,
- evidence relevant to sentence,
- the dichotomy between verdict delivery and sentence,

- relationships between the judge and legal professionals,
- relevance of the victim,
- communitarian concerns in sentencing,
- transparency in sentencing,
- impact of legal principle and normative guidance, and
- processural abuse.

In general terms the analysis has allowed us to explore the comparative historical contexts of two contrasting procedural styles of sentence decision-making, and facilitated an understanding of the impact of procedural norms on sentencing. It has also provided insights into the respective pressures and common themes within these processes, particularly the unique problems posed by the developing hybrid jurisdiction in Italy. Finally, it has enabled us to sense particular issues which have significance across the two jurisdictions. This might allow limited observations and critiques at the jurisdictional level and speculations as to the appropriateness of fair trial paradigms, more particularly since the notion of internationalisation provides an important perspective from which to explore the extent to which domestic and international sentencing practice conforms with particular rights paradigms that might be taken as measures of criminal justice, and to test the adequacy of such paradigms.[49]

FURTHER READING

J. Bell, *French Legal Cultures* (London: Butterworths, 2001).

R. B. M. Cotterrell, 'Why Must Legal Ideas Be Interpreted Sociologically?' (1998) 25 *Journal of Law and Society* 171.

R. B. M. Cotterrell, 'Seeking Similarity, Appreciating Difference: Comparative Law and Communities', in A. Harding and E. Orucu (eds) *Comparative Law in the 21ˢᵗ Century* (London: Kluwer Academic, 2002).

A. Crawford, 'Contrasts in Victim-Offender Mediation and Appeals to Community in France and England', in D. Nelken (ed.), *Contrasting Criminal Justice: Getting from Here to There* (Aldershot: Ashgate, 2000).

M. Findlay, *The Globalisation of Crime* (Cambridge: Cambridge University Press, 1999).

M. Findlay and R. Henham, *Transforming International Criminal Justice: Retributive and Restorative Justice in the Trial Process* (Cullompton, Devon: Willan, 2005).

R. Henham, 'Theory and Contextual Analysis in Sentencing' (2001) 29 *International Journal of the Sociology of Law* 253.

R. Henham, *Punishment and Process in International Criminal Trials* (Aldershot: Ashgate, 2005).

R. Henham and M. Findlay, 'Criminal Justice Modelling and the Comparative Contextual Analysis of Trial Process' (2002) 2 *International Journal of Comparative Criminology* 162.

R. Henham and G. Mannozzi, 'Victim Participation and Sentencing in England and Italy: A Legal and Policy Analysis' (2003) 11 *European Journal of Crime, Criminal Law and Criminal Justice* 278.

J. Hodgson, 'Comparing Legal Cultures: The Comparativist as Participant Observer', in D. Nelken (ed.), *Contrasting Criminal Justice: Getting from Here to There* (Aldershot: Ashgate, 2000) 139.

P. Legrand and R. Munday (eds), *Comparative Legal Studies: Traditions and Transitions* (Cambridge: Cambridge University Press, 2003).

D. Nelken (ed.), *Comparing Legal Cultures* (Aldershot: Dartmouth, 1997).

D. Nelken, 'Legal Transplants and Beyond: of Disciplines and Metaphors', in A. Harding and E. Orucu (eds), *Comparative Law in the 21st Century* (London: Kluwer Academic, 2002).

D. Nelken D and J. Feest (eds), *Adapting Legal Cultures* (Oxford: Hart Publishing, 2001).

F. Pakes, *Comparative Criminal Justice* (Cullompton, Devon: Willan, 2004).

P. Roberts, 'On Method: The Ascent of Comparative Criminal Justice' (2002) 22 *Oxford Journal of Legal Studies* 539.

R. Vogler, *A World View of Criminal Justice* (Aldershot: Ashgate, 2006).

L. Zedner, 'In Pursuit of the Vernacular: Comparing Law and Order Discourse in Britain and Germany' (1995) 4 *Social & Legal Studies* 517.

NOTES

1. Developed in the context of international trial process in M. Findlay and R. Henham, *Transforming International Criminal Justice: Retributive and Restorative Justice in the Trial Process* (Cullompton: Willan, 2005).

2. First examined by the authors in M. Findlay, *The Globalisation of Crime* (Cambridge: Cambridge University Press, 1999).

3. See A. Norrie, 'The Limits of Justice: Finding Fault in the Criminal Law' (1996) 59 *Modern Law Review* 540; R. Henham, 'Theory, Rights and Sentencing Policy' (1999) 27 *International Journal of the Sociology of Law* 167.

4. R. Henham, 'Theory and Contextual Analysis in Sentencing' (2001) 29 *International Journal of the Sociology of Law* 253.

5. A. Norrie, 'From Law to Popular Justice: Beyond Antinomialism' (1996) 5 *Social and Legal Studies* 383.

6. The trial setting was chosen because it provides a stage common to all jurisdictions where the purposes and power relations of penality are given

public expression through the rituals of punishment. Whilst recognising the significance of pre-trial decision-making, the project's trial focus is deliberately chosen as the *locus* where the ideological and policy dimensions of penality are played out, and hence where issues of synthesis and difference can best be explored.

7. The reason why this approach provides a crucial technology for understanding process is that it collapses the fact/value dichotomy implicit in the analysis of process as social reality at both the epistemological and methodological levels. Consequently, objective (that is, contextualised descriptions of what is happening and why) and subjective (that is, phenomenological accounts of the meaning and significance of 'objective' facts) descriptions are generated and evaluations are facilitated through the comparative contextual modelling of trial process.

8. R. Henham and M. Findlay, 'Theory and Methodology in the Comparative Contextual Analysis of Trial Process' (2001) (unpublished working paper).

9. See especially, A. Giddens, *Central Problems in Social Theory* (London: Macmillan, 1979); A. Giddens, *The Constitution of Society: Outlines of a Theory of Structuration* (Cambridge: Polity, 1984).

10. See further, D. Layder, *Understanding Social Theory* (London: Sage, 1994) ch. 8.

11. B. Vaughan, 'Handle with Care: On the Use of Structuration Theory within Criminology' (2000) 41 *British Journal of Criminology* 186.

12. Giddens (1984), see note 9 above, 326.

13. The 'sensitising' concept is designed to convey the notion of a perspective very open to reflecting changes in the situational contexts of discretionary decision-making and their implications for the manufacture of trial process.

14. 'Context' is employed here as a central concept within the analysis in preference to overworked notions such as 'community', 'society', or 'culture'. The interactive and actual connotations of 'context', along with the often artificial and extreme notions of community, society and culture within representations of criminal justice promote contextual analysis. Consequently, as an object of contextual analysis, the trial is not limited to rules, institutions, people, situations, or reactions. The trial is more effectively understood as relationships which develop within the dynamics of its selected context.

15. Giddens (1984), see note 9 above.

16. See further, Henham and Findlay, note 8 above.

17. B. Z. Tamanaha, *Realistic Socio-Legal Theory* (Oxford: Clarendon Press, 1997).

18. R. Henham and G. Mannozzi, 'Victim Participation in Sentencing in England and Italy: A Legal and Policy Analysis' (2003) 11 *European Journal of Crime, Criminal Law and Criminal Justice* 278.

19. D. Nelken, 'Understanding Criminal Justice Comparatively', in M. Maguire, R. Morgan and R. Reiner (eds), *The Oxford Handbook of Criminology* (3rd edn) (Oxford: Oxford University Press, 2002) ch. 6.

20. Thus, the methodological validity of comparative contextual analysis might be asserted in the following way:

    (1) The methodology satisfies a desire for adequate description of basic needs, desires, wants, interests, expressed individually or collectively, within, between or transcending state entities.

    (2) Not *needs* in the sense of justifications for action alone, but also referring to those contextual imperatives or motivators which inform and drive discretion to act.

    (3) Concerning the normative and principled existence of context, needs in the sense of fundamental human conceptions such as rights, community, and the means of their fulfilment.

    (4) The methodology is validated by each social context accounting for needs in its own terms.

    (5) The task of method is to understand these terms and what they describe against existing, modified or emerging theoretical understandings.

    (6) For our methodology the tools for comparable descriptions and explanations of human behaviour are directed at understanding the negotiation of needs through process.

21. R. Henham and M. Findlay, 'Criminal Justice Modelling and the Comparative Contextual Analysis of Trial Process' (2002) 2 *International Journal of Comparative Criminology* 162.

22. In other words, the model is designed to test and verify propositions through deconstruction of specific contexts of decision-making within the trial. The analysis of each micro-context adds a different dimension to our overall understanding of the trial as an interactive and interdependent social process.

23. For example, J. Bell, *French Legal Cultures* (London: Butterworths, 2001).

24. Ibid, 22.

25. Henham, see note 4 above, 272.

26. Henham and Findlay, see note 21 above.

27. Whichever of these analytical approaches is preferred will depend on a determination of the initial reasons for the analysis, which may be to:

    (1) test hypotheses regarding law, procedure and policy;

    (2) apply a normative paradigm as the preferred ideological framework for 'knowing' the trial;

    (3) provide some validation for pre-conceived notions about the trial and make meaningful comparative generalisations about the process of the trial (and thereby explore differences in different processes);

    (4) impose some objectivity onto the consideration of more subjective (or value-oriented) evaluators of trial context; and

    (5) move from higher to lower levels of abstraction, getting closer to individual decisions in order to understand the inclusive levels of decision-making within the site, their different contexts and outcomes (Henham and Findlay, see note 8 above).

28. This is not the same as theoretical determinism since the outcome is dependant on the independent variables generated through the deconstruction of context.

29. As the model for analysing trial decisions indicates, the interaction is of such a nature as to allow for levels of analysis including normative, institutional and discretionary environments.

30. S. Sarantakos, *Social Research* (Hampshire: Macmillan, 1993).

31. W. Twining, 'Narrative and Generalizations in Argumentation about Questions of Fact' (1999) 40 *South Texas Law Review* 351–365.

32. B. Bix, 'H L A Hart and the "Open Texture" of Language' (1991) 10 *Law and Philosophy* 51.

33. I. Parker, *Discourse Dynamics* (London: Routledge, 1992).

34. W. L. Bennett and M. Feldman, *Reconstructing Reality in the Courtroom* (New Brunswick, NJ: Rutgers University Press, 1981), cited and discussed in T. Anderson and W. Twining, *Analysis of Evidence* (London: Weidenfeld and Nicolson, 1991) 170.

35. This is in fact what the reinterpretative construction of trial decision-making (building one decision on another) is all about.

36. B. S. Jackson, *Law, Fact and Narrative Coherence* (Roby: Deborah Charles Publications, 1988).

37. See, for example, D. Sudnow, 'Normal Crimes: Sociological Features of the Penal Code in a Public Defender Office' (1965) 12 *Social Problems* 255.

38. Findlay and Henham, see note 1 above, ch. 3.

39. Henham and Findlay, see note 8 above.

40. Findlay and Henham, see note 38 above.

41. Henham and Mannozzi, see note 18 above.

42. Access in particular, as a feature of fair trial, suggests a critical interrogation of the limited justice outcomes the trial provides for, and how these can be transformed to reflect victim interests.

43. This is explained in detail in Findlay and Henham, see note 1 above, ch. 6.

44. The notion of integrated decision-making as it relates to sentencing was invoked to reflect the prevailing view that victims should participate fully and have a significant input into the sentencing process.

45 It should be noted that the victim can intervene at earlier stages in the

criminal process; for example, Article 90 of the Code of Criminal Procedure 1989 includes rights for the victim to present evidence and object to any proposed dismissal of the charges laid against the accused. Although the existence of these independent rights for the victim undoubtedly influence the nature and quality of the evidence available for trial and sentence, procedural practice and a judicial culture which tends to discourage victim participation in trial proceedings largely counterbalances this positive effect.

46. For example, during the early modern period in England the divisions of function in sentencing matters between trial and post-trial, and judge and jury were far less distinct. See, J. H. Langbein, *The Origins of Adversary Criminal Trial* (Oxford: Oxford University Press, 2003) 57.

47. See Henham and Findlay, see note 8 above.

48. See Tamanaha, see note 17 above, 240.

49. See further, M. Findlay, 'Internationalised Criminal Trial and Access to Justice' (2002) 2 *International Criminal Law Review* 237; R. Henham, 'Conceptualising Access to Justice and Victims' Rights in International Sentencing' (2004) 13 *Social & Legal Studies* 27.

CHAPTER 6

Researching the Landless Movement in Brazil

George Meszaros

INTRODUCTION

E very research setting poses its own problems. Ideally, research methodology has the dual task of first accurately conceptualising and then overcoming them. Failing the latter (which in many respects is a natural part of
the research process, as initial options are discarded), methodology should at
least try to account for the difficulties. The present chapter is just such an
account. It examines some problems commonly arising from overseas
research in so-called 'developing' countries, the context being a project
looking at land struggles in Brazil. The chapter's main aim is to sensitise
readers to challenges posed by fieldwork, especially those associated with
power relations. Power relations, it is argued, pervade the field and thereby
define key aspects of the researcher's relationship to it, and vice versa. Not
only may these relations affect the way a project is constituted (for example,
sold to prospective funders) or justified to participants themselves; but they
will affect the terms of access to so-called gatekeepers; the sorts of questions
posed to interviewees; their perceptions of the researcher; the types of
answers given; and thereby conclusions reached. For all these reasons, and
others discussed in the course of this chapter, power relations (also referred
to as the politics of research) are of vital significance to both the development
of a project and, potentially, its very sustainability. Readers, are therefore
invited to think carefully about the implications of entering the field, not so
much in the belief that all difficulties can be overcome – indeed the chapter
concludes by suggesting the highly contingent nature of research – but in the
belief that it is essential to be aware of those contingencies and their potential impacts.

RESEARCHING THE LANDLESS MOVEMENT IN BRAZIL

In 1971 a relatively inexperienced socio-legal researcher from Portugal, Boaventura de Sousa Santos, was unceremoniously expelled from a Rio slum at gunpoint after being accused of spying on behalf of the police. To say the least, this was a major setback for someone who not only was sympathetic to the plight of *favela* residents, but whose fieldwork totally depended upon their co-operation. The fact that the incident seemed to arise from a linguistic mis-understanding compounded the irony, since both researcher and residents shared a common language, Portuguese. Writing ten years later, de Sousa Santos explained events thus:

> When I said that I was doing research on *favelas* I used the word *'investigação'*. In Portugal's Portuguese the term research can be rendered both as *'investigação'* or as *'pesquisa'*, though the former is more commonly used. However, in Brazil's Portuguese and particularly in ordinary language *'investigação'* means police investigation.[1]

What lay at the heart of this failure to find common ground? Was it simply a matter of cultural or linguistic difference? From the above citation it is pretty obvious that this was significant. Indeed, the difficulty of entering any given community, whether that happens to be a professional one (judges, lawyers, practitioners) or, as in this case, a neighbourhood and class based one, is so commonly faced by researchers that specialists often refer to it as the 'outsider' problem. Was this yet another example of the outsider problem? Insofar as cultural, linguistic and other differences, including the researcher's identity, played a part the answer is yes; but that is only part of the picture. In many senses these were manifestations of something deeper at work, a structuring principle or variable that had the capacity to transform an innocent word into something akin to a minor diplomatic incident. That variable was politics: de Sousa Santos' semantic "error" had revealed the presence of power relations between *favela* residents and police, and between himself and his research participants.

Power relations, whether in the field or between it and the researcher, constitute the main theme of the present chapter, what I loosely term the politics of research. This complex subject can be (and has been)[2] approached from many angles. I do so from a decidedly practical perspective, through detailed analysis of a socio-legal research project (conducted in the year 2000) that explored the relationship between law and rural land struggles in Brazil. Before dealing with this in more detail, a couple of preliminary observations regarding the significance of politics are in order.

Some researchers hold to an ideal typical notion of research that emphasises its ideological neutrality and eschewal of the political. There are multiple variations of this theme (extensively discussed elsewhere in the literature), but in effect its main claim is to be more rigorous and objective and to produce findings that more closely correspond to scientific method (or a certain view thereof).[3] I take the view that in the real world this amounts to little more than denial or, worse still, ideological mystification. Research does not take place in a vacuum. Again, while these issues are discussed extensively elsewhere in the literature, one of the major criticisms of supposedly value-neutral approaches is that they fail to adequately take account of power imbalances and the way these are played out in practise.[4] It is suggested that these dynamics have major implications for the research process that call into question the very viability of value neutrality as a strategy. One implication of this view, however, is that researchers are constantly faced with ethical and political choices.

A brief look at our earlier example illustrates the sorts of problems *routinely* encountered. It will be obvious (albeit to persons more familiar with the Brazilian situation), that the moment de Sousa Santos entered the field he was not just likely to be a 'marked man', but *bound* to be so. Although this partly had to do with his identity (in comparative terms, socially and economically privileged), it mostly had to do with the constitution of the social field prior to his arrival, a field characterised by colossal imbalances of power (that happened to take the form of open conflict between residents and police). De Sousa Santos's subjects were slum dwellers: people with very little formal education or power, who were the habitual victims of police brutality. The key point for our purposes is that de Sousa Santos's subjects quickly came to see him not just as an outsider, or person of status, education and privilege, which he clearly was, but as a threat. In terms of the research, once this potentially disastrous diagnosis was reached, any possibility of a neutral strategy evaporated. Indeed, it seems fair to ask what such a strategy might ever have consisted of. Would it have entailed equidistance between victims and perpetrators, and what might that have meant, practically speaking? To reiterate a point made earlier, the politics of research was not confined to power relations between residents and police (and how these might be negotiated or understood), but encompassed relations between those subjects and de Sousa Santos himself. Momentarily it appeared that he was utterly powerless to control the situation, let alone develop his own agenda.

The above case is significant not just because it provides a forceful illustration of the politics of research, but because it does so within a so-called developing country context. The connection is anything but accidental. By this I do not mean to say that the problems posed are exclusive to developing countries. On the contrary, conflict is a central feature of all societies, of law in particular and therefore of much socio-legal research in general. Issues such as researcher identity, identification with research subjects, overcoming the problem of being an outsider, accessing, gathering, establishing and maintaining data integrity, and so on are inherent to the discipline (as to so many others). However, there is little doubt too that the juxtaposition of precarious legal institutions alongside (or within) societies under tremendous social pressure puts colossal reciprocal strains on both, and that this in turn presents major problems for researchers investigating those relations.

Clearly, one should neither become carried away with nor over-schematise differences between so-called developing and developed countries. Many criminal justice systems, in Europe and the United States for instance, are under immense strain, and this poses problems for researchers. Nevertheless, the sheer scale and intensity of social conflicts in developing countries together with their reverberations throughout the justice system tend to raise the research stakes and consequently put field researchers under much greater pressure. In effect, Becker's question, 'whose side are you on?' is not merely raised, but is done so at a societal level, more aggressively, and more frequently.[5]

As mentioned previously, this chapter addresses the politics of research against the background of a project exploring rural land struggles in Brazil. Given that dozens of people are assassinated every year, that the issue concerns the ownership, use and distribution of land in one of the world's agricultural superpowers, and that land has been both inequitably distributed and a bulwark of power at the highest levels of Brazilian society, we may safely say that the stakes are very high indeed. The project itself had a distinctly socio-legal focus. It attempted to analyse the legal dimensions of social movement struggle for more equitable land distribution together with the State's legal responses to the problem. Rather than looking at the informal and largely hidden politics of residents in an urban shanty town (de Sousa Santos's focus), I was interested in a highly collectivised and politicised nationwide rural struggle conducted by one social movement, the Movimento dos Trabalhardores Rurais Sem Terra, or Landless Workers' Movement (hereafter referred to as the MST). Its direct action tactics, especially mass land occupations, regularly brought it into conflict with the law. This, together with the movement's size and success, made it a particularly attractive research subject. One thing I was certainly not looking to examine was a 'law of the oppressed'[6] or distinctive types of legality away from or in competition with the State. On the contrary, I was keen to explore interactions between State law and society, hence my interest in a second organisation, the Ministerio Publico, or Public Ministry (hereafter referred to as MP). This was the State's prosecutorial arm, at the apex of which stood the Attorney General. What made the MP a particularly attractive research subject was the role ascribed to it by the 1988 civilian constitution. In effect, this had done two important things. Firstly, it had set out an impressive social agenda for prosecutors, over and above more traditional prosecutorial functions; and secondly, it had made the development of that agenda a possibility by complementing it with far-reaching powers. What impact, I wondered, might this have in an area like land reform where the problems had festered so long and where attention was so desperately needed?

In truth, the development of a research subject neither happened in quite this order, nor with this degree of precision. It emerged organically, in fits and starts, with particular problems refined and reconsidered in the light of earlier developments. The following section deals with the project's emergence, including issues like access to funding; access to key informants; my own role as an outsider; and how I sought to structure the investigation. Again, it should be emphasised that these are overlapping issues rather than self-contained stages, hence the discursive rather than compartmentalised nature of the following discussion.

PROJECT DEVELOPMENT

Background

From a research perspective I was a true outsider: a Scot living and working in an English law department who then set out to investigate Brazilian socio-legal problems. It seems reasonable to ask, therefore, what might qualify me to undertake such an investigation. After all, while the differences between England and Scotland's legal systems might have been debated at length and are relatively well understood, those between Brazil and England were neither debated nor understood, let alone meaningfully comparable. Comparisons between Brazil's civil law system and the United Kingdom's common law system might be useful for typological purposes, or those of quick approximation, but they could hardly scratch the surface as far as the operational dynamics, or the problematic nature, of the relationship between Brazilian law and society were concerned. A far more useful insight into that system's operation, and indeed the potential difficulties I might face, was provided by the old Brazilian adage: '*a lei é para o ingles ver*'; literally meaning the law is there for the English to see, meaning law is mere window dressing.

The origins of this saying are not entirely clear. One plausible suggestion is that it arose from an 1831 law (introduced under pressure from the English) prohibiting the traffic of slaves to Brazil. Crucially, it is said that the law's object was not to put an end to the trade, but merely to be *seen* to put an end to the trade in order that it might continue (which it did). The result: law with considerable historical and symbolic significance but no substantive content. Perhaps what is most striking about the expression ("*a lei é para o ingles ver*") is its continued use in popular discourse. Clearly it is an indictment of the legal system, touching upon the latter's susceptibility to manipulation by powerful self-serving interests. Inadvertently, though, it also serves as a useful warning to legal researchers of the danger of concentrating too much on the formal aspects of institutions and laws, instead of the conditions of their operation. The failure to pay attention to these dynamic or organic laws – social, economic and political – is just one reason why legal transplants so frequently go wrong and are either rejected or subverted by their host.

Through previous research, conducted in Brazil the late 1980s, I already had some appreciation of this fact (a partial answer to the question about qualifications). In the course of my PhD, which looked at the relationship between the Catholic Church and trade unions in São Paulo[7], I had come across the profound impact law can have upon social movements. For decades Brazilian trade unions were amongst the most highly regulated in the world. They were socially engineered along lines explicitly inspired by Mussolini's 1930s labour laws (Carta del Lavoro). The aim was to produce consent. When, in the mid-1970s, this complex and largely successful system of social engineering began to break down under the weight of its own contradictions, in other words when workers engaged in mass strike action, the most repressive aspects of law came to the fore. Indeed, it is because of his activities as a union leader that Luis Inacio Lula da Silva, now President of Brazil, was imprisoned in 1980. The rest, as they say, is history. The strikes of the late 1970s or early 1980s dealt the military dictatorship a blow from which it never recovered. What tends to escape the attention of many observers, but is particularly interesting from a socio-legal perspective, is that key pillars of this legislation that had proved so crucial to those in power over decades were progressively drained of all content and reduced to an empty shell. The legislation remained on the statute book, but over time the judges did not enforce it and neither the State nor employers had the stomach to test it. The law was effectively overtaken by events and therefore marginalised.

In the light of these social struggles it was hardly surprising that in my new area of interest, land struggles, I felt that possession might well be nine-tenths of the law. Indeed, it turned out to be the case, for although land reform law had been on the statute books for decades, much of it remained a dead letter. The reasons for this were complex and can only be touched upon here. For many legislators this was law intended to forestall rather than bring about reform – 'lei para o ingles ver'. Thus it was flawed from the outset (depending, of course, upon one's perspective). Secondly, instead of a successful peasant confrontation either propelling or underpinning reform, significant parts of the legislation had been introduced by a military dictatorship (1964–85) keen to curb the relatively mild land reforming instincts of its civilian predecessor, the government of Joao Goulart. In other words this was a top-down (highly authoritarian) model of law making. As for its implementation, the last thing on the minds of judges was a reform in property relations.

They were culturally and politically attuned to the status quo – especially nineteenth-century notions of property – and could, if they wished, seize upon legislation that allowed them to maintain it. Such factors, combined with absence of an effective movement of contestation, were a recipe for legal paralysis until the early 1980s.

Outlining these profoundly negative features is important because they both set the scene for readers and would critically affect the construction of the research project itself. But they are only part of the picture. Law was not simply a cipher for other interests, even if it was mediated by them. Indeed, it was a realisation of the potential power of legal institutions (alongside their weaknesses) that led me to undertake the project in the first place.

The immediate catalyst, although I did not know it at the time, was a speech I listened to in 1992 in London. It was given by Brazil's Attorney General, Aristedes Junqueira. His stated intention was to impeach Brazil's president, Fernando Collor, on charges of corruption. Was this, quite literally, yet another case of '*a lei é para o ingles ver*'? My feeling at the time was that if he really meant what he said, he was unlikely to succeed and might even pay with his life. Collor's backers were too powerful. In the event, however, I was proved wrong. Collor was impeached, his political career was dealt a mortal blow, and the profile and prestige of the MP was dramatically enhanced. To be sure, Collor had succeeded in alienating many of his backers, but it was equally clear that the tenaciousness of the Attorney General played a significant role in his exit. It seemed that there was scope, after all, for decisive legal interventions.

Perhaps this was a unique moment in history, an ungeneralisable even if highly significant case. Certainly the events were exceptional. I was therefore further and pleasantly surprised when some years later Junqueira's deputy, Alvaro Augusto Costa Ribeiro, came to speak in a committee room of the UK Parliament on the subject of Brazil's human rights record and the role of the legal system. Personally speaking, this proved the more significant occasion, since it was the moment at which I sensed the presence of a pattern. Rather than hearing a polished justification of the status quo, we were treated to a devastating forensic analysis of its failures. Undoubtedly this partly had to do with the aforementioned intensity of problems besetting legal institutions in developing countries. In other words, for some practitioners it is hard *not* to take a critical public attitude towards the police and refer, as he did, to their corrupt and criminal practices, when there is overwhelming evidence of this and its disastrous social consequences. It is also probable that his criticisms had to do with inter-institutional rivalries, an area of natural tension, but one that is often brought to breaking point in developing countries because an effective modus operandi, or understanding, either has not been reached or is in the process of being redefined under antagonistic circumstances. That was certainly the case with the MP and police, since the former was expected to exercise external control over aspects of police conduct and investigation.

Returning to Costa Ribeiro's speech, what struck me as significant was its sense of social commitment, and its coupling to a legal project designed to address social issues. One of the country's highest-ranking legal officers was not just suggesting that reforms were urgently required (itself welcome given the extremely conservative nature of Brazilian legal culture)[8], but that there was a project inside the MP designed to bring this about. From a socio-legal research perspective, this seemed like a very attractive combination. It raised many potentially weighty questions, including: how had this sector of the state developed a critical legal perspective? How significant was this strand of legal thinking? What were the prospects of and obstacles to implementation? What impact was a radical project likely to have? And so on.

Accessing informants: A hard bargain?

My curiosity was aroused and I expressed the desire to investigate some aspect of the MP's social impact (I was not sure precisely which, but the land question was a possibility). At this stage, being an outsider was, if anything, an advantage. I came with no immediately recognisable baggage, and was willing to shed light on a developing aspect of the MP's work. Indeed, my status as an academic at Warwick University's Law School probably helped. Whatever one's view of social status, it can carry weight in these settings. Back in 1987, and without a letter of introduction, I found that attempting to set up interviews as part of my PhD fieldwork was extremely difficult. My girlfriend at the time explained that I was approaching things in entirely the wrong manner. She upped my social status by ringing interviewees on my behalf, pretending to be my secretary and explaining that I was in the country for a brief visit just before flying back to England. Now I was in short supply! Within a matter of hours all the interviews were set up. In the process I had also been taught a simple lesson, so obvious in hindsight: different people must be approached in different ways, and status can be important.

I was more fortunate with the new project inasmuch as I met a key informant (the Deputy Attorney General) in a relatively open setting (an overseas visit to the UK, where there was a greater willingness to engage directly and spend time with the public irrespective of status). I secured a promise of co-operation. I adopted this approach on a couple of other occasions, for example a visit to London by the then Minister for Agrarian Reform, Raul Jungmann, who also agreed to be interviewed. It may be that neither expected an obscure researcher from England would appear some months later in Brazil. That did not really matter, I had secured the promise of an interview at source, without the mediation of gatekeepers, and if those gatekeepers (administrative assistants, civil servants and so on) were unco-operative, I had some sort of leverage and the confidence not to be brushed off easily. In the event there was no problem of access.

Although, theoretically speaking, approaching members of the MST would be easier, since I had a couple of academic and legal contacts, I also knew that success would ultimately depend upon establishing a sufficiently high level of trust. Readers should be aware that over the years the movement had been under sustained attack from a variety of quarters and that members had been assassinated, imprisoned and vilified in the media. There was a danger, therefore, that I could be perceived as the wrong kind of outsider – as a threat. I could not allow that sort of impression to develop. Indeed, I had already experienced a more nuanced version of the problem first-hand in the course of my PhD fieldwork. Towards the end of those researches one of my interviewees told me that he and other interviewees had debated whether I was working for an intelligence agency of some kind. This is not as fanciful as it might sound. Indeed, if anything was implausible, it was my story. After all, why should someone from England be so interested in the fortunes of a comparatively obscure opposition union movement, within Latin America's largest union, and their relations with the Catholic Church? Who would want to pay for this research and why? To academics it might make sense – even common sense – but to militants it did not, since it was so far removed from their experience. Sense or not, I failed to dispel, or even seriously consider, their impressions until well into the project. I was not about to make the same mistake with the MST. I therefore decided to nail my colours to the mast at the outset, making no secret of the fact that I was sympathetic to the aims and methods of the MST. I regarded their cause as just. Having said that, though, my intention was to explore quite a distinctive and undervalued area of their activities, namely their relationship to the legal system in all its aspects, rather than just the explosive aspects routinely covered in the media and MST pamphlets.

Should I have nailed my colours to the mast in this way? This sort of question, which occasionally took the form of a dilemma, recurred many times during the research. On virtually every occasion I met or made contact with an interviewee or gatekeeper, I would be asked the purposes of my research. I knew that the answer I gave could affect the kind of responses I got to my own questions, and yet I also knew that interviewees had markedly differing, sometimes opposing, agendas. Could and should I be consistent? We return to this theme in the conclusion. The short answer to the MST question, though, is that I took the view that without some kind of clarification of where I stood, and a firm clarification at that, the project would lose too much, if not prove a non-starter altogether. Establishing trust was an essential prerequisite to success, and was more likely to maximise the flow of information, including that which might not necessarily put the movement in the best light.

My decision was similar to one I took with colleagues some years earlier when, in order to research judicial review in England and Wales and gain access to records, we signed a confidentiality agreement with the Lord Chancellor's Department (LCD). Formally speaking, we were merely gaining access to records. In truth, though, much was happening besides. This had everything to do with the politics of research and associated power relations. Among other things, the LCD was seeking to retain an element of control. The issue concerned more than the privacy of individual records (since the data would be anonymised anyway): it was about our analysis of their collective significance, the sorts of connections and inferences we would make, and how these would impact upon the department. Ultimately, it was about whether we were a safe pair of hands. Thus, signing with the LCD was both an act of consummation and a point of departure. It was a way of saying 'we trust one another' – a highly value laden proposition.[9]

Despite the obvious differences, the situation with the MST was analogous. Indeed, most organisations and individuals that are used to being the objects of research seek codified or informal assurances. With the MST I was simply attempting to establish some basis of engagement that included giving them a sense of safety (since our interests did not clash) whilst preserving my own room for manoeuvre. I was a free agent and not prepared to subordinate my methods or findings to anybody else's agenda. Clearly, this attitude revealed quite a bit about my own working assumptions. My feeling was that my project was unlikely to throw up many – if any – skeletons. Indeed, I genuinely believed that shedding light upon the movement's work was likely to help its cause. Effectively I was asking them for something they could probably afford to give, much as we had done with the LCD.

Accessing funding: A harder bargain

Arguably, the most challenging account of research one provides is to funding bodies, at least insofar as they demand a systematic account at a very early stage, in contrast to interviewees who are generally satisfied with a more impressionistic rendition at a much later stage, when ideas have really begun to crystallise. Certainly this was a problem I faced, made worse by the fact that I had relatively little to go on except very fragmentary accounts and my own hunches. I had already put out feelers but reached numerous dead ends. As a consequence it was difficult to formulate all but the broadest questions. How could I put problems into perspective, and formulate an effective proposal, if others had failed to take even the most basic measure of the issues? I was at an impasse.

Eventually the problem was overcome by means of a small grant (approximately £5,000) provided by the Nuffield Foundation. Technically speaking, the funding went towards a pilot project; practically speaking, they gave me money to explore my hunches. To be sure, they were based on educated guesses, past research experience, and the fact that all available avenues prior to application had been exhausted. I also knew that funders have their agendas, and therefore argued that examining one of the world's largest social movements and most powerful prosecuting authorities was a weighty one that stood well within the Foundation's remit. Ultimately, though, the grant conditions were flexible, and that flexibility proved invaluable for gathering preliminary data and establishing a more tightly defined research agenda.

My experience with the Economic and Social Research Council (ESRC), to which I would apply for full funding was far more difficult. To a large extent this stemmed from my own attitude towards the ESRC and its funding arrangements. The ESRC's agenda had been progressively subordinated to the State, a shift most notably symbolised in the early 1980s when the Secretary of State for Education, Sir Keith Joseph, took the science out of the Social Science Research Council (SSRC) renaming it the ESRC.[10] Such a blatantly ideological move was only to be expected from Mrs Thatcher's chief ideologue, especially given his long-standing scepticism towards the role of social science in Britain, and her own doubts about whether there was such a thing as society at all. More serious than this onslaught, however, was the internalisation by many academics of the seemingly more neutral language of 'value for money' and 'policy relevance', which became watch-words under both Conservative and New Labour administrations. This top-down approach poses serious problems for any academic community. At the very least, it begs questions regarding whose value for money or policy relevance one is referring to. In characteristically defensive fashion (possibly borne of years of attack and financial cuts) the ESRC now defines itself and the research it funds in terms of how these are 'of importance to business, the public sector and government'.[11] Many, myself included, would regard this not just as a schematic and highly restrictive world-view of research's purpose, but as a questionable set of justifications. Indeed, when it came to justifying my own research, the connection between these categories (they are hardly concepts) and my own interests were not readily apparent. I might have argued, albeit somewhat tortuously, that a movement challenging the role of big business and government policy in the field of Brazilian land reform ought to be of vital interest to business and government, much as, unfortunately, Islam belatedly appears well worth studying because of the perceived threat posed to a variety of vested interests. These were arguments I was not prepared to run, although they would have saved me time and effort (it took six weeks to construct the proposal). Instead, thankfully, I was able to fall back on a somewhat evasive category, 'social justice', which seems to exist quite happily alongside the ESRC's other commercial and other world-beating concerns. None of this represents ingratitude on my part. On the contrary, the research would not have been possible without the organisation's support. Rather, my intention is to highlight the fact that official research priorities and attendant categories come and go; that they are almost invariably products of their time – ideological constructions, no less – and that for researchers wishing to access funds, navigating these frameworks may pose real personal and political dilemmas. Quite simply, accessing funds remains one of the most fundamental aspects of the politics of research. Indeed, if anything it has become more significant than ever, as the pressure to attract funds has permeated university culture and become directly linked to the prospects of individual career development.

Entering and managing conflict in the field

With funding and contacts in place (on what I was sufficiently content were my terms), it was now a question of entering the field, of testing the waters. One year was allocated to this phase and a variety of techniques were employed in order to access material. Because I knew that relations between the MST and the Brazilian justice system were so controversial, part of the study was historical. In other words, I felt that interviewing militants, lawyers, administrators, and academics about events that had already taken place would be easier than attempting to discuss unfolding conflicts where the stakes were higher (because of their immediacy), and where it was difficult for people to stand back from events. This does not imply that a retrospective approach was problem-free. I had chosen a region, the Pontal do Paranapanema (located in the most westerly part of São Paulo state), where a great deal of mytholigising had taken place; where reputations and personalities had been built up; where people had been repeatedly interviewed; where they had almost become case-hardened and their own recollections had solidified. The Pontal was regarded (rightly) as a great success story for the MST. My approach, however, was different. I was not going over old ground. Instead, I wanted to try and understand events in terms of a new set of concerns, from a fresh perspective. How, for instance, had the MST understood and employed law? Had it done so in a purely defensive fashion, in order to forestall the imprisonment of militants, or had it done so in a proactive manner as well? To justice officials I was asking what impact the MST had had on aspects of their work. Although I did not immediately ask them this question, I was interested in finding out whether the movement had had a discernible impact on the operation of the justice system; had old legal battles over land been given a new twist; in short had the movement deliberately or inadvertently aided the legal system in coming to terms with historic injustices that it had hitherto been unable to effectively embrace?

 These are big questions, and only at a later stage, and then only in certain instances, were they discussed with interviewees. My questions were of a more immediate nature – what had happened, when, how, why, involving whom, with what consequences and so on, from which broader questions/conclusions developed. The point, though, is that people were willing to talk, and did so in a relatively spontaneous way. This was partly because time had passed, but also, I believe, because this was not material about which they were frequently approached despite the power of the issues.

This point brings us back to the matter of how I explained my project to different parties – especially as they were frequently on different sides of a divide. Prosecutors from the MP were involved in taking militants to court; judges were involved in either negotiating or imposing settlements; administrators within the land agency could find themselves supporting aspects of the MST's actions at one moment, for example attempting to acquire land, while opposing its methods (occupation of land agency premises as well as land in dispute) and assertions in the media the next. Where did I fit within this complex picture? In this regard my identity as an independent researcher, as an 'outsider', was if anything a positive factor. In other words, however much I might sympathise with the MST, I was clear in my own mind that I was not acting on the organisation's behalf. Instead I was, so to speak, there on behalf of the imperatives of my project, as I had designed it, from which, I had little doubt, the movement could derive positive results. The distinction may appear slight, but it is an important one, since it gave me room for manoeuvre, that is, a critical distance. Indeed, to a large extent this notion of positive detachment applied to all the other groups, or rather strands, I dealt with. If we take the MP, for instance, my argument to prosecutors was that their dealings with the MST represented an aspect of their work that should better be understood and systematised (albeit in a manner of my choosing).

Before expanding upon this point, however, some clarifications are in order, especially as regarding the issue of strands. The MP was anything but a homogenous entity. A battle over its identity was taking place. It was, and remains, a divided institution. Such divisions would come out most forcefully at election time, every four years, when prosecutors were invited to choose their leader and the decision / democratic recommendation was either ratified or rejected by the state governor, or in the case of the Brazilian Attorney General, by the President himself. For the rest of the time, though, heated debates took place over who was prosecuted and why, who was promoted within the institution and why, what resources were placed at the disposal of prosecutors and why, and so on. The institution was deeply politicised in a non-party political sense. Ironically, perhaps, this was, to a large extent, sanctioned by the constitution itself. It gave individual prosecutors a remarkable degree of autonomy and discretion in making their decisions. As a consequence, most of the time I was not approaching an institution capable of presenting a clearly worked-out or homogenised version of its operation for public consumption (whatever its spokespersons might say), but individuals – personifications, so to speak – who were fighting for differing visions of its role.

In this context of multiple and evolving visions, the question posed by Becker – that is, whose side are you on? – can appear somewhat simplistic or overdrawn. His fundamental point, though namely, getting researchers to think about power relations and their implications for research remains as timely as ever. Nor could the nuances of individual positions get me around the potential difficulty of taking a stand in relation to those positions. My own sympathies clearly lay with those prosecutors who were attempting to develop a vision of the MP that embraced law's social dimension, a substratum of which was a sympathy towards struggles for land reform. Incidentally, their support was not far-fetched, since key sections of the 1988 constitution were devoted to advancing land reform. Other prosecutors, however, were culturally maladapted to these provisions, ignoring them altogether. Instead they opted for a positivist, or minimalist, legal interpretation that, formally speaking, eschewed both politics and linkages between law and society. Quite simply, many had not been trained in this way. One substratum of their approach was a highly formalised defence of property rights to the exclusion of all other considerations, including, ironically, what the constitution specifically refers to as property's 'social function'. We need not detain ourselves with the details of this debate here. The point is that when it came to approaching them about my research, I was far more circumspect. One case stands out in particular, that of a prosecutor who took militants of the MST to court, but who was, in turn, badly burned as the case became a *cause celebre*, and the MST won a major victory in the Supreme Court. Among some colleagues he had become a figure of ridicule or pity because of his perceived failure to play a sufficiently flexible political game, and because of major tactical errors (for instance, his attempt to barter the liberty of prisoners in custody, for militants who were on the run). Under other circumstances he would have been rewarded and respected, but because this was the Pontal do Paranapanema, where the MST was determined to secure a victory and where the State government had taken a strategic decision to challenge the power of entrenched landed interests, and because his tactical errors were caught on tape by the MST's lawyer, he became isolated. When I approached him, therefore, it was with a view to understanding his side of the story. Few people were interested in a perceived loser, and that chapter of history had already been written. I did not mention the fact that I felt that his defeat represented an important, necessary and historic victory for the MST, or that his actions in seeking a prisoner exchange for fugitives had been foolish, to say the very least. To this extent, it can be argued that I was omissive, but I was genuinely interested in his side of the story and the interview proved extremely productive as a result.

These representations of one's core position often gave me food for thought, for part of my task was to establish a degree of trust with research subjects – many of whom I profoundly disagreed with – that would allow for the freest flow of information. It was not simply a question of agreeing to disagree, but of trying to get them onside, and of doing so ethically.

Whatever apprehension I might have felt beforehand, most of the time my fears proved unfounded. Early on in the fieldwork, for example, I went into what I saw as the lion's den to talk with administrators from the federal land agency, the Instituto Nactional de Colonizacao e Reforma Agraria (INCRA).[12] Its job was to implement land reform, that is, to acquire and then redistribute land on a meaningful scale. Because it had conspicuously failed to do this over decades, I took a critical view of the institution. In a British context, for example, such colossal failures of public administration would have been the subject of judicial review and the public body would, if necessary, have been mandated to act. Additionally, the debate about INCRA's role had become highly polarised. It was constantly attacked by the MST for its failures to keep promises, while the minister ultimately in charge of the institution, an extremely capable and combative individual, put the best spin on its activities he could whilst attacking the MST for its direct action tactics. How was I going to explain my work to these sorts of people?

It quickly became apparent, however, that my picture of the institution, administration staff, and the dynamics of operation was too simplistic. For a start (as now seems obvious in hindsight), many within its ranks were profoundly committed to land reform. For all the public hostility that regularly accompanied land occupations (an extra-administrative attempt at a solution), many staff were supportive of the MST's actions. Even the minister himself, who frequently reserved his harshest words for the MST, acknowledged that the movement had transformed the debate positively, in as much as land reform was now at the top of the political agenda. To be sure, he also felt that the MST had become a victim of its own success and lacked a truly effective project (a criticism made by former close associates of the movement itself). In the event, therefore, explaining myself to these people proved remarkably easy. I wanted to try and understand what had gone wrong. Why, with all the imaginable legislation at its disposal, had INCRA so conspicuously failed in its basic task? What were the primary causes of failure? Was it a lack of political will? Was it corruption? It was known, for example, that some lawyers working for the agency were openly hostile to reform, and that legal papers were sometimes filed with such glaring errors that the courts had little choice but to strike out the case.

Once again I chose a closed case (the failure of land audits in Bagé in 2000)[13] as a means of exploring extremely controversial issues in the belief that people would be more willing to talk and might have a better sense of perspective. The assumption proved correct. Key players, the minister, the former head of INCRA in Rio Grande do Sul, individual administrators, the federal prosecutor, were happy to talk. Indeed, it is worth noting that they did so on the record, and on tape. Perhaps this also reflected a greater cultural openness on the part of Brazilian officials. Certainly the culture of secrecy was nowhere near as strong as that which still surrounds the British civil service.[14] I was not asked to sign any privileged access agreements; I was able to see individual files; I was even able to take photocopies and consult databases. Such access would be unthinkable in a British context without multiple preconditions. In the Brazilian case, though, access was based upon more informal relations of trust, including expectations about how researchers were likely to handle information.

Regarding the related issue of whether to tape or not, a friend had advised me against it, suggesting that nothing of any real substance would go on tape, and the sight of a recorder could put interviewees off. These were real dangers, but my own feeling was that more information could be captured this way; that I was unlikely to concentrate on the issues if I was concentrating on note taking in a second language; that I was likely to edit out as the interview progressed for the sake of shorthand convenience; and that in any case, as I made clear to interviewees at the outset, we could switch the tape off. Although the latter happened from time to time, usually interviewees ended up forgetting entirely about its presence as the conversation went on, so much so, in fact, that I was careful not to exploit potential indiscretions. These might be the stuff of newspaper reports, but they were hardly of great significance in the context of a large-scale research project covering events over comparatively long time scales.

CONTEMPT BREEDS FAMILIARITY: CONSENSUAL DEMANDS OF CONFLICTED FIELDS

At the outset of this chapter I suggested that the intensity of conflict poses significant challenges when entering the field, that these conflicts often take a more visceral form in developing countries, and that Brazilian land conflicts constituted a good example of this. Conflict, however, is only one part of the picture, for other critical variables are also at work. A couple of brief examples may serve to illustrate the point. The most obvious of these was the constant need for key parties to the conflict to negotiate.

For all their declared hostilities, the fact was that the MST and the State constantly needed to negotiate with one another. Bargains of one kind or another were constantly being struck. The MST might be an autonomous organisation that guarded its independence jealously, but in terms of its key objective, land reform, it ultimately found itself in a dependent relationship with the State. After all, only the latter had the power – both legal and financial

– to expropriate property, and then provide the material conditions (loans, equipment, training, and so on) for stable occupation. The MST knew this. Equally, the state recognised that the movement was a key player, if not *the* key player (although we should not overlook the role played by rural unions which still constitute a formidable force). When, for example, one looks at the pattern of land reform instituted so far, the extent to which land acquisitions have followed occupation is quite striking.[15] To a significant degree, state policy has been driven by and forced to respond positively to social movement pressure. There is, in other words, a mutual recognition of each other's power. I will not go so far as to suggest that they need one another, although plausible arguments could be made along these lines, but it is clear that they do need one another's co-operation for securing interim objectives. There is an oscillation between these grey spaces of power and open conflict.

Even relations between the movement and the police, which generally speaking are hostile, provide striking examples of these oscillations. As is well known, one of the worst massacres of landless workers in recent times was carried out not by landowners, but by police in the northern state of Para.[16] However, in conflicts I examined, it became apparent that many police officers were drawn from the ranks of rural families. For many officers, facing women and children of families they knew created real personal dilemmas. These ambiguities were usually overcome in the heat of the moment by the imperative to obey. Others, however, remained. It was evident, for example, that naked repression, getting landless workers off land by force, was not a solution to the problem, since they would have to move elsewhere with the potential for more conflicts further down the line. In some states of the federation, therefore, a greater awareness of the social implications of policing developed. In Rio Grande do Sul the government of the Workers' Party (PT) refused to send in military police to carry out court orders, seeking negotiated settlements instead. The fact was that grey spaces of power existed as well as the polarised ones we are accustomed to seeing portrayed in the media.[17] A similar attitude to the PT's prevailed in one of my other case studies, Parana State. Its governor, Roberto Requiao, had courageously (in the face of judicial opposition) refused to carry out court orders and implement rapid evictions of both urban and rural squatters. He had also invited the MST's leader, Joao Pedro Stedile, to address the military police, to sensitise them to the issues of land reform and the implications of their actions. For sure, the address was an unusual occasion, brought about by unusual circumstances, and it was not going to change relations overnight either, but it is entirely typical inasmuch I came across numerous such grey spaces on the ground.[18] Precisely because the episode runs counter to type (after all, the leader of the MST accepted the invitation) it highlights the importance of individual circumstances and contingencies. Much of my research was devoted to exploring these contingencies.

GENERALISING FROM DIVERSITY

A colleague once told me how some years earlier he was teased by an Indian parliamentarian for speaking of India. How could one sum up a nation of 750 million people in just one word? In many ways I feel much the same way about Brazil, a country of 180 million people with an astonishing degree of social, cultural and racial diversity. Against such diversity all generalisations can either appear to be doomed to failure or the mere products of hubris on the part of the writer. During my own researches I well recall legal practitioners, politicians and activists referring to the seemingly insuperable contrasts between one region and another. The comments of one judge immediately spring to mind:

> I think anyone who isn't Brazilian must bear in mind above all else that Brazil is very heterogenous. Each region, the north, the south, the south east, is enormously different from the other. On average the judiciary is extremely precarious: even if it works reasonably well in São Paulo and southern states, it is extremely precarious the further north you go. I think, without exaggeration, that in terms of institutions the north and northeast are still at a medieval stage.[19]

OK, the term medieval may be an exaggeration, but his point about heterogeneity was essentially valid, applying as much to politics as it did to law. By contrast, Britain appears a small, slow-moving, even dull corner of the world (perhaps on account of which it has ideas well above its station that it seeks to replicate elsewhere as the best in the world).[20] Certainly references to both the State and law in Britain do grasp a more homogenous, neater and intelligible reality than the fuzzy dynamics and remarkable juxtapositions found in Brazil and many other so-called developing countries. Indeed, discussions of legal pluralism partly reflect an attempt to come to grips with precisely these differences and realities.

Grasping the myriad specificities while developing valid generalisations is undoubtedly one of the most daunting tasks facing researchers. It can appear all the more so when one considers the record of individual scholars: if, for example, it took an 'insider' of Darcy Ribeiro's calibre some thirty years to write a book on the Brazilian people,[21] what chance for an outsider of coming to grips with problems in a relatively short space of time? This tension, between a field researcher's necessarily limited immersion in the subtleties of a particular locale, and simultaneously abstracting or standing back from it, surely constitutes one of the main challenges of overseas work. That can manifest itself in all sorts of ways, in overload, for instance.

At one stage during the fieldwork, for example, I had collected a number of in-depth interviews (often an hour or two long), but realised that there was a danger of becoming overwhelmed by the sheer volume and detail of material generated (even allowing for the fact that I had budgeted for transcription). How was I going to make sense of data that was accumulating exponentially – especially in relation to my desire to make ongoing connections and feed these back into the project as it progressed? After a few weeks I devised a simple database consisting of a few basic categories: date, place, organisation, biographical notes of interviewees, and so on. Additionally, I added a summary of how I felt the interview itself had proceeded, together with notes about the circumstances in which it had occurred. The most crucial category, though, was the summary itself (usually a few paragraphs). Through word searches this became the effective gateway to the material – both to the individual interview and, when the search was repeated across the database, to similar concerns expressed in other interviews that I had either entirely forgotten, or whose significance I had never appreciated. This also permitted the cross-referencing and further validation of data, and the generation of ideas, even theories, in a more systematic manner.

Although this proved a good way of overcoming an aspect of access that is all too frequently overlooked, namely accessing one's own data and finding ways of theorising it, it was only a partial solution. In other words, there was a sense in which no matter how systematic I might attempt to be, I was bound to be overwhelmed by raw data, that is, codes of behaviour, signals, practices, motivations, of which, even with the best will in the world, I would never be aware, or which it would take me years to understand.

A couple of examples may serve to illustrate the point. Several of my interviews, upon which much of the research was constructed, were utterly dreadful. For whatever reason, interviewees did not respond to my questions as anticipated. A note was made to this effect at the time. Later analysis, however, revealed that although they may have been unforthcoming on my pet topics, they were, in fact, supplying useful information. I simply could not appreciate it because I was, quite understandably, engaged in an act of discrimination, based upon specific (albeit evolving) research priorities.

Being systematic, therefore, is not always the answer since by definition it also excludes. When considering methodology it is perhaps tempting to view challenges that invariably arise simply as a matter of rationality and technique, as if the application of enough thought and force to a problem will compel it to give way. And yet it is clear, to me at least, that other factors outside our control, like luck and time, can play a decisive role in research outcomes. Again two interviews that went badly – because the answers I received were either superficial or evasive – illustrate this point. The people involved (a leading politician and a leading lawyer) were extremely capable individuals for whom getting to the heart of the matter was a genuine concern. From a methodological perspective I had pretty well done all that I could in preparing the ground. Quite simply, though, they were not ready to talk. Fate subsequently intervened and I was forced to suspend my studies for some years. When these were resumed, I returned to the two interviewees. Somehow the scene was utterly transformed. They were ready to talk – candidly and at length.

We could speculate over why they had been so reluctant and why their attitudes had changed. Was it the fact that I had published material in the meantime, that my identity as an outsider had been clarified; or that they were slightly removed from events; or that certain political battles were going on that made them more ready to talk? In a way it does not matter. The fact is that although there are occasions when one can try and control for factors of this kind, frequently one cannot. Uncomfortable as it may sound, it may be a question of luck, time, or factors that one is unaware of. Who knows, they may happen to have been unwell when I first encountered them. Returning to Darcy Ribeiro, for instance, one is struck by the fact that for all his work's erudition and technique, it was also profoundly affected by seemingly extraneous events, albeit historic ones, like the military coup of 1964 and forced exile. Ironically, these gave him time to consider issues at greater length and thereby profoundly affected his conclusions.

CONCLUSION

If any single over-arching theme emerges from this chapter, it is the contingent nature of research. This expresses itself in many forms; we happen to have focused upon one these, the politics of research. Arguably the real point of departure in the politics of research lies not with external contingencies, powerful though these are, but with researchers themselves, that is, in their deeper motivations, biases, and so on, and in the sorts of choices they make when setting objectives or confronting difficulties. A research question often says as much about those who pose it, as it does about those under investigation. This theme is part of a long discussion, but Darcy Ribeiro's comments, in his preface to *O Povo Brasileiro*, set the tone:

> Do not delude yourself with me, reader. Over and above an anthropologist, I am a man of faith and of party. I engage in politics and engage in science because of ethical and patriotic reasons. Don't look, here, for value free analyses. This is a book that wants to be participative, that aspires to influence people.[22]

My own research interests stemmed from a desire to see social change, coupled with the sense that earlier accounts had failed to do justice to significant problems in terms that I had proposed. Thus, while land reform might be back on the agenda, relations between the state (legal and administrative institutions especially) and social movements were all too often treated superficially, if discussed at all. They were, in effect, marginalised and I felt they should come centre stage.

However significant one's own 'centre of gravity', there is little doubt that a researcher's relationship to the social setting of research is vitally important, particularly as the relationship is, essentially, a dependent one (even if the conclusions are one's own). It has been suggested that working in a so-called developing country context poses additional problems: because the stakes are generally so high, the politics of research (an aspect of all projects) assumes particularly acute forms. Rather than feigning neutrality when researching the MST, for instance, my actions had to correspond to the reality encountered. Had I not proactively nailed my colours to the mast, they would have been placed there by default, through expectations and assumptions generated by subjects themselves. The power of expectations, and the relationship of dependency, is well illustrated by the case of de Sousa Santos, discussed at the beginning of this chapter.

Conflict undoubtedly poses difficult problems. It raises questions, often in quite aggressive forms, about the nature of the researcher's identity. Under such pressured circumstances it is essential to be prepared for those questions, as success almost invariably depends upon research subjects' co-operation, and failure to prepare may lead to its withdrawal. Of course, co-operation should not come at any price – the compromising of one's own research objectives or ethics, for instance – but to lose it through naivety or ignorance would be foolish. When, therefore, I interviewed the head of Parana's land agency on what turned out to be the same day as the MST decided to occupy its offices, the juxtaposition (opposing parties in the same room) may have left me fairly uncomfortable, but I was secure about the fundamentals. The research was not threatened. Indeed, one way of overcoming potential conflicts like this was to trail the fact that I would be interviewing 'the other side'. Occasionally, one side would even ask what the other was thinking, for instance when the Minister for Agrarian Reform asked me what the MST was thinking in relation to the impending trial of a leading militant. Provided no confidence was violated, I did not have a problem answering these sorts of questions.

This brings us to another issue, the fact that researching conflict may not necessarily be as difficult as one might expect. Much depends upon the precise forms that conflict assumes rather than upon some abstracted notion of conflict. It is ignorance of the details that can make the problems look more daunting than they actually are. The circumstances I faced, for instance, were deeply affected by the fact that the parties had been engaged in conflict for so long: they knew one another, how they operated, when they could talk, through whom, and so on. There was, in other words, an element of regularity, predictability, even mutual recognition, that accompanied better known features, like mutual hostility. One is reminded of the periodic, localised and informal cessation of hostilities during early phases of the First World War that culminated in the Christmas Truce of 1914. Paradoxical though it appears, this event was, quite literally, a function of entrenched positions. In some respects, the two sides had gotten to know one another through combat, even earning a grudging respect. Similarly, in the absence of complete victory by one side or the other, what I earlier termed grey spaces of power had developed between the MST and its opponents or its negotiating partners. Thus, a researcher moving between these fields was not as strange as it might first appear, since individuals from all these organisations had already engaged in these activities themselves.[23] And although Becker's 'whose side are you on?' question might appear simplistic in such a context, it was, nevertheless, essential that I consider my relationship to the different parties. This was partly because they talked to one another, and could form a collective profile of a researcher (including any glaring inconsistencies on my part); but also because, like the 1914 Truce itself, these grey spaces were aspects of what, essentially, was a conflictual situation – the normality to which they, and I, would return.

Lastly, since this is a chapter about research methods, it is important to emphasise that method is much more than a matter of applying technique. It is also about empathising or engaging with one's research subjects, of immersing oneself in the field. Clearly, thinking about methodology is essential to the early stages of the research enterprise, before mistakes are made, so to speak, but, paradoxically, it is also a product of that work, an organic development. Ultimately, method is inseparable from, and defined in relation to, its social setting; new methods are one result of these interactions. Just as one must be aware of the exciting new possibilities that advances in research methods bring, we must also be alive to the fact that associated categories are bound to constrain our horizons. At the end of my studies, for example, I became aware of just how limited they were, how, for instance, an anthropological dimension would have shed light on key issues. This is not a problem as such, merely a recognition of the necessarily incomplete and contingent nature of the research enterprise itself.

FURTHER READING

L. Blaxter, C. Hughes and M. Tight, *How to Research* (3rd edn) (Maidenhead: Open University Press, 2001).

A. Bryman, *Social Research Methods* (2nd edn) (Oxford: Oxford University Press, 2004). See especially 'Ethics and Politics in Social Research', pp. 505–20.

C. G. Christians, 'Ethics and Politics in Qualitative Research', in N. K. Denzin and Y. S. Lincoln (eds), *The Landscape of Qualitative Research: Theories and Issues* (2nd edn) (London: Sage, 2003).

M. Fine and L. Weis, 'Writing the 'Wrongs' of Fieldwork: Confronting our own Research/Writing Dilemmas in Urban Ethnographies' (1996) 2 *Qualitative Inquiry* 251.

C. Seale (ed.), *Researching Society and Culture* (2nd edn) (London: Sage, 2004). See especially C. Seale, 'My Research Practice', pp. 463–73.

L. T. Smith, *Decolonizing Methodologies: Research and Indigenous Peoples* (London: Zed Books, 1999).

M. Weber, *The Methodology of the Social Sciences* (trans. and ed. E. A. Shils and H. A. Finch) (Glencoe, IL: Free Press, 1949). See especially 'The Meaning of Ethical Neutrality in Sociology and Economics', pp. 1–49; and 'Objectivity in Social Science and Social Policy', pp. 50–112.

NOTES

1. B. de Sousa Santos, 'Science and Politics: Doing Research in Rio's Squatter Settlements', in R. Luckham (ed.), *Law and Social Enquiry: Case Studies of Research* (New York: Scandinavian Institute of African Studies, Uppsala & International Centre for Law in Development, New York, 1981) 272.

2. Arguably the main focus of the Critical Legal Studies movement of the 1970s and 1980s was precisely about power relations in the context of law. In a very useful survey of the movement, Jírí Príbán notes that, 'The primary target of the critical method is the political neutrality and objectivism of the Western liberal rule of law. This critique is accompanied by a radical critique of the legal science which supports such a value-free and neutral concept of law.' (Jírí Pribán, 'Critical Legal Studies and the Sociology of Law' in R. Bankar and M. Tavers (eds), *An Introduction to Law and Social Theory* (Oxford: Hart Publishing, 2002)) 120. Although the Chapter's main emphasis is upon critical legal theory, issues of method are close to the surface, as they have been for decades: 'Karl Llewellyn in the mid 1930s criticised the American system of legal education for being empty and effectively blinding those seeking to enter the legal profession. Instead of studying the legal texts and rules expressed in them, law professors and students should focus on studying the actual judicial decision-making process, behaviour and social and political motives behind judicial reasoning' (Ibid. 126–7). For a further discussion of theoretical aspects of power relations and law and their implication for method, see also from the same collection M. R. Madsen and Y. Dezalay, 'The Power of the Legal Field: Pierre Bourdieu and the Law'.

3. A relatively recent and especially problematic example of value-neutral approaches to research is offered by Bolanle Akande Adetoun in her chapter on 'The Role and Function of Research in a Divided Society: A Case Study of the Niger Delta region of Nigeria', in E. Portyer, G. Robinson, M. Smyth, A. Schnabel and E. Osaghae (eds) *Researching Conflict in Africa: Insights and Experiences* (New York: United Nations University Press, 2005).

4. G. Meszaros, 'Taking the Land into their Hands: The Landless Workers Workers' Movement and the Brazilian State' (2000) 27 *Journal of Law and Society* 517.

5. H. S. Becker, 'Whose Side Are We On?' (1967) 14 *Social Problems* 239.

6. This is a reference to Boaventura de Sousa Santos's work, 'The Law of the Oppressed: The Construction and Reproduction of Legality in Pasagarda' (1977) 12 *Law and Society Review* 5.

7. G. Meszaros, *The Catholic Church and Trade Unions in Brazil: A Case Study of the Relationship Between the Dioceses of São Paulo and Santo André and the Metalworkers of Greater São Paulo, 1970–1986*, unpublished PhD thesis, London School of Economics, 1991.

8. Conservatism and authoritarianism are amongst the most powerful and enduring features of Brazilian politics and legal culture – especially when it comes to dealing with issues of social class. President Washington Luís Pereira de Sousa's (1926–30) dictum, that the 'the social question [that is, labour movement] is a matter for the police' clearly still held force in 1980, when Lula was imprisoned along with other strike leaders. See, for a discussion of this contested phrase, Célio Debes, 'Washington Luis e a Questão Social'? (2004) 41 *Revista Brasileira* 89–100. In the new millennium too, the way in which the legal system deals with those engaged in land struggle is highly repressive. These practises and attitudes are hard to convey in such a short space as this chapter, but one case that stands out was of six labourers held in prison for six months because they had *allegedly* stolen eight goats.

9. See L. Bridges, G. Meszaros and M. Sunkin, *Judicial Review in Perspective* (London: Cavendish, 1995).

10. For a brief account of developments see I. Gaber, '1965–2004: Forty Years of Social Science Research' (2005) *Social Sciences* Issue 60, available at: http://www.esrc.ac.uk/ESRCInfoCentre/about/CI/CP/Social_Science s/issue60/fortyyears_1.aspx?ComponentId=10788&SourcePageId=112 18

11. Available at: http://www.esrcsocietytoday.ac.uk/ESRCInfoCentre/about/

12. Extensive details of this agency's work, structure and functions, as well as wide range of its publications, are available at its website: http://www.incra.gov.br/

13. For a brief summary of events in Bagé, see Meszaros, note 4 above, 535–8.

14. For decades, even the most trivial aspects of administration in Britain were governed by a culture of secrecy. This was most potently symbolised in the Official Secrets Act, which as a hapless student postman even I was compelled to sign before doing the Christmas rounds! Despite the Freedom of Information Act 2000 reluctantly introduced by New Labour, it seems that a culture of secrecy still prevails. See, for example, R. Evans and D. Hencke, 'Whitehall Finding it Hard to Give Up Secrets', *Guardian Unlimited*, 24/6/2005, available at: http://www.guardian.co.uk/freedom/Story/0,,1513475,00.html

15. The overlap between occupation and subsequent acquisition is brought out to striking effect in the work of B. Mancano: 'Approximately 77 per cent of settlements set up in the South and Southeast regions, in the states of Mato Grosso do Sul and Goias, and in the states of Ceará, Alagoas, Sergipe and Pernambuco in the period 1986-1997, had their origins in land occupations' (p. 299). B. M. Fernandes, *Contribuição ao Estudo do Campesinato Brasileiro: Formação e Territorialização do Movimento dos Trabalhadores Rurais Sem Terra – MST – 1979-1999*, unpublished PhD thesis, Universidade São Paulo, 1999.

16. In April 1996 protesting landless workers blocked a motorway near the town of Eldorado dos Carajás. For months they had urged state authorities to appropriate a ranch as part of the land reform programme, but to no avail. The response of the state government to this act of civil disobedience was swift and brutal. It sent in heavily armed police. Nineteen workers were shot dead, a number in the back at point blank range, and sixty-six others were injured. A recent Amnesty International press release, issued to mark the tenth anniversary of the massacre, notes that the failure of the legal system to bring the perpetrators to justice is symptomatic of the culture of impunity that still exists in Pará state. See: 'Brazil: The Eldorado dos Carajás massacre ten years on', available at: http://web.amnesty.org/library/Index/ENGAMR190192006?open&of=ENG-2AM

17. Ironically the much looser compartmentalistion or separation of legal and political power found in Brazil means that its government is often far more 'joined up', to use a fashionable phrase, than European counterparts.

18. I could refer to yet another of my case studies, the State of São Paulo, and to the actions of its governor, Mário Covas, who came from the same party (the PSDB Partido Social Democratico Brasileiro) as the then President of Brazil, Fernando Henrique Cardoso. He too – not to mention his Secretary of State for Security – was not adverse to the adoption of more flexible policing and legal approaches to the issue of land occupations and reform.

19. Interview with Judge Urbano Ruiz, 2 September 1999.

20. Let us leave aside the issue of military force, democracy and human rights altogether and look at the UK government's Department for International Development (DFID). It asserts that: 'Given Brazil's middle-income status, our role is to provide access to international best practice, promote lesson learning' (available at http://www.dfid.gov.uk/countries/caribbean/brazil.asp). Here is one 'lesson learning' [sic] experience it offers: 'Brazil has made significant progress in tackling macro-economic weaknesses in recent years, particularly in controlling inflation and tightening public spending. The Fiscal Responsibility Law imposed tight discipline on public spending and, for the first time, a requirement for transparency and accountability on regional and local government spending.' Presumably this is good and yet it stands at odds with the assertion made two pages later in the same document that: 'Mechanisms, including local councils, exist to enable civil society to have a role alongside government in both the allocation and monitoring of expenditure at state and municipal level. However, in practice many of these councils lack the resources, both human and financial, to enable them to be effective' (source: *The Development Challenge for Brazil*, available at Ibid. pp. 2 and 4 respectively).

21. Ribeiro was a leading anthropologist and intellectual, who set up Brazilia University, served in the administration of Joao Goulart and faced a period in exile. He has written extensively on politics and anthropology. The particular work I have in mind is his *O Povo Braileiro: A formação e o sentido do Brasil*, Compamhia das Letras, São Paulo, 1995.

22. Ibid. 17.

23. Paradoxically, these grey spaces have become simultaneously more intertwined and frayed in recent years as the MST's political ally, the Worker's Party (PT), has moved into political office. The accession of Lula to the Presidency illustrates these contradictions. His election raised the thorny issue of what State power really meant for the MST and those of its sympathisers (activists and intellectuals) promoted to high office. Notwithstanding waves of occupations, the answer of the MST to this question has been ambiguous to say the least – almost as if, like the PT, it too was taken by surprise. Perhaps this ambiguity is attributable to the scale of the investment made in the PT over the course of two decades; to the limited availability of alternative options; and to the sheer power of the State. In other words, to a very particular form of inertia. However distinctive the circumstances, it is a pattern replicated elsewhere – and across the globe.

CHAPTER 7

Non-empirical Discovery in Legal Scholarship – Choosing, Researching and Writing a Traditional Scholarly Article

Michael Pendleton

There are many areas in or touching law worthy of further examination by those trained in it. Such further examination usually takes the form of scholarly articles in law reviews, journals, chapters and books, though some contemporary schools of jurisprudence would suggest social action programmes.[1] Scholarly articles and the like may begin life as vague ideas over coffee with colleagues, flashes of inspiration in the middle of the night, mere drafts or seminar, conference and symposium papers. There are also many ways of classifying legal writing. Before discussing the sense in which it is used in this chapter, it is instructive to survey possible definitions.

One attempted definition was put forward as follows:

> 54. Research in and on the law takes many forms. Apart from the substantial research undertaken in connection with the teaching of courses, the major types of research are:
> (i) research which provides a systematic exposition of the rules governing a particular legal category, analyses the relationship between rules, explains areas of difficulty and, perhaps, predicts future developments ('doctrinal research');
> (ii) research which intensively evaluates the adequacy of existing rules and which recommends changes to any rules found wanting ('reform-oriented research'); and
> (iii) research which fosters a more complete understanding of the conceptual bases of legal principles and of the combined effects of a range of rules and procedures that touch on a particular area of activity ("theoretical research").[2]

It is important to note that the definition of legal writing has in recent times responded to university funding models for law which have largely adopted a single model for all disciplines – the science model of discovery through empirical research. This has had serious negative effects for traditional scholarship.

ON THE CONTEMPORARY DOMINANCE OF EMPIRICAL LEGAL RESEARCH

In a country representative of many Anglo Commonwealth jurisdictions – Australia – the universities, under pressure from federal tertiary funding ministries in various incarnations and corporate styles, the most recent of which is the Department of Education, Science and Training (DEST), insisted that all disciplines, be they physics, law or theology, embrace and emphasise empirical research as a form of academic endeavour. Under this definition a law textbook will rarely even count as a publication, no matter how frequently cited in the courts. What matters is the dollars brought in by empirical research funding. The legal academic has little in the way of equipment or materials (other than a good library) that he or she requires – unlike the physicist or indeed most of the scientific community. The notion that legal scholarship primarily involves reflection on what is the doctrine inherent in the law and what policy underlies the doctrine, or its appropriateness, is foreign to the contemporary definition of legal research.

Present-day legal research grants invariably involve calculating teaching buyout and travel allowances. Aside from research assistance, what other expenses are there for a legal academic? Thus a very inexperienced part time teacher would take over the researcher's undergraduate teaching. The law school had to live with the inherent unaccountability of part-time teachers and ignore the foundational importance to student development of good teaching at undergraduate level. Many of us, the author included, compounded our involvement by consenting to become research assessors, applying the very criteria we knew to be flawed. One size fits all always creates problems, and shoehorning lawyerly, arts or humanities scholarship under the umbrella of empirical research is no exception. ·

THE DISCOVERY ELEMENT IN LAW

The Pearce Report[3] refers to the submissions of the Australian Law Deans submission which succinctly states why law does not fit the empirical research definition of the funding models:

> *The nature of academic research in Law*
> It follows from what has just been said that, in Law, the 'discovery'
> element in academic research is not as immediately apparent as it is, for

instance, in the natural sciences. In Law, and in the humanities and social sciences generally, it may seem that one does not 'discover new truths' but that one merely reviews and analyses (or synthesises) past and present social phenomena.

This view is however based on a fundamental misconception. Law is a highly sophisticated human construct that is constantly changing. A large part of legal research therefore consists of formulating hypotheses to give meaning to detailed legal rules already created (whether by statute or judicial decision) and projecting these hypotheses so as to create new patterns of rule-making. Often the most profound 'discoveries' are in fact those that give new coherence to familiar legal phenomena. For this reason, the process of ascertainment and synthesis of existing legal principles constitutes original research, as also does coming to terms with the dynamic of past, present and future legal development.

When one uses the term 'research', as a key aspect of 'scholarship' the former term must accordingly be interpreted widely enough to cover a whole range of investigative, analytical, critical, theoretical and/or synthesising intellectual activity by academic lawyers. In addition, any implicit requirement that there be some obvious and dramatic element of 'discovery', such as might win a Nobel prize in a scientific field, cannot apply in Law.

Regrettably, the above wisdom is lost upon many funding models for law in many jurisdictions, and law as a discipline is considerably impoverished for it.

TRADITIONAL LEGAL DOCTRINAL CRITICISM

Legal writing inevitably reflects the writer's jurisprudential assumptions and beliefs. Their legal philosophical or theoretical assumptions and beliefs is a more contemporary way of saying the same thing. So this writing not merely reflects the various schools of analytical jurisprudence such as the positivist, realist (American and Scandinavian), critical legal studies, post-modernist, various justice theories such as economic analysis of law or sociological conceptions of law, but all the unpublished variants of jurisprudential theory which make up your and my understanding of what is law. Clearly then, this chapter, like all chapters on law, reflects elements of the writer's jurisprudential assumptions and beliefs.

The classification of legal writing adopted in this chapter is temporal. Traditionally, legal writing in common law jurisdictions predominately concerned examining decisions of judges and identifying matters of concern to the author and his or her audience. That audience consisted of practitioners of law, judges and fellow academics. Often these matters of concern were of a technical nature: what is the true *ratio decidendi* of the decision; is there an implicit overruling of a previous decision; is this decision really in line with previous authority; is the reasoning subject to criticism in terms of formal, deductive or inductive logic; does or should the principle of *stare decisis* allow a superior court in a judicial hierarchy to depart from its own previous decisions; and other related criticisms. In this chapter this area is termed traditional legal doctrinal criticism.

Later, perhaps beginning in the 1960s and 1970s, reconciling judicial decisions with perceived public policy became a predominant theme of legal writing in Anglo Commonwealth common law jurisdictions. The current concern with sustainable environmental practices has spawned a large tract of legal writing. For the purposes of this chapter, this area is designated public policy legal writing.

Most recently, much legal writing in these jurisdictions has concerned empirical research into matters involving or related to law. Reconciling crime recidivism rates with stated purposes of sentencing policy; making a film about newly established legal concepts such as native title rights; and examining methods to free up access to information by imaginative copyright licensing arrangements are all examples. This latter area is termed 'empirical legal writing'. It has become a dominant area of legal writing today. Its growth, in the author's opinion, is related to the single model for funding of universities which accords with the science models whereby scholarly writing always begins with empirical research.

This chapter concerns the first area of legal writing: legal doctrinal criticism. The term legal research is much bandied about in present times and is inevitably linked to empirical legal writing as defined above. Legal doctrinal criticism of course involves legal research but is only one, and a relatively minor, component. Traditional legal research concerned finding the law. Perhaps the traditional sense of the term legal research was, but is no longer related to, the old discredited declaratory theory of law:[4] that law is out there, in the clouds as it were, waiting to be divined. It suggested one answer to the research and we have certainly moved beyond this. Those seeking to do traditional research are usually practitioners of law, solicitors, barristers and judges, and their participation is limited by the dispute between the parties. The writer of legal doctrinal criticism joins this group but legal research is where he or she begins to do legal writing, it is not the enterprise itself. I find it inaccurate, certainly inappropriate, to refer to myself as a legal researcher. It is just a small step in my work as a legal scholar.

Traditional legal doctrinal criticism of course requires identifying, reading and digesting the area of concern to the author – cases or statutes, preparatory material, and subsequent commentary, for example – but this is relatively straightforward and involves a minor proportion of time devoted to the whole enterprise.[5] Most of the time is devoted to reflection on the law and applying one's imagination to gain new insights. Without imagination, reflection in any area of human knowledge may render technical results, yet will be sterile – it will create nothing new. The writer of legal doctrinal criticism is not unrelated to the sociologist, theologian, or philosopher – much of their work is about one's world-view and what, therefore, is desirable societal regulation. The research task is relatively straightforward. The reflection process is the major part of the work and is particularly conducive to original and lateral thought.

CHOOSING A TOPIC

There are many ways to choose a topic as the subject of a scholarly article. One of the best is through exchanges with colleagues in informal settings, in the staffroom over coffee, for example. Teaching is a wonderful way to get ideas for articles. You leave the room uneasy with a solution you have proposed to students. A student raises a point you had never thought of before – a very common experience and one reason why teaching can keep you young. There is the famous example of the author of the 1970s seminal article on sustainable development and standing to bring suit to protect the environment, '*Should Trees Have Standing?*'[6] The author recites how a student asked in class why a river should not be invested with legal personality so it could sue via the medium of representatives.

For me, most ideas about subjects for legal articles came from imagining, proposing, accepting, refining and testing over time a theory of my subject – intellectual property (IP). I was lucky to start at a time before even the subject title – IP – had any currency. Everything I read on the subject, consciously or unconsciously, is tested against the theory and the theory is modified or the development criticised after this reflection. I imagine most of us do this in normal conversation about anything much beyond the weather and we probably have theories on this too, with greater or lesser degrees of scientific content!

WHERE TO PUBLISH – CHOOSING A LAW JOURNAL

Generally speaking it is best to try a refereed law journal, though this is principally for reasons of academic credit with the university rather than for any intrinsic reason.

A major distinction which must be adverted to immediately which exists between law and many other disciplines relates to the issue of refereed journals, to which so much importance is attached in science and technology. The process of refereeing and assessment is altogether more diverse, varying considerably from journal to journal, than it seems to be in other areas. There are very many journals which have considerable influence in legal circles which would or might not fulfil the generally required science criteria, but it would be wrong to ignore them especially as they deal with matters relating to the practising legal profession. Methods of quality control are different but no less rigorous that in other disciplines.[7]

A further comment may be added about publication in law journals that are edited by students. It is sometimes assumed that for an academic journal to have student editors is a mark of low scholarly content and repute. Yet this is a characteristic of some of the leading law journals in the world, in particular, the *Harvard Law Review*, which is one of the most prestigious law journals in the United States. In such journals, submitted articles are assessed, if not formally refereed, by leading academic lawyers in the particular field.

OMITTING OR BLURRING THE WRITER'S RELEVANT ETHICAL PREMISES – AN UNFORTUNATE NEW FASHION IN INTELLECTUAL DISHONESTY

Silence or omission has always struck me to be as dishonest as a positively false statement. It certainly creates as much damage, perhaps no more so than in the pursuit of knowledge. When you write, I believe you must identify and go equipped with your world-view and make it apparent and upfront to the reader what that world-view is. It is ironic that much contemporary scholarly writing, not just in law but across the humanities and social sciences, is deliberately dense and impenetrable when it comes to discovering the world-view of the writer – a key concern for most of us. Rightly so too, because generally speaking we will not be prepared to discard major platforms or assumptions in our own world-view without substantial argument addressed to these very assumptions. The fact that Professor X, of prestige to the power of twelve, rejects by implication a key premise in our own world-view, for example, the desirability of a market system, is unlikely to have much persuasive effect on us. The postmodernist position must bear considerable responsibility here. While a philosophical position may question the very meaning and sanity of even contemplating a world-view, like all world views it should state the position upfront.

In my view, the ethical and normative major premises on which an argument is advanced, or indeed the rejection of such a concept, should be apparent and made transparent at the beginning of a piece of scholarly writing. If I read an article on IP which advances a technical criticism of an element of copyright law, I am very annoyed when I find after reading it that hidden in the text is the major premise that the author rejects one of the two key justifications for IP. For example, the utilitarian market failure argument – that is, that without legal rights, information can not be traded and thus there is a lack of incentive to invest resources of labour and time in creating the information. Had the author stated the article was a minor premise and conclusion to this major premise, I would have seen the point immediately and formed my response. I regard this as dishonest writing, all the more so from the perspective of the student reader who may not always be able to identify the unstated major premises in such articles.

Thus, if the underpinning of the argument in a scholarly legal article rests on a moral premise of universalist, relativist, logical positivist, nihilist, post-modernist or other position, it should be stated at the outset.

LAW IN CONTEXT APPROACH TO LEGAL WRITING

I had never really thought through the meaning of the phrase 'law in context' aside from the literal and jurisprudential genre until the first editor of this volume explained one meaning of it to me. He suggested it meant to identify social problems by attempting to put out of mind current legal characterisations of problems and their solutions and then to suggest solutions anew. Once it was so explained, I realised I always, at least for the past twenty-five years, begin a course on IP by asking students to imagine a scenario which takes place in their own kingdom, where they have total freedom to interpose their own perceptions and solutions to problems.

I ask them to imagine a society where a large number of deaths and injuries have resulted from driving on unlit sections of road at night. One night a person sees a cat racing across an unlit section of road, its eyes reflecting back at the driver. Instantly, and thinking laterally, the person sees the solution to driving on unlit sections of road by using clear glass reflecting domes affixed to the centre lines of roads. In one scenario she thinks to herself, 'Ah well, I have done it again with my rare lateral capacities', and promptly forgets it, as she did her previous idea of yellow 'post it' notes and the paper clip. In another scenario, she begins manufacturing these 'cat's eyes' as she calls them and makes a profit for six months until a competitor starts manufacturing cat's eyes with a dull chemical light. These have the advantage of not only reflecting back a car's headlights but also indicating which direction the road will take beyond the straight-line direction of the headlights. The competitor calls these 'tiger's eyes'. I then ask the student if the originator of the cat's eyes deserves or needs any reward and if so what form it might take. If there is to be a restriction on other people's access to the cat's eyes how long should this extend and from when? I ask them a great many other questions including whether the competitor's tiger's eyes should be held to transgress the cat's eyes rights, if any, and whether the tiger's eyes should enjoy a reward in their own right.

The scenario inevitably requires the students to state the justification or lack of justification for what we in the present day call IP, to identify interest groups and to propose balances of interest. Just for your interest, in my experience, the students are always roughly equally divided in a straw poll I habitually take of whether the 'tiger's eyes' should be held to transgress rights in respect of 'cat's eyes'. Along the way they usually anticipate most of the present-day patent regime including priority date based on the date of filing, as in the Anglo Commonwealth, or date of invention as in the USA.

A step back from the present-day law to this law-in-context approach can always be illuminating for legal scholarship. It is not just the solution which needs to be considered in this context but the identification and classification of the problem. It may well be that once the problem is expressed in a certain way, the solution automatically suggests itself. Remember in the example above, the role of the cat in the 'discovery' of 'cat's eyes'. More importantly, people who have the ability to think laterally are rare, and rarity is by definition of economic value.

THE COMPARATIVE APPROACH – LAW REFORM COMMISSION MODELS

Law teachers often remind themselves that we all teach from a comparative perspective these days. But what does that mean and what especially does it mean for legal scholarship? I must admit it was only after I became chairman of the Law Reform Commission of Western Australia that I really came to appreciate the comparative method. This was despite having taught comparative law in terms of the doctrine of functional equivalents and its application for many years across major legal families (not just civil and common law), and having taught and researched outside my home jurisdiction for much of my professional life. It was through the habitual routine of drafting a law reform commission issues paper, then drafting the answers paper as a summary of submissions received, and then finally drafting the formal report that I came to appreciate the role of comparative law. A reference to the Commission which I remember well was whether there should be a privilege against being compelled to testify as witnesses for journalists, clergy and others. The comparative research on the position in other jurisdictions illustrated the value of the comparative method. It was not so much the solutions in those jurisdictions as to how the functionally equivalent need was perceived and addressed. As regards the privilege reference, some jurisdictions – made no distinction as to the calling of the witness – journalist, clergy, and so on but rather grouped together anyone who received confidential or deeply personal information from another for example, a spouse, a social worker, an academic. These jurisdictions also considered that the issue of compellability ought to be deferred to a consideration of how relevant and necessary the information was likely to be in the case before the court as against the damage done by forcing the disclosure of confidential information. Once this research uncovered these approaches, and their workability in their home jurisdictions was established, the solution to our reference suggested itself.

In a similar vein, when I was a member of the Australian Federal Attorney General's Copyright Law Review Committee, we had a reference entitled Copyright and Contract. The key issue was whether contracting out of fair dealing and other defences and exceptions to copyright infringement should be permitted. It has become common place for websites to require users to click on a licence term whereby the user agrees to give up any fair dealing (fair use in the USA) and other defences and exceptions under copyright legislation. Comparative research demonstrated that fair dealing and the like can either be regarded as defences, privileges or exceptions to infringement, or they can be characterised as positive rights of users which balance the rights of copyright owners. Expressed in this way, and again so stated on the basis of comparative research, the answer is apparent. Fair dealing and the like are part of the balance of interests which copyright law represents, a user right, and as such not to be put aside by individual contracts. Having so concluded, we were then reminded of our limitations due to the nature of modern information society, namely whatever one country's law prohibits in terms of internet usage, anothers might permit. Thus in the absence of an international convention, a prohibition on contracting out of fair dealing and such like was likely to be of limited utility.

A RESERVOIR FOR ACADEMIC WRITING – A THEORY OF YOUR SUBJECT

My abiding interest in IP over the past twenty-five years has been in large part sustained by a theory of the subject which has to date managed to explain (at least to me) most new developments, twists and turns. I developed this theory before, during and after writing my first book in 1984 on the subject of IP. I describe it now, perhaps at unconscionable length, because it may assist you in developing your own theory of your subject.

It occurred to me then and still seems so now that IP is about legal rights restricting access to aspects of information. All IP at base concerns an aspect of information. Trade names, patents, designs, trade secrets, domain names, copyright, plant breeder's rights, silicon chip topography are all information at base. To this information, the law ascribes legal rights to restrict and allow access. The justification for law's interposition of legal rights is twofold. First, a kind of natural rights proposition is extended to the effect that the innovator's own self flows into their creation, and as an extension of self ought not to be freely appropriated by others. An identical justification underpins the academic convention against plagiarism. Secondly, unless legal rights attach to information it cannot be sold or traded; thus there is no incentive to invest time and money in creating new forms of information. This utilitarian or market failure justification is frequently cited.

At least three groups have interests, and conflicting interests at that, in the law's ascription of legal rights to information. The innovator wants as much protection of the information and for as long as he or she can get. Competitors want limited rights to the information so they can compete but, should they succeed, they do want some rights they themselves can enjoy. We the public want unlimited access to information, at least until we have to address the consequences of lack of incentive for creators. Further the law in common law and civil law jurisdictions has, over the centuries, steadfastly refused to recognise legal rights in information as such, fearing unjustified monopoly. Rather the law developed ad hoc as separate species of highly technical rights – patent, copyright, trade marks and the like – many of which were and are today heavily overlapping each other.

I was not then and have never been persuaded by the danger of monopoly – a very real danger of course – being of itself reason to reject a law protecting all information. I have argued, repetitively perhaps, over the past twenty-five years that we need a general principle of liability, easily understood and respected by the person on the street, to protect aspects of information which come into existence through the expenditure of labour, skill, effort, time, money and imagination.

Call it a law against misappropriation, unfair competition or slavish imitation, it does not matter but such a law has the potential to replace most of present-day IP. In so doing, I would argue the reasoning applied would be virtually identical to what is applied in many hard cases under the present regime. Although the doctrine on copyright, patent, trade secrets is complex, you find the familiar refrain throughout the IP cases in most jurisdictions of 'has the defendant cashed in on the labour, skill effort investment of time and money of the innovator, has he ridden on the back of the plaintiff, has he misappropriated the plaintiff's work'. The key to avoiding unjustified monopoly is to limit the innovator's rights by the extent to which the defendant has contributed its own labour, skill and effort or lateral thought and brought about some new information demonstrably different in kind to that of the plaintiff.

None of this is new today but when I put it together in an article published in *European Intellectual Property Review* (*EIPR*) in 1985,[8] there was little written about which even justified why we were now using the term IP as a compendious term for all the causes of action which hitherto had been referred to simply as patent law, or copyright law, or trademark law, and so on. However, the latter hypothesis about the law conferring rights in information as such is far from accepted, and I suppose this will keep up my interest in IP as I seek to champion this position or perhaps am persuaded that I have been in error.

The above theory of my subject and the following are examples drawn from my own legal writing, and they illustrate a type of traditional legal doctrinal criticism.

EXAMPLES OF WRITING LEGAL DOCTRINAL CRITICISM

I will give three examples of legal doctrinal criticism from my own writing. The first example is an article involving the proper scope of IP[9]. This article was very much informed and moulded by the formation of a theory of my subject IP, referred to above. That world-view came out of my book on IP in Hong Kong, according to one commentator only the second book published anywhere in the world to treat IP as one coherent subject matter.[10] That observation is not meant as a pat on the back but rather to illustrate that the experience of researching, and then trying to make sense of the research, caused me to conceive a theory of IP which has remained with me for twenty-five years.

My book did not contain a thoroughgoing statement of my theory of IP. It was still developing. That was articulated later, in again truncated form, in the article referred to above in *EIPR* (see note 8). Another reason for the omission in the book and for a full-blown account in the article was hesitation and, I hope, some intellectual humility. A more fully articulated form of my theory of IP came in the latter part of the proper scope of an IP article which forms the third example of traditional legal doctrinal criticism in this chapter.

The second example is from an article[11] about interpreting the words of a patent in cases of so-called non-literal infringement.

EXAMPLE I: ENDORSING FAULTY LEGAL REASONING – MEANS, ENDS AND *CROCODILE DUNDEE*

Passing off is a tort which evolved from the tort of deceit to protect business reputation and goodwill. It constitutes the law of unregistered trademarks. In order to succeed the plaintiff must prove reputation or goodwill attaching to a badge of consumer recognition, for example, a brand name, a device, get up or trade dress. Next it must prove a relevant misrepresentation, for example, the defendant is using an identical brand name. Finally the plaintiff must prove damage or its likelihood. For example, if the plaintiff sells pot plants under the brand Acme, and the defendant uses Acme at a much later date for aircraft, it is unlikely, though not impossible, that a court would be persuaded damage to the plaintiff results.

In the *Hogan v Pacific Dunlop*,[12] the *Crocodile Dundee* case, the actor Paul Hogan, who played the *Crocodile Dundee* character, sued in passing off a multi-national company that made shoes, *inter alia*. The defendant made a television advertisement which featured a scene reminiscent of the knife scene in the film where the hero is set upon by muggers who brandish a knife. The hero then draws a veritable sword and says 'you call that a knife'. In the defendant's shoe commercial the hero looks down at the mugger's shoes and says, 'you call those shoes', at the same time proudly exhibiting his own shoes of the defendant's manufacture. The plaintiff succeeded.

The judge, Justice Gummow, Australia's leading IP judge and now ensconced in its highest court, prefaced his opinion by quoting a decision which was binding upon him, and which roundly condemned evolving the mis-representation-based tort of passing off towards an expanded remedy for mis-appropriation. It is impossible to discern approval or disdain for the precedent from the words of the judgment because there is simply no comment on it. Gummow J. then constructed an argument based upon a thorough compara-tive analysis across at least five major jurisdictions of the law of passing off applied to fictional characters.

In a telling passage at the outset of the case, Gummow J. stated:

> But the advertising campaign was conceived and carried through with an intention, to put it shortly, to 'cash in' on the success of 'Crocodile Dundee' and the fame attending the performance of Mr Hogan in the title role.

When experienced IP lawyers read words like these, it is clear that whatever doc-trine stands in the way, the result is almost always in favour of the plaintiff.[13]

In my article (see note 9), I argued that the ultimate basis of most decisions in the character merchandising cases (and, by a similar line of reasoning, to the personality and sponsorship cases) is that where the public believes a 'com-mercial arrangement' should exist between a plaintiff who is known to have created a fictional character and a defendant character merchandiser, and in fact no such arrangement exists, the defendant is found guilty of an actionable misrepresentation in passing off. If this is accurate, there are substantial logical difficulties with the reasoning adopted in some of these cases. However, there

is little doubt that the judicial motive is to prohibit objectionable misappropriation, and rightly so in my view.

Why might the public assume the existence in a character merchandising
case of a commercial arrangement (and licence fee) between plaintiff and defendant, invariably wrongly, otherwise a case will not arise? One might guess that
it is because the public assumes the law requires the defendant to acquire a permission from the plaintiff. Yet in the *Crocodile Dundee*[14] case the court utilised
a public belief in what the law requires as the basis for finding a misrepresentation in cases which in reality were about what the law of passing off does or,
more accurately, should require.

On any objective analysis, the law on this question was moot, at least for
lawyers, if not for the public. Thus I argued there is an inevitable circularity in
pressing into service a public perception of what the law of actionable misrepresentation requires as the benchmark of what is in fact an actionable misrepresentation. This is only a short step from saying any representation not
according with what the public perception of what the law of actionable misrepresentation requires is itself an actionable misrepresentation. Amongst the
various judges responsible for developing this area of the law, Gummow J. was
fully mindful of this criticism and in the *Crocodile Dundee* case refers to it as the
doctrine of 'erroneous assumption'.[15]

Gummow J. observed on the basis of the evidence, and partially perhaps by
way of judicial notice, that there is a widespread practice in Australia and elsewhere generally referred to as character merchandising, whereby those who
create fictional characters licence others for reward to manufacture or deal in
products in association with a representation of these fictional characters.
This is also true of famous personalities licensing their names and likeness.
His Honour then made a finding which was to become crucial to the result in
this case:

> I infer from this evidence that the purchasing public would be aware in
> a general way of this practice.
>
> What is also interesting is the likelihood that a misrepresentation
> cannot stand unless the public conviction of the need for a commercial
> arrangement is, in theory, proven in every case. But, in reality, as cases
> of this type multiply, proof may well become a mere formality. The
> requirement of misrepresentation in character merchandising cases
> may, as a result of these cases, become akin to a legal fiction, a time
> hallowed device for courts to work justice when there are apparent
> doctrinal restraints.
>
> The evidence introduced by the defendant in Crocodile Dundee in
> respect of the television advertisement and certain advertising posters
> tended to suggest that the viewers did not think the actor was Mr Hogan

nor did they address their minds to whether there was a business connection between the defendant and Mr Hogan. The evidence introduced on behalf of the plaintiff suggested that the actor in the television advertisement and the posters was intended to imitate Mr Hogan and further that they imagined some authorisation had been given by Mr Hogan to the defendant to make the advertisement and posters. Evidence introduced by both parties suggested that the advertisement and posters was a send-up of the Crocodile Dundee film.[16]

Gummow J. dismissed the argument that parody was a sufficient disclaimer on the present facts, though apparently he left open situations in which parody might amount to such a disclaimer.

Thus my article on the *Crocodile Dundee* case was at base a criticism of the fallacious logic in the character merchandising cases as well as an endorsement of the results in those cases. It is circular reasoning and thus illogical to commence an inquiry into the existence of a legal right when the first step in that process is to inquire what the public believes as to the existence of that self-same legal right, and then to proceed to say the public were deceived because the legal right they presumed should exist in cases of this type – that is, character merchandising – did not in fact exist. Much better, I argued, as indeed with most forms of IP, is to allow misrepresentation to evolve to a remedy against misappropriation of labour, skill and effort, investment of time and money.

EXAMPLE 2: THE MEANING OF WORDS – PATENT INTERPRETATION

My first published academic article[17], was on the interpretation of patents. I was working at Bird & Bird, a law firm in Grays Inn Square, London, after leaving teaching at the University of Sydney Law Faculty when I read an as-yet-unreported recent House of Lords decision which was causing some comment. The decision was *Catnic v Hill & Smith* [18] which continues today as the leading case on patent interpretation in Anglo Commonwealth jurisdictions.

How to interpret words is of the essence of law. So, too, how to interpret literature, an enterprise which is as old as law. It is appropriate that some jurisprudential theory talks of law as literature. Interpretation arises with statutes, judicial decisions, contracts and other written documents including patents.

The facts in *Catnic* were of startling simplicity. A lightweight lintel of wooden box girder construction for supporting brick courses above door cavities had a back plate which extended at ninety degrees from the base plate. The patent claim described the back plate as extending 'vertically' from the base plate. The defendant inclined the back plate in one lintel model at six degrees off vertical and in another model at eight degrees off vertical. The simplicity of these facts plus the finding that six or even eight degrees off vertical was still comprehended by the word 'vertically' in the patent gives the decision its impact and perhaps partly explains its longevity.

The court's decision that the defendant's variant infringed the claim was equally startling at the time. A little research uncovered that the judge concerned had pioneered purposive construction of statutes against an English heritage of strict literalism. His efforts had been fiercely opposed by brother judges but by the time of *Catnic*, purposive construction was firmly ensconced in the English legal and other Commonwealth jurisdictions.[19]

The judge recited the previous law in terms of a literal approach but where a defendant had taken the 'pith and marrow' of an invention, used a mere 'mechanical equivalent' (the basis of present-day US law is the doctrine of equivalents), or been guilty of 'colourable evasion', the courts would abandon literalism to assist the patentee. The difficulty with this approach, Lord Diplock implies in his speech, is that it is entirely subjective.

In delivering the unanimous decision of the House of Lords, Lord Diplock declared that there is only one method of patent construction and interpretation: the purposive approach:

> My Lords, in their closely reasoned written cases in this House and in the oral argument, both parties to this appeal have tended to treat 'textual infringement' and infringement of the 'pith and marrow' of an invention as if they were separate causes of action, the existence of the former to be determined as a matter of construction only and of the latter upon some broader principle of colourable evasion. There is in my view no such dichotomy; there is but a single cause of action and to treat it otherwise, particularly in cases like that which is the subject of the instant appeal, is liable to lead to confusion.[20]

Like so much in law the prescriptive and the descriptive can become muddled especially when the court writes, as it often does, as if it is describing, when in fact its power and function is to prescribe. The declaratory theory of law has much to answer for. Lord Diplock was really saying that from this case forward there is to be one cause of action in regard to patent interpretation and that is purposive construction as he had defined it.

Lord Diplock and Lord Denning had formed the avant garde in reforming the interpretation of statutes away from literal interpretation to interpretation that had regard to the legislative history of the drafting of a statute and its progress through parliament, an approach they coined as 'purposive construction'. Despite rebukes from the House of Lords, which Lord Denning left in order to move down to the Court of Appeal where he was less often in dissent, purposive interpretation has established itself as the mainstream. The attack on literalism in regard to patent interpretation has proved as, if not more intractable than its counterpart: statutory construction. The key to interpretation of both statutes and patents is an aid outside the four corners of the document to aid interpretation. With legislation, the aid is the preparatory material. With patents, it is, at its most basic, the understanding of what a hypothetical person skilled in the art would have understood the patentee to have wanted to claim at the priority date of the patent by looking at the feature in question ('vertically' in *Catnic*) in the context of its importance to how the invention works as a whole. Thus in *Catnic*, the hypothetical skilled person was chosen as a builder, and the evidence showed that a builder who would understand the patentee in respect of the lintel would have wanted to include variants of the lintel with a back plate extending eighty two degrees from the base plate. Why, because the evidence showed a builder would know eighty-two degrees would work in a lintel even though the physicist could point to some diminution in strength as the back plate leaves vertical from the base plate.

I wrote in my article in *EIPR* that, in *Catnic*, Lord Diplock sought to explain the law in terms of decided cases. Lord Diplock observed that all members of the Court of Appeal in *Catnic* agreed that the applicable law was to be derived from *Van der Lely NV v Bamfords Ltd (Van der Lely)*[21] and *Rodi & Weinenberger AG Henry v Showell Ltd (Rodi)*.[22] Both cases split the House of Lords and Court of Appeal respectively, and contain powerful dissents.

In both cases the intention of the patentee to claim a feature as an essential integer of the invention was held by the majority to be the test of whether an infringement had occurred. For infringement to exist, there had to be copying of each and every such integer. This was the traditional formulation of the pith and marrow doctrine. However, this intention was to be imputed whenever a feature was included in a claim in clear language deliberately chosen. The essentiality of the feature in relation to the working of the invention as a whole was not considered as an aid in determining the patentee's invention.

The test of essentiality was then set out by Lord Diplock in a rather circumlocutious paragraph, which outlines the application of the new functionally orientated test of essentiality to circumstances where the effect of a variant is uncertain, having regard to the state of the art at the date of the specification.

> Where it is not obvious, in the light of then existing knowledge [presumably whether a variant will have a material effect on the way the invention worked], the reader is entitled to assume that the patentee thought at the time of the specification that he had good reason for limiting his monopoly so strictly and had intended to do so, even though subsequent work by him or others in the field of the invention might show the limitation to have been unnecessary.[23]

It seems that in these circumstances the limitation will be held essential. It is hard to see how it could mean otherwise. But Lord Diplock says objective reasons will be required to confine narrowly the scope of the patentee's monopoly.

> No plausible reason has been advanced why any rational patentee should want to place so narrow a limitation on his invention. On the contrary, to do so would render his monopoly for practical purposes worthless, since any imitator could avoid it and take all the benefit of the invention by the simple expedient of positioning the back plate a degree or two from the exact vertical. [24]

However, it would appear from the sentence immediately following the above quotation that a superfluous limitation will be held inessential in the following circumstances:

> It [the question of essentiality] is to be answered in the negative only when it would be apparent to any reader skilled in the art that a particular word or phrase used in a claim cannot have been intended by a patentee, who was also skilled in the art, to exclude minor variants which, to the knowledge of both him and the readers to whom the patent was addressed, could have no material effect upon the way in which the invention worked. [25]

Hence it appears that for the first time the Court will protect what the patentee might have claimed, provided that both the patentee and his readers would recognise, had they directed their minds to it at the priority date, that the minor variant was incapable of having any material effect on the way the invention worked.

I submitted in the *EIPR* article that it was implicit in Lord Diplock's analysis of the decision in *Van der Lely* that the Court should have had regard in their judgment to expert evidence as to whether the defendant's machine utilising dismountable foremost wheels could have a material effect upon the way the patented hay-raking machine worked. Once it was established that there could be no material effect, the court should then ask the relevant expert whether, either hypothetically or in fact, any rational patentee would have intended to exclude the defendant's variant from the scope of his monopoly. If not, it is a mere minor variant and will be held to infringe.

I suggested that in similar circumstances where the patentee has failed to think through the effect of minor variants which, to his and patent specification readers' knowledge at the priority date, can have no material effect on the way the invention works, the Court should, if Lord Diplock's principle is accepted, lend its assistance.

EXAMPLE 3: REPLACING MOST OF PRESENT DAY IP LAW WITH A MISAPPROPRIATION LAW

The above topic is my most ambitious piece of legal doctrinal criticism to date and is built upon my theory of IP discussed above under the heading 'A Reservoir for Academic Writing – A Theory of Your Subject'. It is traditional legal doctrinal criticism because it is about the best legal vehicle for the task and builds upon existing law. There is no radical agenda, such as getting rid of property rights.

It argues that the current law assumes that property is the appropriate conceptual legal device to give expression to these competing and legitimate interest groups yet property is an entirely exclusionary device. It is primarily designed to exclude trespassers. It is not inherently adapted to giving expression to a conception of a positive rights of access, let alone a balancing of competing interest groups. Various far from radical writers have suggested that the legal device of property is no longer appropriate for structuring rights in information in the way that the present law of IP does.

Roger Cotterell[26] points out that it is essential to recognise that most IP forms are at their base concerned with the protection of ideas, aspects of ideas or at the very least information. This creates difficulties for a law based essentially on property.

The possibility of explicit recognition in the law of a right to protect the fruits of any more than *de minimis* expenditure of labour, skill, effort, investment of time and money, and a countervailing right to legitimately take the labour, skill, effort and investment of another where sufficient *additional* labour, skill, and effort and investment are expended, ought to create a new balance of rights for competitors with flow-on benefits to consumers. Many of these competitor rights already exist in our present law but are largely unarticulated in this form. What is sufficient additional labour, skill, effort and investment of time and money to avoid what would otherwise be an infringement is a difficult but not insoluble problem.

Unfortunately, this crucial problem is largely ignored in an otherwise very important but little known article by D. F. Liebling, *The Concept of Property: Property in Intangibles*.[27] He argues that the basis of proprietary rights is the expenditure of time, effort, labour and money, and therefore the creation of valuable information so brought about should vest in the creator property rights to commercially exploit the information. This result, he argues, not only should be the case but is the case under the present Anglo Commonwealth law once certain hard cases have been explained (which he seeks to do). According to Liebling, those cases which have denied property rights to the creators of valuable commercial information brought into being through the expenditure of time, effort, labour or money were wrongly decided, given a Dworkin-like assumption that law does not consist of the decided cases *per se*, but rather of principles of which the cases are evidence.

Certainly there is a crucial problem of what might be sufficient additional labour, skill, effort and investment of time or money to escape the initial protection which accrues to the fruits of any more than *de minimis* investment of labour, skill, effort and expenditure of time and money. But it is not a question which can be addressed here for reasons of space and complexity. However, the key to this difficult problem might just lie in an analogous concept to the copyright notion that *de minimis* independent labour, skill and effort expressed in a material form gives rise (subject to conditions) to a copyright work, yet the degree of protection is proportionate to the contribution of labour, skill and effort.[28] Thus a few meaningless lines on a page might qualify as a work of artistic copyright, yet there will be no infringement unless the work is reproduced in virtually identical form and dimensions.[29] Changing the shape or dimensions of the few lines could be considered sufficient additional labour, skill and effort to take it outside the protection available to the earlier contributor of labour, skill and effort.

One matter is, however, clear. Any such expanded law of unfair competition or misappropriation as that discussed here could never substitute for all existing IP forms and actions, particularly patent law. Some immensely valuable information will always be discovered by lateral thinking and accident and without expenditure of even *de minimis* labour, skill, effort, investment of time or money.[30] Under present patent laws, information products devised are, and in the writer's view should remain, as protectable[31] as the products of years of labour, skill, effort and investment of time and money. It would seem the patent system, or at least its general principles, will be with us for a long time.

Critics may suggest the approach outlined above will create enormous uncertainty, but how many IP practitioners would view such a regime as all that different from what obtains under the present law? It would be interesting to know how many practitioners would be prepared to admit that at root his or her advice to a client, and in his or her experience with a judge's response to an IP claim, is in large measure influenced by whether the defendant has attempted to 'cash in' (as Gummow J. termed it in the *Hogan* case) on the plaintiff's labour, skill, effort or investment of time, money or imagination, without adding any or sufficient of his or her own.

CONCLUSION – DEVELOPING A LEGAL IMAGINATION

Traditional legal doctrinal criticism is what the common law is all about. It is discovery in the non-empirical sense and no less valuable than the discovery of new knowledge in the natural or social sciences. Developing a theory of your subject, of which the above are but examples, will provide some stimulus for writing. So too will applying a law in context framework. Perhaps most important of all is developing a legal imagination, a way of reconciling, rejecting or modifying the law in the light of your own personal pre-existing world-view.

FURTHER READING

J. Barzun, *Simple and Direct: A Rhetoric for Writers* (revised edn) (Chicago: University of Chicago Press, 1994).

J. Barzun and H. F. Graff, *The Modern Researcher* (6th edn) (Belmont, CA: Thomson/Wadsworth, 2004).

C. Chatterjee, *Methods of Research in Law* (2nd edn) (Horsmonden, Kent: Old Bailey Press, 2000).

E. Fajans and M. R. Falk, *Scholarly Writing for Law Students: Seminar Papers, Law Review Notes, and Law Review Competition Papers* (2nd edn) (St Paul, MN: West Group, 2000).

B. A. Garner, *A Dictionary of Modern Legal Usage* (2nd edn) (Oxford: Oxford University Press, 1995).

B. A. Garner, *The Elements of Legal Style* (2nd edn) (New York: Oxford University Press, 2002).

H. Meeker, 'Stalking the Golden Topic: A Guide to Locating and Selecting Topics for Legal Research Papers' (1996) 3 *Utah Law* Review 917.

Melbourne University Law Review Association, *Australian Guide to Legal Citation* (2nd edn) (Melbourne: Melbourne University Law Review Association, 2002).

NOTES

1. Critical legal studies (CLS), or critical race theorists, for example.
2. Submission of Australian Law Deans (April 1986) to the CTEC Assessment Committee for the Discipline of Law published in Dennis Pearce, Enid Campbell and Don Harding, *Australian Law Schools: A Discipline Assessment for the Commonwealth Tertiary Education Commission, vol. III* (Canberra: Australian Government Publishing Service, 1987) vol. 2, para. 9.15 (Pearce Committee Report).
3. See note 2 above; the submission is an appendix to the Pearce Report at vol. 2, para. 9.15.
4. Leaving aside Ronald Dworkin's theory that the right answer to a legal problem is always there to be found in the literature of law. See R. Dworkin, *Law's Empire* (Oxford: Hart Publishing, 1998), for the most

recent reformulation of a recurrent theme in his earlier books and publications.

5. One useful work on legal research technique is C. Chatterjee, *Methods of Research in Law* (2nd edn) (London: Old Bailey Press, 2000).

6. C. D. Stone, *Should Trees Have Standing?: And Other Essays on Law, Morals and the Environment* (Dobbs Ferry, NY: Oceana Publications, 1996).

7. The Council of Australian Law Deans' Statement on 'The Nature of Law Research' points out that a hard-and-fast distinction between refereed and unrefereed journals does not exist in Law. See note 2 above.

8. M. Pendleton, 'Intellectual Property, Information Based Society and a New International Economic Order – the Policy Options' (1985) 2 *European Intellectual Property* 3.

9. 'Character Merchandising and the Proper Scope of Intellectual Property' (1990) *Australian Intellectual Property Journal* 242.

10. S. Stewart LLD QC, 'Review of The Law of Intellectual and Industrial Property in Hong Kong' (1985) 34 *International & Comparative Law Quarterly* 658. The first such book was W. R. Cornish, *Intellectual Property* (London: Sweet & Maxwell, 1980).

11. 'Catnic: Signpost to Where' (1982) 3 *European Intellectual Property* 79.

12. (1987) 12 IPR 225 per Gummow J. upheld on appeal to the Full Federal Court of Australia at (1989) 14 IPR 398.

13. Lord Scarman's decision in the Judicial Committee of the Privy Council in *Cadbury Schweppes v Pub Squash* (1981) RPC 429 is a rare exception. In that case Lord Scarman found clear misappropriation but denied a remedy.

14. *Hogan v Koala Dundee Pty Ltd* (1988) IPC 90 per Pincus J. *Pacific Dunlop v Hogan* (1987) 12 IPR 225 per Gummow J. approved by the Full Federal Court of Australia at (1989) 14 IPR 398.

15. (1987) 12 IPR 225, 253.

16. (1987) 12 IPR 225, 246.

17. 'Catnic: Signpost to Where' (1982) 3 *European Intellectual Property* 79.

18. (1982) RPC 183.

19. Purposive construction was a term first coined by Lord Diplock in *Kammins Ballrooms Co Ltd v Zenith Investments (Torquay) Ltd* (1971) AC 850 at 881.

20. (1982) RPC 183, 187.

21. [1963] RPC 61 (House of Lords).

22. [1963] RPC 369 (House of Lords).

23. *Catnic* (1982) RPC 183 at 187 at 66. Author's words in brackets.

24. See note 24 above, 67.

25. See note 24 above, 66. Author's words in brackets.

26. R. Cotterell, 'The Law of Property and Legal Theory', in W. Twining (ed.), *Legal Theory and Common Law* (Oxford: Basil Blackwell, 1986) 88.

27. [1978] 94 *LQR* 103.
28. But in this respect refer to the interesting Privy Council decision in *Interlego v Tyco* [1988] 3 WLR 678, on appeal from the Supreme Court of Hong Kong. There, redrawing, not mere tracing, of designs for the famous Lego children's building blocks in different dimensions and style plus the addition of explanatory material and dimensions was held not to attract artistic copyright protection as an original work.
29. As was suggested in the early seminal case on artistic copyright: *Kenrick v Lawrence* (1890) 25 QBD 99.
30. For example, the product 'cat's eyes'; multiple, small, reflecting marble like domes for marking unlit sections of road at night might well have been discovered by an individual who while driving at night on an unlit road catches the reflection from the eyes of a cat running across the road and reasons by analogy so as to envisage 'cat's eyes'.
31. The 'cat's eyes' in the case referred to under the heading 'Law in Context Approach to Legal Writing' might well have been patentable.

CHAPTER 8

Researching International Law

Stephen Hall

THE LEGAL ACADEMY AND INTERNATIONAL LAW

International law is now a ubiquitous course offering at law schools throughout the developed world. Even in relatively recent times this was not always the case, especially in common law jurisdictions. As recently as twenty years ago, many law schools in the Commonwealth and the United States did not even include international law in their curriculums. By contrast, there is now an increasing trend to make international law a compulsory component of the basic law degree. It is also now a mandatory course for entry to the legal profession in a number of significant jurisdictions (for example, China and India).

The rise to prominence of international law in the legal academy has occurred in parallel with the rapid development of technologies which facilitate international travel, communications, financial transfers and economic production and exchange. Furthermore the end of the Cold War following the implosion of Europe's totalitarian regimes in 1989–91 created a political climate much more conducive to international contacts, exchanges and co-operation. These developments have in turn magnified the international importance of issues concerning migration, national and public security, human rights, trade, investment, environmental protection and a host of other matters. The world is undoubtedly now a more closely interconnected place than it was in 1980.

In considering options for research topics in international law, the prospective research student is likely to be spoiled for choice. Because it regulates primarily relations among states, the material scope of international law is co-extensive with the whole spectrum of international relations. This can cover laws regulating activities as diverse as international mail delivery to nuclear disarmament. Indeed, the emergence of international human rights and international criminal law means that international law's material scope extends even into areas which were, until a few decades ago, considered sensitive matters of exclusive domestic jurisdiction.

RESEARCH METHODOLOGY IN INTERNATIONAL LAW

The single most striking feature of the international legal system is its decentralised, consensual, and relatively primitive character. This has profound consequences for the conduct of research in the field of international law, and requires approaches markedly different in many ways from those which predominate in researching domestic law. Once it is understood that the sources of international law are significantly different in character from the sources of law in most domestic systems and that there is no very clear hierarchy among the various sources of international law, it becomes apparent why there are frequently such divergent views among publicists working in even well trodden territory.

On the international legal plane, and in contrast to domestic legal systems, it is not possible to point to institutions endowed with readily identifiable legislative and executive functions. Further, such international judicial organs as exist are not endowed with compulsory jurisdiction. Indeed, it is not even possible to point to international legal instruments which possess the unambiguously normative character of domestic constitutions or statutes. In this limited sense, there is no international government and no system of international legislation.[1]

The absence of an international legislature does not, however, result in international society being without the means of generating and modifying international legal rules. International law is primarily a system of customary law, increasingly supplemented by rules and principles which are agreed upon in treaties. These two sources of law are 'positive international law' in the sense that the norms which they generate have been chosen or agreed upon by States in their dealings with each other. Positive international law co-exists with, and is conditioned by, numerous general principles of law which also find expression in most of the world's domestic legal systems. Although there is no doctrine of *stare decisis* in international law, decisions of international and domestic courts and tribunals are often highly persuasive evidence for determining the content and scope of international norms derived from custom, treaties and the general principles. These judicial and arbitral decisions, as with the writings of eminent publicists, may be used to shed light on the existence, scope and applicability of norms based in custom, treaty and the general principles.

This schema is reflected in Article 38(1) of the Statute of the International Court of Justice, which provides as follows:

The Court, whose function is to decide in accordance with
international law such disputes as are submitted to it, shall apply:
a. international conventions, whether general or particular, establishing
rules recognised by the contesting states;
b. international custom, as evidence of a general practice accepted as law;
c. the general principles of law recognised by civilised nations;
d. subject to the provisions of Article 59, judicial decisions and the
teachings of the most highly qualified publicists of the various nations,
as subsidiary means for the determination of the rules of law.

The term 'evidence' has a somewhat different meaning in international law
from that which it normally bears in discourse about domestic law. In domestic legal systems, lawyers usually speak of material tending to establish facts as
'evidence' of those facts. In international law, 'evidence' is usually material
which tends to establish the content and scope of particular norms derived
from custom, treaties or the general principles. Thus, the text of a treaty is evidence of what a treaty requires and a historical incident may be evidence of a
customary norm's requirement. By contrast, it would be most unusual for a
lawyer in a common law jurisdiction to speak of a statute as constituting 'evidence' of what the legislature requires. Occasionally, international lawyers will
also use the term 'evidence' in the fact-establishing sense familiar to domestic
lawyers, so that attention to context is needed in order to determine the sense
in which the term 'evidence' is employed.

Treaties

Treaties are the real workhorses of international law because they are used for
an array of indispensable tasks ranging from the creation of commercial com-
mitments, the regulation of technical matters and the establishment of universal norms of conduct, through to founding international organisations. Most
States are parties to numerous treaties: Australia, for instance, is party to more
than 900 of them.

Especially since the end of the Second World War, treaties have assumed
an increasingly important place in international law. Unlike custom, whose
evolution can take long periods of time and whose precise requirements can
frequently be unclear, treaties are capable of furnishing States with instant
and more or less clearly defined rights and obligations. Treaties are, thus,
essential tools for keeping international law abreast of the requirements of an
increasingly interdependent world society. An ability to find, interpret and
update treaties, and a knowledge of the law relating to the operation of
treaties, is a fundamental requirement for any effective research in international law.

As the language of Article 38(1)(a) of the Statute indicates, treaties may be either 'general' or 'particular'. When a multilateral treaty is widely adhered to and represents the views of the States parties as to universal substantive legal principles, it may be regarded as possessing a general character. More commonly, such treaties are said to be 'legislative' or 'law-making' (*traités-lois*). This means that they lay down standards of conduct which are common to all the States parties.

Multilateral treaties are also sometimes described as 'legislative' or 'law-making' when they create rules binding on all States whether or not they are parties to the treaty. While it is entirely possible for States to be bound by rules which have their origins in multilateral treaties to which they are not parties, it would be a mistake to regard such a treaty as being a legislative act in the same way as a legislative act in a domestic legal order. It is possible for a multilateral treaty to reflect an existing customary norm, to crystallise an emerging customary norm, or to generate a new customary norm where certain conditions are met.[2] Whatever the precise relationship between the multilateral treaty and the parallel customary norm which it reflects, crystallises or generates, States that are not party to the treaty are bound by the customary norm and not by the treaty. The point is not entirely moot as the treaty may possess a procedural, institutional or enforcement dimension which will be inapplicable to the parallel customary norm.

A 'particular' treaty is one in which States undertake obligations in relation to specific matters around which wide or universal agreement would be unattainable, or in relation to which States would not be willing to commit on a multilateral basis. Such treaties are usually bilateral, and most closely resemble a domestic law contract (*traités-contrat*). Treaties relating to extradition and reciprocal enforcement of judgments are common examples, although these matters have been dealt with largely on a multilateral basis among many of the member States of the Council of Europe.

Particular attention must be paid to the existence of reservations or declarations, especially when dealing with multilateral treaties. It is in this area that some of the most easily avoidable research solecisms most frequently occur. It cannot be assumed (although it too frequently is by inexperienced researchers) that because a State has become party to a treaty, it is bound by all the treaty's terms. Where a State has made a valid reservation to a treaty, its legal relations with other parties to that treaty are modified to the extent of the reservation, and the other parties may also rely on the same reservation in their dealings with the reserving State.[3]

For instance, Article 14(6) of the International Covenant on Civil and Political Rights provides that where a convicted criminal has been pardoned or had his conviction overturned because newly discovered evidence demonstrates a miscarriage of justice in his case, he shall be 'compensated according to law'. Australia is party to the Covenant, but with the reservation that 'the provision of compensation for miscarriage of justice . . . may be by administrative procedures rather than pursuant to specific legal provision'. Other State parties that have not objected to that reservation are bound to accept that Australia is not obliged to pay compensation according to law, provided such compensation is administratively available. Conversely, Australia is precluded from claiming that any other State party is in breach of the Covenant where the other State makes compensation available only administratively, even where the other State has not made a reservation concerning Article 14(6). The other State may, however, be in breach of its obligations to all other parties to the Covenant that have not made a reservation similar to Australia's.[4]

The current position is that when 'a State objecting to a reservation has not opposed the entry into force of the treaty between itself and the reserving State, the provisions to which the reservation relates do not apply as between the two States to the extent of the reservation'.[5] This well established rule can sometimes lead to paradoxical results. In the context of our example, it means that where another State has objected to Australia's reservation to Article 14(6), no part of that provision forms part of the two States' obligations towards each other. Consequently, Article 14(6) would impose *no* obligations between the two States with respect to the payment of compensation to convicted criminals where they have been pardoned or had their convictions overturned because newly discovered evidence demonstrates a miscarriage of justice.

The researcher must also bear in mind that making a reservation which is inconsistent with a treaty's object and purpose will prevent the reserving State from becoming a party to the treaty. A State which objects to another State's reservation on the basis that the reservation is incompatible with the treaty's object and purpose may, until such incompatibility is authoritatively determined on the judicial plane, unilaterally regard the reserving State as not being party to the treaty at all.[6]

These rules exist because, according to classical theory, a State is bound by a treaty only by virtue of its free consent, and its reservations form part of that consent. If the reservation turns out to be invalid, then an essential component of the State's consent to be bound is missing.

It has sometimes been suggested, however, that human rights treaties are an exception. According to this view, an invalid reservation to a human rights treaty can simply be severed from the reserving State's consent, thereby leaving the State bound by the treaty without the benefit of the reservation.[7] Where the reserving State wishes to be bound notwithstanding the invalidity of a reservation, there would appear to be no issue.[8] Where, however, the reserving State regards the validity of its reservation as an essential component of the original consent to be bound, it is very hard to reconcile this alleged exception for human rights treaties with the idea that States are bound only by those treaty obligations to which they have freely consented. Several States – including notably France, the United Kingdom and the United States – have expressly rejected an exceptional regime for reservations to human rights treaties. Researchers should be aware that this important area impacting upon the effectiveness of human rights treaties remains contentious.

CUSTOM

Although customary law has played a prominent role in relations between different political communities since antiquity, it was not until the twentieth century that international law developed a definite doctrine sharply defining the requirements for a practice to qualify as a customary legal norm.

The first important step in this direction was the adoption in 1920 of the text of Article 38 of the Statute of the Permanent Court of International Justice. In 1945, this provision was readopted almost verbatim as the text of Article 38 of the Statute of the International Court of Justice. Article 38 specified international custom as one of international law's sources, and described it as 'evidence of a general practice accepted as law'. It is on the basis of Article 38 that the doctrine was elaborated that customary international law consists of two distinct elements: (1) general practice (or *usus*); and (2) *opinio juris sive necessitatis* (or *opinio juris et necessitatis*), usually referred to as simply '*opinio juris*' and meaning a belief that the practice is required as a matter of legal right or obligation.

International law has evolved in such a way as to treat States as the basic units of the system. States are simultaneously the main subjects of international law and the entities whose choices and conduct generate positive international law. The choices and conduct of States are their 'practice', and the general practice of States is an essential element in the emergence, evolution, decline and disappearance of norms of customary international law.

A State is a legal person. As with all legal persons, its will is necessarily expressed through the choices and conduct of natural persons whose activities are legally attributable to it. In the case of States, this means their governments – broadly defined to include their executive, legislative and judicial branches and any other person, organ or institution exercising official public authority or exercising public functions at a national, regional or local level.

The choices and conduct of persons who are not officials of a State, or who are not acting on the instructions or under the control of State officials, cannot be regarded as evidence of State practice. Consequently, the choices and conduct of private natural persons, entities incorporated under domestic law for commercial or charitable purposes and non-governmental organisations

(NGOs) do not ordinarily furnish practice which is relevant to determining the existence or scope of a putative norm of customary international law. According to Judge McNair, 'the independent activity of private individuals is of little value unless it can be shown that they have acted in pursuance of a licence or some other authority received from their Government or that in some other way their Governments have asserted jurisdiction through them'.[9]

Subject to this limitation, however, State practice may be evidenced by reference to a wide array of materials. Essentially, anything that demonstrates the choices and conduct of persons acting in their capacities as State officials, or under the instructions or control of State officials, will provide evidence of State practice. Examples include:

- speeches by State officials and diplomats;
- transcripts of parliamentary proceedings;
- domestic legislation;
- decisions of domestic courts and tribunals;
- diplomatic correspondence;
- historical records;
- press releases and communiqués;
- policy statements;
- reports of military and naval activities;
- comments by governments on the work of international bodies (for example, the International Law Commission);
- voting records in international forums (for example, the United Nations General Assembly);
- official manuals issued to diplomats and armed forces; and
- treaties.

These and other instances of State practice may be evidenced by official documents or, where appropriate, unofficial documents, such as newspaper reports and academic works.

It is sometimes argued that mere statements and declarations by States are insufficient to establish State practice, and that they must be supported by actual conduct directed at physically exercising or defending claimed rights.[10] This remains, however, a minority view and the International Court of Justice and other international tribunals regularly accept statements as evidence of State practice. The weight to be attached to such statements may, however, be diminished where a State fails to take action in enforcement of its claims and no reasonable explanation exists for such failure.

State practice can also include omissions. This type of practice is particularly relevant where a customary rule involves a prohibition or requires forbearance, such as the obligation not to harm diplomatic personnel.

The State practice element of a customary norm is not established merely because some States occasionally behave in a way which is approximately consistent with that putative norm. Article 38(1)(b) of the Statute specifies that the practice must be 'general'.

In the *Lotus* case,[11] the Permanent Court of International Justice rejected a submission that the infrequency with which States sought to prosecute criminal offences committed on the high seas aboard vessels flying another State's flag was proof of a customary law rule forbidding criminal prosecutions in those circumstances. In rejecting this submission, the Court was impressed by several reported cases which contradicted the alleged rule and which drew no protest from the flag State.

In the *Asylum* case,[12] the International Court of Justice observed that, in order for a *usus* to help constitute custom, it must be 'in accordance with a constant and uniform practice'. The court found that the State practices raised before it were too uncertain and contradictory to establish a general practice. Similarly, in the *Anglo-Norwegian Fisheries* case,[13] the International Court of Justice rejected a submission that customary international law precluded drawing baselines longer than ten miles across bays for the purposes of mapping the territorial sea; there was too much State practice which was inconsistent with the asserted rule to regard it as reflecting a general practice.

Does this mean that there needs to be an absolute conformity among States before a practice can be regarded as 'general' for the purposes of establishing a customary norm of international law? According to the American Law Institute:

> A practice can be general even if it is not universally accepted; there is no precise formula to indicate how widespread a practice must be, but it should reflect wide acceptance among the states particularly involved in the relevant activity.[14]

In the *North Sea Continental Shelf* cases[15] the International Court of Justice remarked that, in order to help establish the existence of a new rule of customary international law, 'State practice, including that of States whose interests are specifically affected, should have been both extensive and virtually uniform'. This suggests that occasional departures from an otherwise uniform practice will not be fatal to the emergence of a new customary rule of international law. As the *North Sea Continental Shelf* cases themselves indicate, however, the fewer the instances of State practice said to support a new customary rule, the more significant will be occurrences of inconsistent or contradictory State practice.

In the *Nicaragua* case,[16] the International Court of Justice elaborated upon what constitutes 'general practice' in the context of discussing the existence of customary international law rules against the use of force and intervention:

It is not to be expected that, in the practice of States, the application of the rules in question should have been perfect, in the sense that States should have refrained, with complete consistency, from the use of force or from intervention in each other's internal affairs. The Court does not consider that, for a rule to be established as customary, the corresponding practice must be in absolutely rigorous conformity with the rule. In order to deduce the existence of customary rules, the Court deems it sufficient that the conduct of States should, in general, be consistent with such rules, and that instances of State conduct inconsistent with a given rule should generally have been treated as breaches of that rule, not as indications of the recognition of a new rule. If a State acts in a way prima facie incompatible with a recognised rule, but defends its conduct by appealing to exceptions or justifications contained within the rule itself, then whether or not the State's conduct is in fact justifiable on that basis, the significance of that attitude is to confirm rather than to weaken the rule.

Thus, occasional departures from an otherwise widespread and uniform practice will not deprive it of its customary character provided such departures are generally either met with protest by other States, or justified by reference to exceptions allegedly forming part of the rule itself (even if such attempted justification is ill-founded).

Protest will be more significant in the case of alleged new rules of customary international law than in the case of established rules. In the former case, protest by just a few other States will weigh heavily against recognising the rule's emergence. In this situation, there will need to be much more evidence in support of the practice in order to establish its 'general' character.

Failure to protest is usually referred to as 'acquiescence', which has been defined as 'silence or absence of protest in circumstances which generally call for a positive reaction signifying objection'.[17] Acquiescence in the face of conduct inconsistent with an asserted new rule will count heavily against its recognition. In the case of an established customary rule, acquiescence in the face of departures from the rule will tend to erode its legal status and may, in time, lead to its disappearance or replacement by a different or modified rule. In the case of alleged new customary rules, acquiescence in the face of practice said to reflect the new putative rule may be treated as implied consent.

Furthermore – and whether dealing with practice, protest or acquiescence – greater weight is given to the attitude of States that are specially affected by the putative rule or that are particularly involved in the activity it is said to regulate. Thus in the *North Sea Continental Shelf* cases[18] the International Court of Justice, in seeking to ascertain the existence of an alleged new customary rule affecting the delimitation of disputed boundaries over the continental shelf, was more interested in the practice of States with extensive coastlines than the practice of landlocked States. Similarly, in the evolution of customary law regulating activities in outer space, the attitudes of the United States, Russia and other States with space programmes are more significant than those of States without such programmes.

As mentioned, it is not necessary for every State to have actively participated in a *usus* for it to assume the status of general practice. It follows that a State is not able to assert the non-application to it of a customary rule corresponding to a general practice merely on the basis that the State did not adopt the *usus* in its own conduct. In the absence of protest against a new or developing *usus*, a State will usually be taken as having acquiesced in its emergence and such acquiescence will count as assent.

If a general practice by States (*usus*) is the necessary objective element of customary international law, a belief that the practice is permitted or required as a matter of legal right or obligation (*opinio juris*) is the necessary subjective element.

A *usus* does not generate a rule of customary international law merely because it has become an extensive and virtually uniform practice of States. Many such practices are not reflective of legal rules but are simply the expression of international 'comity', that is, courtesy among States. For example, the practice of greeting visiting heads of State with military honours and displays of the visitor's national flag is an expression of international comity, but does not involve a legal obligation. Such practices may be expressive of a custom in the social sense, but are not required as a matter of customary law. It is the presence of an *opinio juris* which transforms an extensive and virtually uniform *usus* into a rule of customary international law.

In the *Lotus* case[19] the Permanent Court of International Justice, after commenting on the inadequacy of the State practice said to sustain a customary rule forbidding the commencement of criminal proceedings in certain circumstances, said:

> Even if the rarity of the judicial decisions to be found among the reported cases were sufficient to prove in point of fact the circumstances alleged by the Agent for the French Government, it would merely show that States had often, in practice, abstained from instituting criminal proceedings, and not that they recognized themselves as being obliged to do so; for only if such abstention were based on their being conscious of having a duty to abstain would it be possible to speak of an international custom. The alleged fact does not allow one to infer that States have been conscious of having such a duty.

The International Court of Justice, in the *North Sea Continental Shelf* cases,[20] considered the significance of adherence by States to a multilateral treaty for the purposes of generating a rule of customary international law. According to the Court, State practice relied upon to support an alleged customary rule 'should . . . have occurred in such a way as to show a general recognition that a rule of law or legal obligation is involved'.[21] In commenting on the conduct of States that were not parties to the treaty but in apparent conformity to its requirements, the Court said:[22]

> [E]ven if these instances of action by non-parties to the Convention were much more numerous than they in fact are, they would not, even in the aggregate, suffice in themselves to constitute the *opinio juris* – for, in order to achieve that result, two conditions must be fulfilled. Not only must the acts concerned amount to a settled practice, but they must also be such, or be carried out in such a way, as to be evidence of a belief that this practice is rendered obligatory by the existence of a rule of law requiring it. The need for such a belief, i.e. the existence of a subjective element, is implicit in the very notion of the *opinio juris sive necessitatis*. The States concerned must therefore feel that they are conforming to what amounts to a legal obligation. The frequency or even habitual character of the acts is not in itself enough.

Where there is reason to believe that a *usus* is motivated by political or other non-juridical considerations, it will be more difficult to establish the existence of the requisite *opinio juris*. In the *North Sea Continental Shelf* cases the International Court of Justice noted that there was 'not a shred of evidence' indicating that States that had applied the equidistance method of drawing international boundaries contained in the Geneva Convention on the Continental Shelf 1958, but that were not parties to the Convention, 'believed themselves to be applying a mandatory rule of customary international law'. The Court also noted that there was 'no lack of other reasons for using the equidistance method, so that acting, or agreeing to act, in a certain way, does not of itself demonstrate anything of a juridical nature'.[23]

There are passages from the judgments in the *Lotus* case, the *Asylum* case and the *North Sea Continental Shelf* cases which indicate that separate evidence is required of the *opinio juris* element, and that it is not permissible simply to infer *opinio juris* from State practice. These findings were made, however, in the context of related determinations that the evidence of State practice fell short of what was required to establish a general practice, and that there was reason to believe that the practice was motivated by political or other non-juridical considerations.

The dissenting opinions of Judge Tanaka and Judge *ad hoc* Sørenson in the *North Sea Continental Shelf* cases, however, point to a different approach to proving *opinio juris* where the evidence indicates that a State practice has indeed become general. Both judges regarded the practice in issue as being sufficiently widespread as to be capable of supporting a customary rule. Judge Tanaka stated:[24]

> [S]o far as . . . *opinio juris sive necessitatis* is concerned, it is extremely difficult to get evidence of its existence in concrete cases. This factor, relating to international motivation and being of a psychological nature, cannot be ascertained very easily, particularly when diverse legislative and executive organs of a government participate in an internal process of decision-making in respect of ratification or other State acts. There is no other way than to ascertain the existence of *opinio juris* from the fact of the external existence of a certain custom and its necessity felt in the international community, rather than to seek evidence as to the subjective motive of each example of State practice, which is something which is impossible of achievement.

Judge *ad hoc* Sørenson quoted with approval Sir Hersch Lauterpacht who wrote that 'the accurate principle . . . consists in regarding all uniform conduct of governments (or, in appropriate cases, abstention therefrom) as evidencing the *opinio necessitatis juris* except when it is shown that the conduct in question was not accompanied by any such intention.'[25]

Although these dissenting opinions are rationally compelling, the International Court of Justice has more recently reaffirmed the necessity of separately establishing *opinio juris* even where the State practice to which it corresponds is widespread and virtually uniform.[26]

There are also occasions when a virtually unanimous and unequivocal *opinio juris* will be capable of sustaining a customary rule even in the absence of an 'extensive and virtually uniform' practice by States. For instance, the customary and *jus cogens* rule against torture retains its legal status notwithstanding that torture is widespread in the practice of States. Torture remains, however, universally condemned as unlawful in the pronouncements of States. When accused of torture, States almost always deny the charge, and never assert that torture is permitted by international law.

General principles

The very existence of the general principles as a source of law indicates that treaty and custom do not provide an exhaustive source of legal norms in international law. The fact that the general principles are described as 'principles *of law*' demonstrates that they do not authorise the International Court of Justice to proceed merely on the basis of non-legal considerations which are thought to be fair and right in all the circumstances.

This conclusion is reinforced by the fact that Article 38(2) of the Statute provides separate authorisation for the court to decide cases '*ex aequo et bono*' – that is, by reference to non-legal conceptions of equity and fairness – if the parties agree.[27] Such separate authorisation would not have been necessary had Article 38(1)(c) already authorised resort to non-legal considerations. The same reasoning precludes the view that the reference to general principles of law in the Statute adds nothing to what is already indicated by the reference to treaty and custom.[28]

The result is that the general principles, which are of a legal nature and not merely manifestations of treaty and custom, are a source of real law for the regulation of international relations.

The general principles are merely 'recognised' by civilised nations, and not enacted or consented to by them. In the Advisory Committee of Jurists on the Statute of the Permanent Court of International Justice, Lord Phillimore, the provision's co-author, observed that: 'the general principles referred to . . . were those which were accepted by all nations *in foro domestico*, such as certain principles of procedure, the principle of good faith, and the principle of *res judicata, etc*'. In particular, he intended the general principles to mean 'maxims of law'.[29] This suggests that those basic concepts and processes of legal justice which are observed in mature domestic legal systems are to serve as sources of international law. Again, what is required is *recognition* of *existing* basic legal ideas, not enactment of, or consent to, measures to be adopted on the plane of international law.

This approach is strengthened by reference to the fact that recognition of the general principles is by 'nations' and not by States. The terminology is not without significance. States are the international legal entities which are still the principal subjects of rights and duties in international law. Nations, by contrast, are the peoples themselves.

What one is dealing with in the general principles of law then, is the *jus gentium*.[30] The term '*jus gentium*' is commonly translated as 'the law of nations', but is perhaps less ambiguously rendered as 'the law common to all peoples', or 'the common law of mankind'.

The *jus gentium* originated in Roman law as a supplement to the *jus civile*, which was the law regulating relations among Roman citizens. As Roman power expanded and Roman citizens had increasing contact with non-citizens, a law was developed to regulate relations among non-citizens and between citizens and non-citizens; this was the *jus gentium*. The Roman jurist, Gaius (c. AD 130–180) provides the following characterisation:[31]

Every people that is governed by statutes and customs observes partly
its own peculiar law and partly the common law of all mankind. That
law which a people establishes for itself is peculiar to it, and is called *ius*

civile, while the law that natural reason establishes among all mankind is followed by all peoples alike, and is called *ius gentium* as being observed by all mankind. Thus the Roman people observes partly its own peculiar law and partly the law of mankind.

The *jus gentium* did not regulate relations among sovereigns (formal equality between Rome and foreign sovereigns was not recognised) and was, therefore, not international law. Rather, it consisted of general principles governing relations among individuals in any civilised society, which principles would find differentiated manifestation as to detail in each society's functional equivalent of the *jus civile*. Accordingly, the '*ius gentium* as defined by Gaius is a comprehensive concept which includes rules and legal institutions . . . found everywhere, such as matrimony, protection of property, or the wrongdoer's obligation for damages; it is a universal law'.[32] It included some principles of an international character, such as the inviolability of envoys and the law on spoils in war, but this was far from establishing an equivalence of the *jus gentium* to international law.

Finnis identifies thirteen inter-related principles which constitute 'general principles of law', and which are (or are part of) the *jus gentium*:[33]

(i) compulsory acquisition of property rights to be compensated, in respect of *damnum emergens* (actual losses) if not of *lucrum cessans* (loss of expected profits); (ii) no liability for unintentional injury, without fault; (iii) no criminal liability without *mens rea*; (iv) estoppel (*nemo contra factum proprium venire potest*); (v) no judicial aid to one who pleads his own wrong (he who seeks equity must do equity); (vi) no aid to abuse of rights; (vii) fraud unravels everything; (viii) profits received without justification and at the expense of another must be restored; (ix) *pacta sunt servanda* (contracts are to be performed); (x) relative freedom to change existing patterns of legal relationships by agreement; (xi) in assessments of the legal effects of purported acts-in-the-law, the weak to be protected against their weakness; (xii) disputes not to be resolved without giving both sides an opportunity to be heard; (xiii) no one to be allowed to judge his own cause.

These *jus gentium* principles really are principles in that 'they justify, rather than require, particular rules and determinations, and are qualified in their application to particular circumstances by other like principles'.[34] This is precisely how the general principles of law function in international law.

The *jus gentium* general principles of law identified by Finnis bear a striking resemblance to the general principles of law and of equity that feature prominently in the work of the International Court of Justice and other tribunals applying international law.[35]

Other general principles of a primarily procedural character, such as *res judicata*, *effet utile* and denial of justice, have also figured among the general principles which international tribunals have applied in cases before them.

The foundational and pre-positive nature of the general principles was emphasised by Cheng Bin in his landmark work on the subject:[36]

> This part of international law does not consist . . . in specific rules formulated for practical purposes, but in general propositions underlying the various rules of law which express the essential qualities of juridical truth itself, in short of Law.

Furthermore, Baron Descamps, President of the Advisory Committee of Jurists on the Statute of the Permanent Court of International Justice, stated that the inclusion of general principles in the text of Article 38 'was necessary to meet the possibility of a *non liquet*'.[37]

Consequently, the general principles of law provide a reservoir from which apparent gaps in the corpus of international law may be filled. They reinforce the view that international law should properly be regarded as a 'complete system', that is, that every international situation is capable of being determined as a matter of law and that international tribunals may not pronounce a *non liquet*. The *jus gentium* general principles do not provide a foundation for any arbitrary or capricious rejection of positive law rules. Rather, the positive law rules from which the general principles are partly derived furnish a basis upon which the *jus gentium* may be employed to fashion a rule to 'fit' the requirements of a case where no directly applicable conventional or customary rule provides an answer.

Because the general principles of law function primarily to fill *lacunae* in positive international law (treaties and custom), their practical significance has steadily declined as the corpus of conventional and customary international law has grown. In its earlier stages, modern international law relied heavily on the extrapolation of rules directly from the *jus gentium*. The role of publicists from the time of Grotius (1583–1645) until well into the nineteenth century consisted largely of reasoning from first principles towards just solutions across the array of international legal problems. It is this feature of the earlier publicists' works which lends most of them a quality ranging from the rigorously rationalist to the flatly speculative, and which makes them seem so remote in style and substance from more recent works.

As conventional and customary law accumulated, the need to engage in reasoning directly from the general principles receded, and publicists began placing greater emphasis upon positive international law. This development was accelerated during the nineteenth century by the emergence of legal positivism as the dominant philosophy of law, according to which positive law is the only variety of law in the true sense. While legal positivism no longer enjoys the near-monopoly on legal theorising which it held in its heyday from the mid-nineteenth to the mid-twentieth centuries, the fact remains that the general principles are only a reserve source from which new rules of international law may be fashioned.

That reserve function should not, however, be undervalued. In the words of a United States-United Kingdom Claims Tribunal:[38]

> Even assuming that there was . . . no treaty and no specific rule of
> international law formulated as the expression of a universally
> recognized rule governing the case . . . it cannot be said that there is no
> principle of international law applicable. International law, as well as
> domestic law, may not contain, and generally does not contain, express
> rules decisive of particular cases; but the function of jurisprudence is to
> resolve the conflict of opposing rights and interests by applying, in
> default of any specific provision of law, the corollaries of general
> principles, and so to find . . . the solution of the problem. This is the
> method of jurisprudence; it is the method by which the law has been
> gradually evolved in every country resulting in the definition and
> settlement of legal relations as well between States as between private
> individuals.

Further, the general principles remain highly significant in providing a ratio for the positive law rules. The interpretation and application of conventional and customary rules will inevitably occur against the background of the general principles, which furnish a juridical foundation for the positive law.

JUDICIAL DECISIONS

Article 38(1)(d) of the Statute specifies that 'judicial decisions' are among the 'subsidiary means for the determination of the rules of law'. This means that judicial decisions are not themselves sources of law, but may be used to ascertain the existence and scope of rules sourced in treaties, custom and the general principles of law.

Moreover, there is no doctrine of *stare decisis* in international law. In the case of the International Court of Justice, the point is driven home by Article 59 of the Statute which specifies that the 'decision of the Court has no binding force except between the parties and in respect of that particular case'. Accordingly, prior decisions of courts and tribunals have no binding force in the determination of disputes before international courts. This is partly a consequence of the absence of a formal system and hierarchy of international courts and tribunals, but it also accords with the legal tradition to be found in most non-common law jurisdictions.

Nevertheless, the tendency by judges to have regard to the reported decisions of prior cases is a recurrent feature of most legal systems, even if it is not formalised in legal dogma. This is a natural product of the rule of law itself, which requires that like cases be treated alike. Accordingly, international courts and tribunals routinely have regard to earlier decisions by dispute-settlement bodies for the determination of rules of international law.

A 'judicial decision' may be the result of a hearing before either national or international courts and tribunals. Generally speaking, decisions of international tribunals are more persuasive, though the most superior courts or tribunals of several States are very highly regarded: for example, the Supreme Court of the United States, the English House of Lords and the French Conseil d'Etat. The High Court of Australia and the Supreme Court of Canada are also well regarded.

The most prominent international tribunals are the International Court of Justice (and its predecessor, the Permanent Court of International Justice), the Court of Justice of the European Communities, the Dispute Settlement Body and the Appeal Body of the World Trade Organisation, the European Court of Human Rights, the Inter-American Court of Human Rights, the Human Rights Committee of the United Nations, the International Tribunal for the Law of the Sea, the Permanent Court of Arbitration, and, more recently, the International Criminal Court. All these tribunals are permanent or 'standing' in their constitution. However, a large volume of frequently important international adjudication or arbitration is conducted by ad hoc tribunals which are constituted, usually by special agreement between disputing States, to determine or arbitrate particular international disagreements of a legal character. Sometimes, ad hoc tribunals, such as the International Criminal Tribunal for Yugoslavia (and the corresponding tribunal for Rwanda), are established by an act of the United Nations or other international organisations. The Special Court for Sierra Leone was established by agreement between Sierra Leone and the United Nations.

The absence of a formal hierarchy among courts and tribunals in international law means that a number of other factors will assume greater importance in determining the extent to which a prior judicial decision is persuasive.

Obviously, relevance to the problem at hand is always the most important consideration. The next most important is the extent and quality of the reasoning. A brief or elliptical judgment generally carries less weight than one that is thorough and well argued. A decision written by a judge or publicist of high repute in international law generally carries more weight than decisions authored by lesser-known figures. Indeed, even a dissenting, but thorough and well argued, opinion by a well regarded judge or publicist can frequently be highly persuasive.

In the case of national courts or tribunals, the extent to which the decision really turns on issues of international law, as distinct from national law considerations, is important. Finally, the age of the decision is significant. Formally, courts and tribunals are merely ascertaining and applying rules sourced in treaties, customs and the general principles of law. As a general proposition, the older the decision, the more cautiously it should be treated as conventional, as customary laws are likely to change with the passage of time.

The formal absence of a judicial hierarchy notwithstanding, decisions of the 'World Court' (that is, the International Court of Justice and the Permanent Court of International Justice) are afforded the very highest respect. Such is its influence in international law that its decisions have frequently had a decisive impact on the practice of States. It is no exaggeration to say that even where the court has probably determined the law wrongly, States have generally accepted the court's view of international law and altered their practice accordingly. The court also routinely makes liberal reference to its own previous judgments in reaching decisions, according them a status which can only be regarded as falling not far short of binding. As Judge Azevedo remarked in the *Asylum* case:[39]

> It should be remembered . . . that the decision in a particular case has deep repercussions, particularly in international law, because views which have been confirmed by that decision acquire quasi-legislative value, in spite of the legal principle to the effect that the decision has no binding force except between parties and in respect of that particular case (Statute, Art. 59).

Teachings of publicists

The 'teachings of the most highly qualified publicists of the various nations' are also among the 'subsidiary means for the determination of the rules of law'.[40] These teachings are frequently referred to as 'doctrine' or 'doctrinal writings'. This means that, as with judicial decisions, the teachings of publicists are not themselves sources of law, but may be used to ascertain the existence and scope of rules sourced in treaties, custom and the general principles of law.

'Publicists' are almost always eminent academic experts in international law, though the published works of diplomats or statesmen may also occasionally feature. Their 'teachings' are generally found in published scholarly books and journals. Analogous to the teachings of publicists, and often regarded as more authoritative, are the published works of bodies such as the United Nations International Law Commission, the Institute of International Law, committees of jurists commissioned by international organisations, and other expert bodies.

With the decline in importance of the general principles of law relative to conventional and customary law, the role of publicists in shaping international law has also declined. Nevertheless, whereas judicial precedent plays a somewhat lesser role in international law as compared to common law systems, academic writings continue to figure more prominently in resolving international legal problems than they do in common law systems and most other domestic legal systems.

The writings of publicists often feature prominently in legal argument before courts and tribunals determining issues of international law. Such writings are only infrequently cited in decisions of the International Court of Justice, in large part because of to collective drafting. However, the greater prominence of doctrinal writings in separate and dissenting opinions probably more accurately indicates the true extent of their influence on the deliberations of international courts and tribunals.

The role of doctrinal writings in the process of international law adjudication before United States courts was described by Mr Justice Gray of the Supreme Court of the United States in the following terms:

> International law is part of our law, and must be ascertained and administered by the courts of justice of appropriate jurisdiction, as often as questions of right depending upon it are duly presented for their determination. For this purpose, where there is no treaty, and no controlling executive or legislative act or judicial decision, resort must be had to the customs and usages of civilized nations; and as evidence of these, to the works of jurists and commentators who by years of labor, research and experience have made themselves particularly well acquainted with the subjects of which they treat. Such works are resorted to by judicial tribunals, not for the speculations of their authors concerning what the law ought to be, but for trustworthy evidence of what the law really is.[41]

Mr Justice Gray's formulation is too narrow for the purposes of adjudication before international courts and tribunals. Not only are the teachings of publicists relevant for the purpose of ascertaining the state of customary international law in relation to a particular point, but they are also helpful in interpreting and applying treaties (subject to the specific requirements of customary international law, the Vienna Convention on the Law of Treaties and the applicability of any relevant general principles of law).

The factors that are relevant in determining the relative persuasive weight to be attached to different doctrinal writings resemble those that apply to assessing the relative weight of judicial decisions. Accordingly, relevance is always the most important factor, followed by the extent and quality of reasoning. The more thorough and well argued the writing, the more weight it is given. As mentioned, the work of a publicist of high repute in international law carries more weight than opinions authored by lesser-known figures. As with judicial decisions, the age of the doctrinal writing can also be significant. Formally, doctrinal writings help in ascertaining and applying rules sourced in treaties, customs and the general principles of law. Again, the older the writing, the more cautiously it should be treated, as conventional and customary laws are likely to change over time.

Generally, doctrinal writings are afforded less persuasive weight than the decisions of courts and tribunals. As the corpus of reported judicial decisions expands, the relative importance of doctrinal writings gradually declines.

This is partly the result simply of judicial habit, but also reflects the fact that judgments, decisions, awards or opinions issued by courts or tribunals are almost always the product of careful and collective consideration after taking into account extensive evidence and legal submissions from the parties. Although eminent publicists frequently make significant contributions to the explication and development of international law, it is:

> obvious that subjective factors enter into any assessment of juristic opinion, that individual writers reflect national and other prejudices, and, further, that some publicists see themselves to be propagating new and better views rather than providing a passive appraisal of the law.[42]

ACTS OF INTERNATIONAL ORGANISATIONS

International organisations established by agreement among States provide forums within which international relations may be conducted. With the exception of certain acts adopted by the United Nations Security Council, none of these organisations are capable of adopting acts which per se create rules applicable to all States in international law. Neither the United Nations, nor any other international organisation, is a world legislature.

The treaty establishing an international organisation is its constitution. Where the treaty provides that the organisation may adopt measures which bind its member States, then, as a matter of treaty law, those States are obliged to comply with any such measures to the extent and in the manner prescribed by the conventional obligation. Usually, authorisation of this kind extends only to adopting measures affecting the organisation's internal operations, such as its finances or procedures.[43] Furthermore, and subject to any contrary provisions in the treaty itself, an organisation's constitutive treaty may be authoritatively interpreted by the practice of States operating within the treaty.[44] Less commonly, a constitutive treaty will empower an international organisation to adopt measures which produce more general legal obligations among the member States inter se.[45] Much more rarely, however, a constitutive treaty might confer on the organisation powers to adopt measures which produce legal effects directly in the territory of its member State.[46] In such a case, international law requires States to give effect to the more extensive obligation as a matter of *pacta sunt servanda*.

Although resolutions and similar acts of international organisations do not directly and per se generate rules which form part of general international law, it is possible for them indirectly to help create such rules. Acts of international organisations can provide useful and easily accessible evidence of *opinio juris*, and may, therefore, contribute to the emergence of rules of customary international law binding on all States. Similarly, the acts of regional organisations, such as the Council of Europe or the Organisation of American States, are capable of providing evidence of *opinio juris* in support of both general and regional customary international law.

In ascertaining the existence of the *opinio juris* element of the customary rule against the threat or use of force in international relations, the International Court of Justice took account of several United Nations General Assembly resolutions, a resolution of the 1928 Sixth International Conference of American States, and a declaration of the 1975 Conference on Security and Co-operation in Europe.[47] Ten years later, the court considered a series of General Assembly resolutions passed since 1961, and said:

> General Assembly resolutions, even if they are not binding, may
> sometimes have normative value. They can, in certain circumstances,
> provide evidence important for establishing the existence of a rule or
> the emergence of an *opinio juris*. To establish whether this is true of a
> given General Assembly resolution, it is necessary to look at its content
> and the conditions of its adoption; it is also necessary to see whether an
> *opinio juris* exists as to its normative character. Or a series of resolutions
> may show the gradual evolution of the *opinio juris* required for the
> establishment of a new rule. [48]

Not all acts of international organisations are equally useful in helping to establish the existence of a customary rule. Among the factors to be taken into account are:

- The extent to which the act is supported by States from different political and economic groupings; support from only one group or bloc tends to militate against its support for a customary rule.
- The extent to which the act is supported by States who are specially affected by the putative rule or who are particularly involved in the activity it is said to regulate.

- The language used in the act itself; language which declares or suggests that it is stating a legal right or obligation is stronger evidence in support of a customary rule.
- The records of any proceedings leading up to the act's adoption; statements by State representatives indicating their view as to the provision's juridical character are important.
- The frequency with which the provision in the act has been reiterated in subsequent acts; a frequently reiterated provision provides stronger evidence in support of a customary rule than a single statement.

The United Nations Security Council possesses under Chapter VII of the United Nations Charter an exceptional, and relatively narrow, power to adopt acts which directly and per se create legal obligations in general international law.

These powers include a power to require, with compulsory legal effect, a State to perform acts or refrain from acts in order that international peace and security might be maintained or restored. Thus, in its Chapter VII resolution of 25 June 1950, the Security Council called upon 'the authorities of North Korea to withdraw forthwith to the 38th parallel', and in resolution 1267 (1999), the Security Council demanded that Afghanistan turn over the terrorist leader Osama bin Laden to face trial.

Chapter VII also enables the Security Council to 'call upon' States to impose a range of embargos and sanctions in the areas of economic relations, transport, communications and diplomatic contacts. This may be done in order to 'maintain or restore international peace and security' where the Council has already determined that the situation to which the sanctions are directed constitutes a 'threat to the peace, breach of the peace or act of aggression'.

It should be emphasised that the Security Council is a political and not a judicial body. When acting under Chapter VII of the Charter, it does not need to make a determination that a breach of international law has occurred, though it will do so where agreement on such a characterisation can be reached. Conversely, not every breach of international law justifies resort to Chapter VII powers. The Security Council's powers to act under Chapter VII are enlivened only when it determines that there is a threat to the peace, breach of the peace or act of aggression.

SOFT LAW

There is also a category of legal materials which is often referred to, somewhat infelicitously, as 'soft law'. The reference is an unfortunate one because the material is not really law at all, and the label 'soft law' has a capacity to mislead the reader into ascribing to the materials a legal significance that they do not really possess.

Soft law is any material which is not intended to generate, or is not per se capable of generating, legal rules but which may, nonetheless, produce certain legal effects. Those effects can range from providing the evidence of the State practice and *opinio juris* required to establish a rule of customary international law, through providing assistance in the interpretation and application of conventional and customary law whose precise requirements remain unclear, to indicating the likely future course of international law's development.

This rather amorphous category of materials is usually taken to mean non-binding instruments, such as declarations, resolutions and guidelines, adopted by international organisations or assemblies of States. Occasionally, it can extend to similar instruments adopted by private associations, such as the International Committee of the Red Cross, where they are endowed with officially recognised functions by virtue of a treaty.[49] Accordingly, although General Assembly resolutions are not usually per se capable of producing legal effects, they may provide evidence of a customary rule or point to the *lex ferenda* (the future development of the law). The same is true of expressly non-legally binding international agreements or declarations, such as the declaration on principles governing the mutual relations of States adopted at the 1975 Helsinki Conference on Security and Co-operation in Europe.[50] These materials may also provide a foundation upon which States eventually conclude treaties.

The most effective research in international law is that which pays faithful attention to its rather peculiar system of sources. A mastery of these sources, and an appreciation of the demands which they place upon the researcher, are essential ingredients for the pursuit of an effective and fruitful research programme in international law.

FURTHER READING

M. Akehurst, *A Modern Introduction to International Law* (6th edn) (London: Allen and Unwin, 1987). (The 6th edition was the last by Dr Akehurst before his death in 1989, and remains the most lucid overview of the subject ever published.)

J. L. Brierly, *The Law of Nations* (6th edn), ed. H. Waldock (Oxford: Clarendon Press, 1963). (Professor Brierly's brief but classic work is an exemplar of impressive scholarship issuing in clear, jargon-free and highly instructive exposition.)

M. Byers, *Custom, Power, and the Power of Rules: International Relations and Customary International Law* (Cambridge: Cambridge University Press, 1999).

B. Cheng, *General Principles of Law as Applied by International Courts and Tribunals* (London: Stevens, 1953).

A. D'Amato, *The Concept of Custom in International Law* (Ithaca, NY: Cornell University Press, 1971).

G. M. Danilenko, *Law Making in the International Community* (Dordrecht: Martinus Nijhoff, 1993).

S. Hall, 'Natural Law, International Order and the Limits of Legal Positivism' (2001) 12 *European Journal of International Law* 269.

S. Hall, *International Law* (2nd edn) (Sydney: Butterworths, 2006).

H. Kelsen, *Principles of International Law* (New York: Rinehart, 1952). (Professor Kelsen forcefully expounds a positivist approach to international law.)

J. Klabbers, *The Concept of Treaty in International Law* (The Hague: Kluwer Law International, 1996).

C. MacGibbon, 'Customary International Law and Acquiescence' (1954) 31 *British Yearbook of International Law* 143.

M. Ragazzi, *The Concept of International Obligations Erga Omnes* (Oxford: Clarendon Press, 1997).

NOTES

1. There are, however, two notable exceptions. First, certain resolutions adopted by the United Nations Security Council will impose legally binding obligations on all States. Second, the European Union, while founded on a number of constitutive treaties, possesses most of the characteristics of a federal legal system so that the Union's legislative organs may adopt laws which are effective in the Member States in such a way that they may be directly relied upon by litigants in national courts and tribunals.

2. *North Sea Continental Shelf* cases *(Germany v Denmark, Germany v The Netherlands)*, International Court of Justice Reports (1969) 3, paras 72–4 of the judgment.

3. Article 21(1), Vienna Convention on the Law of Treaties.

4. Ibid. Article 21(2).

5. Ibid. Article 21(3).

6. *Reservations to the Genocide Convention case*, International Court of Justice Reports (1951) 15.

7. See, for example, General Comment No. 24 of the Human Rights Committee established by the International Covenant on Civil and Political Rights, CCPR/C/21/Rev.1/Add.6, (1995) 15 *Human Rights Law Journal* 4 64 , (1995) *International Human Rights Reports* 10, (1995) 34 *International Legal Materials*.

8. See, for example, *Weber v Switzerland*, European Court of Human Rights (1990) Series A, No. 177.

9. *Anglo-Norwegian Fisheries* case *(United Kingdom v Norway)*, International Court of Justice Reports (1951) 184.

10. For example, Judge Read's dissenting opinion in the *Anglo-Norwegian Fisheries* case, ibid. 191.

11. *France v Turkey*, Permanent Court of International Justice Reports (1927), Series A, No. 10.

12. *Colombia v Peru*, International Court of Justice Reports (1950) 276.

13. See note 9 above.

14. *Restatement (Third) of the Foreign Relations Law of the United States* (1987), Vol. 1, § 102, 25.

15. See note 2 above, para. 74 of the judgment.

16. *Case Concerning Military and Paramilitary Activities in and Against Nicaragua (Nicaragua v United States) (Merits)*, International Court of Justice Reports (1986) 14, para. 186 of the judgment.

17. I. C. MacGibbon, 'Customary International Law and Acquiescence' (1954) 31 *British Yearbook of International Law* 143.

18. See note 2 above.

19. See note 11 above, 28.

20. See note 2 above.

21. Ibid. para. 74 of the judgment.

22. Ibid. para. 77 of the judgment.

23. Ibid. para. 76 of the judgment.

24. See note 2 above, 177.

25. Ibid. 248.

26. *Nicaragua* case, see note 16 above, para. 188 of the judgment.

27. *Frontier Dispute* case *(Burkina Faso v Mali)* International Court of Justice Reports 1985, 6, paras, 27–8.

28. See the contrary Soviet view expressed by G. I. Tunkin, *Co-existence and International Law*, Rec Acad, Vol. 95, 1958, III, 25–6.

29. Permanent Court of International Justice, Advisory Committee of Jurists, *Procès-verbaux of the Proceedings of the Committee*, 1920, 335.

30. See, for example, D. P. O'Connell, *International Law* (2nd edn) (London: Stevens, 1970) 10–14; compare Judge Tanaka (dissenting) in the *South West Africa* cases *(Ethiopia v South Africa, Liberia v South Africa* (second phase)) International Court of Justice Reports (1966) 6, para. 296.

31. Gaius, *Institutiones*, as translated by H. J. Wolff in *Roman Law: An Historical Introduction* (Norman: University of Oklahoma Press, 1951) 82–3.

32. A. Nussbaum, *A Concise History of the Law of Nations* (rev. edn) (New York: Macmillan, 1958) 14.

33. J. Finnis, *Natural Law and Natural Rights* (Oxford: Clarendon Press, 1980) 296.
34. Ibid. 288.
35. See, for example, R. Jennings and A. Watts (eds), *Oppenheim's International Law* (9th edn) (London: Longman, 1992), §12, 36–40 and §15, 43–45; I. Brownlie, *Principles of Public International Law* (6th edn) (Oxford: Oxford University Press, 2003) 15–19, 25–27. See also *Chorzow Factory (Indemnity) (Merits)* case (*Germany v Poland*), Permanent Court of International Justice Reports (1928), Series A No. 17, 47–48; *River Meuse* case *(Netherlands v Belgium)*, Permanent Court of International Justice Reports (1937), Series A/B No. 70, 76–77.
36. B. Cheng, *General Principles of Law as Applied by International Courts and Tribunals* (London: Stevens, 1953) 24.
37. Permanent Court of International Justice, Advisory Committee of Jurists, *Procés-verbaux of the Proceedings of the Committee* (1920), 336. To pronounce a *non liquet* (a Latin phrase meaning 'not clear') is to invoke the absence of clear legal rules applicable to a dispute as a reason for declining to give judgment.
38. *Eastern Extension, Australasia and China Telegraph Co Ltd*, 6 Reports of International Arbitral Awards (1923) 114–15.
39. See note 12 above, 332.
40. Article 38(1)(d), Statute of the International Court of Justice.
41. *The Paquete Habana* 175 US (1900) 700–1.
42. J. L. Brierly, *The Law of Nations: An Introduction to the International Law of Peace* (6th edn) (Oxford: Clarendon Press, 1963) 24.
43. For example, Articles 17 and 18 of the United Nations Charter.
44. *Reparation for Injuries Suffered in the Service of the United Nations*, International Court of Justice Reports (1949), 174.
45. For example, the power of the International Civil Aviation Organisation to adopt legally binding standards for air navigation under the Chicago Convention 1944.
46. For example, Article 249 of the Treaty establishing the European Community 1957.
47. *Nicaragua* case, see note 16 above, paras. 188 and 189.
48. *Legality of the Threat or Use of Nuclear Weapons*, International Court of Justice Reports (1996) 226.
49. See H. McCoubrey, *International Humanitarian Law* (2nd edn, 1998), at 52–3.
50. *Nicaragua case*, see note 16 above, para. 189.

CHAPTER 9

Development of Empirical Techniques and Theory

Mike McConville

INTRODUCTION

This chapter explores research methods for law through a journey that has been an unfinished part of my life's work. It seeks to frame some of the choices that are open to empirical researchers and the political and ethical dimensions to which these choices in turn give rise. It does not provide pro forma solutions but rather is intended to illustrate possible ways forward in terms of method and in terms of encouraging prospective researchers to reflect upon their role and the role of potential respondents. It is as subjective as all research with the strengths and weaknesses that this implies. It is not meant to be a model for others but an example of how one individual negotiated part of his research life. It is premised on the basis that law cannot be considered apart from other aspects of social organisation and is worthy of study because of its intimate relationship to social control and the regulation of disputes.

THE INITIAL EXPLORATION

My first empirical research project, carried out with my colleague John Baldwin, provides a salutary example of the excitement and demoralisation confronting the researcher, of the unavoidable politics and ethics of research, and of the values and limitations of attempts to reach a wider understanding of how individuals are treated within institutional settings. It is a cautionary tale but one that I believe also illustrates how lone scholars can make a contribution and through the process itself learn from the experience of research so as to enrich later projects.

Our initial research project, started in 1974, had a relatively closed objective. Considerable political controversy centred upon the jury, an institution that

excited great passion among both its supporters and detractors and, in particular, the allegation that it was acquitting far too many people who were, it was
alleged, guilty of serious crime. The then Metropolitan Police Commissioner,
Sir Robert Mark, had delivered a withering attack on the jury system in his
Dimbleby Lecture in 1972[1] in which he accused juries of acquitting too many
criminals who were, he alleged, assisted by lawyers who were often more
wicked than the clients they represented.

The jury had become a concern of government politicians (or at least the
Home Office) since the Morris Committee report of 1965.[2] The Morris
Committee had recommended democratisation of jury service, thereby sig-
nalling the replacement of blue-ribbon property-owning juries hitherto
deemed in official circles to be safe, that is, panels of citizens who would reli-
ably convict defendants drawn mainly from the lower classes. Extending jury
membership to all those on the electoral register[3] caused concern in official
circles and immediate steps were taken to lessen the predicted impact.[4] We
applied for funding to the Home Office, our application was approved, and we
established a Consultative Committee (including representatives of the Home
Office, Police, Law Society and Bar Association) to help oversee the project and
assist in access.

The Home Office was an arm of government not known, as we shall see, for
unconditional support of independent researchers. So, we suspected that its
willingness to fund our proposal to undertake research into the workings of the
jury at a time of active public discussion of the institution was substantially on
the basis that it was looking for results which would enable restrictions to be
placed upon the right to jury trial. This impression was soon reinforced by the
recommendations of a Departmental Committee under Lord Justice James to
take away the right to jury trial in many cases involving theft or criminal
damage.[5] We did not, however, give any undertakings other than that we would
show a pre-publication draft of any report to the Consultative Committee and
consider any comments offered.

This highlights one important point about the independence of research.
We were acutely aware that government bodies could impose or seek to control
the findings of researchers that they had funded where the results of the
research were not to their liking. Any concession on our part to allow the
Home Office or others a veto on publication would not only have compromised
our independence but also that of other researchers in the future who would
then be subjected to the same constraints supported by precedent. We had the
earlier example of Stanley Cohen and Laurie Taylor's study of long-term confinement in prisons which was published in the face of strong opposition from
the Home Office and the consequent 'blackballing' of the two academics from
further government-funded research.[6] Additionally, we had the immediate
example of the Home Office obstruction of research on prisons by Roy King

and Kenneth Elliot[7] whose book was long delayed through Home Office obstruction.

We decided to accept the grant and to undertake the research with full awareness that its findings might encounter resistance even though we had ensured that no restrictions were placed upon us at the outset. In an effort to ensure co-operation and access from the potential respondent organisations, we established The Consultative Committee with representatives from the Home Office, Law Society, Bar Association and Police. We used the committee to further our purposes, gained their trust and through their good offices secured access for the research in the chosen field sites.[8]

As the fieldwork progressed, it became increasingly clear to us that most of the cases in our samples, selected at the charging stage, were being disposed of without going before a jury. Indeed, such was the seepage of cases that we were having difficulty in gathering an adequate sample of jury trial cases. This was contrary to our prior expectations since the cases chosen were of some gravity where a 'not guilty' plea and jury trial had been anticipated by the Crown Court authorities on the basis of information supplied in advance of the intended trial date by the defendants' solicitors. Why were cases routinely diverting from the path set out by defence lawyers?

We decided that this occurrence was sufficiently important to investigate in its own right, notwithstanding that the principal focus of the research had originally been the jury. To this end we selected a sample of 150 defendants whose cases were being disposed through the entry of a guilty plea in the Crown Court and prior to the empanelment of a jury. We went ahead with this ancillary study without the involvement of barristers whose representative body, the Senate of the Bar, withheld co-operation, and we did so without bringing it to the notice of the Consultative Committee since no additional resources or consents were involved and, whatever we were to discover, it would have a direct bearing upon our understanding of the jury within the criminal justice system.

Whether we were right to go ahead is a question on which individual researchers should reflect. On the one hand, it would be fair to say that whilst our research plan as originally put to the Home Office did mention guilty pleas, this was not the focus of the study and, however generously read, guilty pleas, though included in the original design, were always a side issue in our plans. On the other hand, research is very often about chance or serendipity. Scientific discoveries, for example, have not uncommonly been made as an unanticipated by-product of some other scientific pursuit: the discovery of the effects of a closed electrical circuit by Luigi Galvani (leading ultimately to neurophysiology and clinical neurology), of the penetration of solid matter by x-rays by Wilhelm Rontgen, vaccination and disease prevention by Louis Pasteur and of penicillin by Alexander Fleming, Ernst Chain and Howard Florey are but examples. Whilst our findings are not of this stature, the main point nonetheless remains.

We went ahead without making special mention of this to the Consultative Committee because the main study was proceeding without interference at its own slow pace and because we thought that we were on to something important. This raises another important issue of research ethics. Our action can be viewed in another way: as being less than candid with, even deceiving, the Consultative Committee in order to preserve the wider research as to which the Committee's co-operation was crucial. Personal ambition and vanity are the other side of a researcher's dedication and it is as well to confront this head on when you embark upon a research career. As long as it drove the research and did not distort it, we felt justified in our 'ancillary' foray into guilty pleas.

What we soon uncovered was the phenomenon now widely known as plea bargaining, a process which involves persuading defendants to enter a guilty plea in return for a reduced sentence. Actually, the details of what we were to find came as a major surprise. The research took place in an age when the police station was a 'no go' area for lawyers as well as researchers, when there were few, if any, enforceable rights for suspects, when people were held in detention without charge for indeterminate periods on the pretext that they were 'helping the police with their inquiries' and thus, in law though not in fact, free to leave at any time, and when widespread allegations were levelled at the police over the use of inducements, violence and threats of violence to secure confessions and thus a guilty verdict outcome. We were quite prepared for suspects and defendants to reinforce this picture and provide further ammunition against what everyone felt was prevailing police practice.

But whilst we expected this, we did not encourage it. Instead, we sought a mechanism which would not induce defendants to castigate the police, or indeed, any other criminal justice actor, whilst allowing for spontaneous narratives to emerge. Respondents were generally willing to co-operate, especially those in prison who welcomed a break from daily routine and the opportunity to smoke our cigarettes.[9] The question was: how to extract their stories without distorting them? What should we do in methodological terms? We settled on a single simple question at the outset of every interview with defendants: 'Tell me about your case?' This formulation permitted defendants to talk about any aspect they saw as important, including what they understood their 'case' to be. Defendants were thus not induced to talk about their experience with the police at the interrogation stage, nor about their evaluation of their solicitor, nor about their experience of their barrister, nor, indeed, about any specific matter that might have led them to plead guilty.

Whilst some focused on the history of their lives and others on the next stage (a possible appeal or complaint), over and over again, unprompted, defendants used this opening question to attack the treatment they had received at the hands of their barrister, almost invariably a complete stranger to them, and to a lesser extent the judge on the day set, they had believed, for trial. In general they had prepared themselves for a trial, their day in court, but had been persuaded by various stratagems to capitulate and plead guilty just before the time set for trial. They were never accorded an opportunity to give their side of the story. The question that Howard Becker[10] asked: 'Whose side are you on?', was quickly answered: we empathised with defendants, irrespective of factual guilt of innocence, and decided that their voice should be heard.

Additionally, the consistency of the stories told by individuals who had never met each other, together with accounts from some solicitors and others, enabled us to be confident about the findings that these guilty pleas were not 'free and voluntary', as required by law, but had instead been induced by various forms of coercion and that 'plea bargaining' was a widespread institutional *practice* and not isolated aberrational behaviour on the part of some maverick lawyers and judges.

The method we chose was also a good example of the value and application of the axiom that, in an ideal state, research should be done *with* people not *on* people.[11] All of the defendants were fully informed about the research (without being told that we were interested in *how* they had decided upon a guilty plea) and all freely gave their consent. However, the ideal cannot always be attained and I would assert that, on occasions, subterfuge is justifiable where the public interest cannot be secured through candid engagement with respondents. It is for each researcher to determine what is right on a case-by-case basis; but few who have engaged in empirical research can honestly assert that a measure of duplicity is never used or can never be justified without distorting or abandoning the project.

The findings of our research were in a 'revelatory' vein and not informed by deep theory beyond the obvious point that defendants unwittingly confronted a 'courtroom workgroup', the members of which held greater allegiance to each other than to the transient population of defendants. We had uncovered a subterranean process conducted by barristers and judges in the privacy of the court corridors[12] or judges' chambers. In graphic terms, defendants told us how they had been coerced into pleading guilty, often at the last minute on the day set for trial, by threats or promises from their own counsel or the trial judge, a process well attested to in the United States of America but believed alien to the British justice system.

THE POLITICS OF RESEARCH

Our interim report to the Consultative Committee, eventually published as *Negotiated Justice*,[13] was met with open hostility, and a concerted attempt was made to prevent publication and discredit the research. The research was leaked to the press and leaders of the legal profession queued up to assail the findings and launch personal attacks on our integrity. On the one hand the research was said to be based on 'unsubstantiated anecdotes' and to be little more than the 'tittle-tattle of the cells'; on the other hand, we were said to have breached confidentiality (what barristers said to defendants) and not to have done anything to assist defendants who had been the victims of alleged coercion. We were even said to have been the cause of the rise in crime. Revealingly, however, in none of the attacks did the legal profession deny the practice of plea bargaining. Using the politics of discreditability, they sought to deflect discussion onto the reliability of 'criminals' and vague and spurious allegations about our own trustworthiness.

After months of press publicity, personal pressure increased when we were summoned to see the vice-chancellor of the university. He warned of the grave risks in publishing and mentioned, in a pointed aside, how parts of the university such as Psychology (then involving large-scale animal experimentation) were in receipt of significant Home Office or other governmental funding. At this meeting we were told that, unless we agreed to stop publication, the university had been given to understand that the then Home Secretary (Merlin Rees) would make a statement to the House of Commons the next day in which he would denounce the research. We told the vice-chancellor that we would provide no such undertaking.

The vice-chancellor then ordered that we could not proceed further until the manuscript had been vetted by three senior figures, all of emeritus professor standing, appointed by him and that we were not to respond to press inquiries until the professors' report had been received. Despite the threats to our careers, barely started, we were determined to go ahead but decided that we had to wait for the report. When the three emeritus professors submitted their report, we were more than relieved to learn that they had given the research a clean bill of health and exonerated us from the wild accusations.

Publication, in turn, was made possible by the good fortune of having an excellent commissioning editor in Edward Elgar, then at Martin Robertson, the support of the series editors, Colin Campbell and Paul Wiles, and the general solidarity of the socio-legal community in the face of unwarranted attacks. Campbell and Wiles in their introductory note to the book pointed up some of the wider questions our research had raised. This included the moral dilemma confronting many researchers who are witnesses to some malpractice or wrongdoing and who have to choose whether to intervene in an effort to correct the perceived wrongdoing (and thereby, in all likelihood, abandon the research project) or, instead, remain detached from individual cases in order to uncover the social processes which give rise to structural injustice.[14] Researchers must confront and resolve this dilemma for themselves.

The way to do this is to anticipate, prior to undertaking the research, the dilemmas that are likely to be encountered and then to decide whether the production of the research is of more long-term value than intervention in individual cases. If it is, the research can proceed; if not, the research should not be started. I know of no research example where the general problem, if not its precise detail, cannot be foreseen in advance.[15] And I know of no generic answer other than the moral framework of the individual researcher which should be openly declared to encourage debate and contest.

Despite the evasions of the profession at the time, over the years it has become clear that what the research uncovered was an endemic practice in which most barristers and judges were deeply implicated. Indeed, although for many years afterwards the Court of Appeal continued to denounce plea bargaining as a practice alien to English justice and to fulminate over instances which came on appeal in an ever-increasing tide, plea bargaining eventually came in from the cold. It is now defended as an essential weapon in the fight against crime and the quest for a cost-effective criminal justice system.

SOME GENERALISABLE RESEARCH LESSONS

For the researcher, however, there are many lessons. First, it is essential that the socio-legal community gives a full account of the natural history of research projects, including the ethical and political dimensions, so that those who come after can be better prepared. This rarely happens in science where the emphasis is upon how the results should be applied, not on how they came to be produced, except, of course, in those all too common occurrences involving scientific fraud where the process of 'discovery' has to be confronted, albeit only after public exposure of the wrongdoing. In socio-legal studies, however, accounts of the process of the production of knowledge are indispensable.

Second, it is obvious that official institutions have great power to influence the production of knowledge by placing constraints on what can be done (for example, denying researchers access to barristers or, in other settings, to judges,[16] to prisons, and so on); persuading researchers to undertake only 'policy-relevant' research, that is, defining the problem in terms seen as appropriate by the dominant institution; and requiring research findings to be expressed in terms of variables over which the institution has a measure of control. The long line of 'administrative criminology' research is a sad testament to the power of dominant institutions and the failures of individual researchers to resist. This has lead to 'research' institutions which are little more than client states of institutional funding bodies and to research which avoids interrogating powerful organisations to concentrate instead upon the powerless in society or, as Paul Rock, in a slightly dated but apposite comment, starkly put it,[17] 'the stripper, dwarves, prostitutes, cheque forgers, the maimed, the blind, the stuttering and the thief'.

Third, it remains possible for researchers to contribute to a deeper understanding of social organisations even where they are forced to conduct their research under considerable constraints. The plea bargaining research referred to earlier gave rise to a spate of other inquiries, and more and more of the criminal justice process was piece by piece uncovered.[18] Though much of the research and commentary may not have been explicitly informed by deep theory, theoretical insights were achieved. For example, plea bargaining can now be seen to provide a classic example of a central problem faced by client-centred organisations (such as law firms and courts), the products of which may be arbitrary rather than, as they would wish to portray, pre-determined according to promulgated 'rules' and 'principles'. The organisational problem is then addressed through various gate-keeping devices designed to exclude outsiders from looking in and at the same time to enmesh members of the organisation in rules, policies and procedures. These policies, in turn, promote secrecy under the guise of confidentiality and, in doing so, create irreconcilable conflicts of interest for the members rationalised, for example, through convoluted lawyers' codes of conduct and the construction of narratives which seek to sanitise actions as inevitable or client-driven and to portray a system no longer tracking the formal or public process as legitimate and in conformity with it.[19]

RESEARCHING AS AN FOREIGNER

After several years of researching other topics, I returned to plea bargaining by chance. The New York City Bar Association had become concerned about the quality of representation afforded to indigent defendants in the City, and it proposed various reforms. Essentially, most cases were dealt with by the Legal Aid Society, a private society in name but a public defender in substance. Where, however, there was an actual or potential conflict of interest between defendants in a multiple defendant case, all but the principal defendant were represented by private lawyers appointed and remunerated pursuant to Article 18-B of the New York County Law and colloquially known as '18-B lawyers'. The New York City Bar Association was of the view that these court-appointed 18-B lawyers were a rag-tag group providing at best inadequate and ineffective assistance, and that the main problem was the Bar Association's inability to control the quality of representation these lawyers offered the poor. To better ensure a thorough reform and the adoption of their recommendation, the City Bar Association agreed to co-operate in research on court-assigned lawyers, and I was invited to lead the research during the currency of my appointment as a research professor at New York University.

At the outset, I was confronted with a choice about how to proceed. On the one hand, I could examine the 18-B lawyers through ethnographic research, by direct observation and through interviews with accredited City Bar Association lawyers and officers and lawyers of the Legal Aid Society, all of whom pledged support for such an approach. On the other hand, I could look at *all* indigent lawyers, Legal Aid Society as well as 18-B. It became apparent that if the latter were chosen, it would be without the active co-operation of the Bar Association and against the resolute objection of the Legal Aid Society. The vehement opposition I encountered from a Society that claimed to be the 'gold standard' in and of itself aroused my curiosity and suggested that the claim being advanced by the Society about their superiority over 18-B lawyers should itself be tested. I accordingly chose to do the study on both sets of lawyers. The question was: how could I do it in the face of such opposition?

The starting point was an alliance with Professor Chester (Chet) Mirsky, Acting Director of the Criminal Law Clinic at New York University. Chet was an experienced trial lawyer who knew every nook and cranny of the City courts but nothing about empirical research. I had substantial empirical research experience but knew nothing about New York. It proved to be a natural alliance: we became friends and research partners for the next twenty years. Luck can thus play a major role in research endeavours. Chet was able to get me a court pass through a friend in the Correctional Services which allowed me to get into the holding pens behind the courtroom where defendants were produced from police custody (without having had a lawyer present at the interrogation) pending court appearance and where they were assigned a defence attorney, either Legal Aid Society or 18-B. Once court officers saw me a few times as I flashed the 'court pass' (good only for use by Correctional Services' personnel), I became accepted by all concerned, a deception that did not need to be actively repeated thereafter, so that I could come and go as I pleased for any purpose. In other words, I soon lost my standing in their eyes as a researcher or outsider, though I continued, of course, in their minds to be a Correctional Services person.

Initial acceptance by judges was assisted by my status as a foreigner who was thereby perceived as peculiarly engaged in some ill-defined pastime. As I served shifts with the lawyers on a rotational basis in this twenty-four-hour, seven-day week system, I was soon seen as part of the furniture, my status and identity having been lost to all court actors. Indeed, in the managed chaos of the court house, I was able to see Legal Aid Society lawyers at work, examine case files, interview defendants, lawyers and judges, review the working notes of judges and do almost everything except represent defendants (much, it must be said, against the occasional protestations of some judges who, in their anxiety to 'clear the calendar', tried to assign cases to me as a 'courthouse regular' when no one else was available in the courtroom to accept assignment).

In this privileged position,[20] we were able to gather a wealth of data on all lawyering activities and thereby lay a foundation for a comparative study of

Legal Aid Society and 18-B lawyers. We discovered a guilty plea system in which poor defendants in state criminal cases received ineffective assistance from lawyers (Legal Aid Society or court-assigned) because the lawyers allied themselves with courts, prosecutors, local government and the organised bar, rather than with indigent defendants, in the interests of cost-efficient disposition.

For their part, the public defender (Legal Aid Society) operated under a massive case overload, resulting in individual lawyers choosing the least serious instead of the most serious cases in multiple-defendant cases and dumping swathes of cases which were picked up instead by 18-B lawyers. Because staff attorneys of the Society often failed to appear on a case on subsequent dates, the Society employed 'catchers', attorneys stationed at a courtroom who would 'stand up' on any case 'belonging' to the Society. Judges would tolerate this practice where the appearance was a pure formality but where issues of substance were involved, they could take the case away from the 'catcher' and re-assign it to 18-B. In fact, staff attorneys of the Legal Aid Society often failed to appear at court, with the result that judges, anxious to move cases forward, would re-assign the case to 18-B which would hold the case thereafter whatever the appearance rate of the private lawyer. Indeed, whilst in theory the Legal Aid Society should have taken between 90 per cent and 95 per cent of cases, such was the extent of diversion to 18-B that the caseloads of the two groups of lawyers were virtually indistinguishable.

FROM DATA TO THEORY

Here we were looking at a system that had achieved a much higher level of cost-effectiveness and contempt for the individual than the British system I had seen when researching for *Negotiated Justice*,[21] and, unlike in the system operating in Britain, this was, at least in part, open and notorious to those who cared to spend time in the courtroom. Despite the posturing of the Bar Association elite and liberal reformers, this clearly was a system that was not susceptible to change, and we needed an explanation that went beyond 'revelatory' description.

The first insight was to break out of the reformist discourse which had persisted for many years without impacting in any degree upon the lived reality of the courtroom. The New York indigent defence system was a system that was fulfilling its goals rather than being a system in failure, and this required an examination of the origins and development of criminal defence services in New York. To explore this, we embarked upon a detailed historical analysis focusing on the Legal Aid Society.

We discovered that for most of the first half of the twentieth century, assigned counsel and institutional defenders served separate interests. Originally established as the sole means of providing representation to the poor in the United

States, assigned counsel (18-B) eventually fell into disfavour precisely because of its adversarial defence techniques which were linked to the solicitation of fees from indigent defendants and were portrayed as a cause of social unrest. Those who feared social unrest created the institutional defender (Legal Aid Society) to eliminate adversarial advocacy for poor people, with attorneys dedicated to a cost-efficient method of representation.[22]

From its origins in 1871, the Legal Aid Society sought to provide aid in civil cases to poor German immigrants in New York City by representing those who were 'worthy' and seeking justice through conciliation in individual cases under a general philosophy of Americanisation of the immigrant classes. This approach attracted the interests of the organised bar who had always opposed socialised legal services by arguing that they would institutionalise adversarial advocacy, increase delays in the processing of cases and serve only to set criminals free. Instead, they promised that elite lawyers would provide free legal services to truly indigent defendants on a *pro bono* basis. Whilst *pro bono* representation never materialised in any significant amount, the Society offered a vehicle through which the Bar Association could retain control over legal services.

To this end, elite lawyers and Directors of the Legal Aid Society joined with prosecutors to form the Voluntary Defenders' Committee which was later absorbed into the Legal Aid Society. In this way, the Society came by 1920 to assume a role in criminal cases and continued its philosophy of compromise and cost-efficiency. As its Chief Counsel stated: '[d]efense in its general acceptance is not always required, as statistics show beyond question that most of the indigent accused are, in fact, guilty'.[23] Upon assuming the role of public defender, the Legal Aid Society counselled defendants to accept lesser pleas and developed strategies for securing compliance including 'laughing at the defence advanced, pouring scorn on the story of the defendant and treating whatever was said with the utmost suspicion' with the consequence that 'defendants who had first asserted their innocence . . . admitted their guilt'.[24]

The establishment of the Defenders' Committee enabled the bar to further a number of objectives: to ensure that control over legal services remained in the hands of the private bar; to maintain public confidence in the administration of justice by facilitating the efficient processing of indigent defendants; and to reduce the potential for social unrest created by the adversarial practices of assigned counsel. In this way, elite lawyers, through membership of the Legal Aid Society, guaranteed private lawyers' control of New York's institutional defender legitimated through the cloak of the Society's 'independent' status. In the pre-*Gideon*[25] era, 'independence' meant that the Defenders' Committee would forego technical defences associated with adversarial advocacy and assist the prosecution in convicting 'guilty' defendants. In the post-*Gideon* era, 'independence' meant that only a private society, even after the shift to full public funding, could carry out the mandate of the state to provide counsel to poor criminal defendants.

Viewed through this lens, the empirical data took on a different meaning, apparent failures turning out to be success stories. The Legal Aid Society had been structured to recruit staff attorneys willing to conform to the indigent defence system's original goals and to accommodate lawyers willing to pursue these goals. As time went by, however, when new staff attorneys energised by the era of rights in the 1960s attempted to assert adversary principles in the face of overwhelming case loads by withdrawing their labour, management imposed a no-strike clause and binding arbitration which was accepted by the union. Staff attorneys were thereafter trapped in a system which guaranteed oppressive case loads and 'burn-out'. The 'shedding' of cases by staff attorneys to 18-B, the failure to accept new case assignments and the low court appearance rate of staff attorneys became standard 'easing behaviour', practices designed to relieve the stress of heavy case loads and of poor working conditions. Such practices could be condoned by management because its case load was measured by the number of cases for which it initially assumed responsibility rather than the number it saw through to completion. This, together with underreporting its budget, enabled it to continue to claim that it discharged its contractual obligations to the City by providing defence services at a cost per case of less than US$200.

One other striking feature of our research was the obvious difference between how plea bargaining was conducted in New York and England. Whereas plea bargaining in England was covert, practised in corridors and judges' chambers, unannounced and undetectable in courts renowned for decorous behaviour and stylised rituals, in New York, by contrast, deals were openly struck amid threats and blandishments, with both defendants and their lawyers subjected to ritual humiliations from calendar judges.

As the most prominent New York calendar judge told us, the encounters with defendants were seen by judges as 'strength-testing exercises'. As part of the testing process, defendants' bail status would be manipulated by gaoling those who refused to plead guilty even where the defendant had been previously released at arraignment and had voluntarily appeared in court on several adjourned dates. By contrast, some defendants who had pleaded guilty were rewarded by being allowed to remain free on bail, although they were now convicted and awaiting sentence. Judges raised the stakes on those who refused to admit guilt by threatening them with a greater sentence on any subsequent court date: initial offers of probation, if refused, would later become fixed gaol time, whereas offers of gaol time once refused would be increased to indeterminate state prison sentences. In the event of a conviction after trial, judges would impose a sentence that greatly exceeded the last guilty plea offer made.

In this setting, it seemed superficially plausible to explain these events through a theoretical approach which confined itself to the courtroom and its principal actors. Indeed, the approach of much socio-legal research had emphasised shared organisational interests and norms in a setting in which, for example, lawyers and judges are 'repeat' players in contrast to the defendant who is often a 'one-shot' player.[26] This laid the foundations for the establishment of 'courtroom work groups'[27] which, at the extreme, engage in 'short-cuts, deviations and outright rule violations' at the expense of defendants.[28]

EXPANDED THEORY

We came to regard that approach as inadequate because it derived from a narrow focus on the professional actors and failed to take into account the wider context, a context which became apparent once the dynamics of the courtroom discourse were more fully documented through the adoption of an ethnographic framework for data collection allied to data on courtroom organisation and policing strategies. The lesson here is to ensure as far as possible that if multiple data sources are available, researchers should use them all and integrate them in the analysis.

Thus, whilst the open-court 'bargaining' encounters at one level placed a premium on the defendant's resolve pitted against the judge's power to control the outcome, at another level, as a careful observer could see, judges were directing many of their remarks to different constituencies. In the absence of witnesses or witness statements, calendar judges reduced cases to skeletal outlines: 'a chain snatch'; 'a buy and bust'; 'an undercover operation'; these precluded substantive case discussion and focused upon sentence underpinned by a naked presumption of guilt. In court, the advice that lawyers gave to their clients took place under the watchful eye of the judge. Should a defendant grimace or otherwise show disdain for the sentence offer being conveyed or utter a dismissive or hostile response, the judge would immediately raise the offer (increase the minimum sentence) and gaol the defendant. All conversations at the bench and all bargaining statements made by judges to lawyers and defendants were 'off-the-record', the stenographer sitting inertly by until the 'formal' stage of bail setting or entry of guilty plea. At that stage defendants were required to have read into the record their 'acknowledgement' that they had received their 'rights' and had not been coerced into foregoing their right to jury trial.

In parallel, as a careful observer could see, lawyers themselves were the butt of coercive pressure from calendar judges. These judges were rated by court administration officials according to their ability to dispose of large case loads without hearing or trial. Those with the highest rate of disposition were fixtures in these guilty plea courts, while judges who compared unfavourably on this disposition scale were routinely assigned to hearing and trial courts in which there was, of course, little business. If a lawyer attempted to take an adversarial position before a calendar judge, the lawyer might be, as we witnessed, summarily dismissed from the case ('relieved') and thrown out of the court, to be replaced by a court-assigned lawyer[29] whose compliance was known to the judge. Lawyers unfit by reason of ability, age or inebriation were routinely assigned to 'represent' defendants to enable him or her to 'cop a plea'. One judge placed an old drunken lawyer in the 'can', the holding spot for drunken defendants and, on his release four hours later, promptly assigned him new cases. All of this was conducted in open court with the more egregious judicial outbursts not recorded by the court stenographer and thus 'off the record'.

Marginalisation and humiliation of defence lawyers and contempt shown for defendants were more than mere indicia of the non-existence of a consensual courtroom workgroup. It was the aberrational displays of power by calendar judges that gave the lie to everyday practice which was held together by the superior power of the judge and the judge's willingness to exercise it whenever it was deemed necessary. Consensual behaviour of lawyers in ordinary cases gave the impression of a courtroom workgroup, but it was no more than an impression.

Moreover, the interactions in court were carefully choreographed events laid on for the education of other defendants and their lawyers awaiting appearance before the judge and for the relatives and friends of defendants sitting in the public gallery. These individuals would thereby learn to appreciate the judge's displeasure at recalcitrance and the power that the judge could bring to bear upon anyone who rejected initial offers or insisted on pleading not guilty.

Viewed through this wider lens, the theorisation of plea bargaining is given new meaning. Guilty plea courts in large urban settings come to be seen as part of a vertically integrated system of imposing control and discipline on highly visible sections of society perceived by official actors as members of the 'dangerous classes'. This system often commences with proactive 'sweeps' by police units (such as drug control units) in which neighbourhoods are subjected to a policy of mass arrests;[30] it extends through the system of assigning lawyers to poor defendants; and it concludes with a highly coercive drama in which defendants are first shown (by being made to watch others) that they will suffer greatly enhanced penalties if they refuse to plead guilty and/or see their lawyer dismissed and replaced by one of the 'on-tap' tame lawyers. That drama is set in courtrooms whose practices might imply, from a narrow focus upon lawyers' interactions, a consensus model of justice but whose real mission, disempowered as the lawyers are by the controlling judge, is to expedite capitulation.

At the same time, members of the defendants' families and other supporters in the audience themselves sometimes attracted the direct displeasure of judges and received contemptuous tongue lashings. In this way, they too learned the futility of challenging police actions and the futility of the promise of 'due process' itself, a message they were expected to carry back to their neighbourhoods. Disciplinary practices thus routinely occurred in the presence of disempowered people who, whilst expecting nothing from a system in which the objectives of policing define the process, become in turn conduits to their own communities, communicating the controlling power hierarchies in a society graphically reinforced by their courtroom experience.

These insights laid the foundation for constructing a 'social disciplinary' model of criminal justice, a form of substantive rationality committed to achieving order through surveillance and control of an urban underclass.[31] Social discipline bears little relationship to traditional notions of crime control which, in theory, enhances the autonomy of the individual and is sought to be achieved through an analysis of the state's burden of proof at hearings or trials. By contrast, social discipline, a vertically integrated system through which control and discipline is exercised, imposes blanket judgments of conviction on those ensnared in police mass arrests without significant restraint on how police power may be exercised against the individual. In this setting, the entry of a guilty plea is without any assurance that criminal activity occurred in the first instance or will cease thereafter. At the same time, routine case processing through guilty pleas reinforces the actions and expectations of the police and defendants, thereby encouraging drag-net arrests and neighbourhood sweeps in a process of institutionalised domination.

WIDENING THE LENS

Now, when we reflected upon this, we could not reconcile what we had seen with the traditional explanations that sought to account for the rise of plea bargaining, the disappearance of the jury and, in practical terms, the elimination of proof in the modern era of criminal justice in the United States. Leading commentators[32] were agreed that early reliance on jury trials until the latter part of the nineteenth century was a function of the presence of amateur actors, while reliance upon guilty pleas, which later came to displace jury trials, occurred because of the advent of professionalisation among police and lawyers. Under this depiction, the new police became capable of producing reliable evidence of guilt, and this brought into the criminal process lawyers with the ability to assess evidence so that courtroom actors could thereafter accurately distinguish between cases where conviction was certain ('dead bang' cases) and those where triable issues remained. In a context of cost-efficiency, it was argued, in which concerns about case load dominated thinking, cases without triable issues gave rise to and became the fodder for plea bargaining.

This traditional theory was widely supported by other commentators[33] and buttressed by authoritative summations, case load data analysis, and technical arguments.[34] The details are not relevant here but a few sample quotations will make the point:

> In the beginning . . . there were no actors in the system who spent all their working lives in criminal justice. There were no police, professional prosecutors, public defenders, prison wardens, probation officers, detectives, social workers and the like. There were also few full-time criminals. Laymen, amateurs, and ordinary judges (some of them without any training in law) ran the system, together with a few lawyers, and a ragbag of constables, night watchmen, and haphazard jailers.[35]

> Frequently, courts were staffed with part-time officers; often prosecutors and judges were not trained in law . . . Police officers often acting as prosecutors in court were unfamiliar with the rudiments of law and cared even less . . . Admissibility of evidence was capricious, points of law were treated with casualness.
> Historically, the modern jury trial emerged when the criminal justice system was staffed by untrained amateurs who were charged with the task of trying to cope with the problem of accusing, trying and convicting or acquitting someone.[36]

None of this fitted with what we had viewed in New York's courts, the aggregate evaluation of which could hardly be described as the capstone of professionalisation, but all of it might have been a sufficient deterrent to further inquiry. After all, if the historical evolution of the jury and plea bargaining system had been subjected to such scrutiny by leading scholars from Roscoe Pound down the generations, what else was there to find out?

This leads on to the next lesson for the prospective researcher: do not take for granted 'received wisdom', no matter who is transmitting the wisdom. Whilst all research in a sense builds upon those who have gone before, accumulated 'knowledge' must always be open to testing and verification. This is particularly so when what the researcher confronts appears inconsistent with what is already 'known'. It is at this point, at the latest, that the researcher should carefully interrogate how earlier 'wisdom' has come into existence and taken hold, and not allow the reputation of those who have gone before to become a barrier to inquiry.

Suffice it to say that upon exhaustive empirical enquiry of historical records from 1800 to 1865, the professionalisation hypothesis of Roscoe Pound and others that the 'formative era' of American law occurred in the nineteenth century, wherein professional practice replaced primitive 'frontier justice', was contradicted by all the available evidence: it turned out to be merely a tenet of a wider ideological view of American legal history uninformed by any systematic analysis and founded in romanticism. The criminal justice system extant in New York City from the outset of the nineteenth century was in every sense a professional system based upon rational considerations, evidence-driven and staffed by trained lawyers and judges who sought to protect defendants from over-reaching by the state. However, and without any 'professionalisation' of the parties, in an abrupt transformation occurring in 1850–65, the system turned on its head with guilty pleas replacing juries in everyday cases. Existing 'top-down' explanations, reliant upon macro-theories unanchored in empirical data, could not account for this, and so we had to develop a new theoretical understanding.

Our strategy here was to engage in 'bottom-up' theory-building in which the building block is the mass of case-related data collected in the field structured and located within the wider socio-political economy. We found that what had happened so dramatically in New York City was not a function of case load or professionalisation of police or lawyers, but instead sprang from wider changes in the political economy resulting in a change in the nature and purpose of criminal prosecutions, the role of courtroom actors and the method of disposition. Criminal prosecutions transformed from disputes between the private parties resolved through a public determination of the facts and law to a private determination of the issues between the emergent state and the individual, marked by greater police involvement in the processing and management of defendants and greater public prosecutorial discretion. As this occurred, the structural purpose of criminal courts changed from individual to aggregate justice, as did the method of case disposition, from jury trials to guilty pleas. All this occurred against the backdrop of a new criminology, with its origins in Europe, when a new ruling class came into being whose legitimacy was derived from the ballot box rather than the paternalism and political sensibility of a class-based elite which marked the earlier era.

In this research process, therefore, the guilty plea system or plea bargaining was no longer understandable through traditional explanations tied to the courtroom. We learned, as we hope others will, that whether one concludes that law and its practice are subordinate to politics or vice versa, the structure of society, including government, and its relationship to law courts must be significant in any searching inquiry. Whilst we hoped that this analysis would encourage others to take on the burden of writing history and interrogating the relationship between the state and the law, we were also deeply aware that other approaches are far from precluded. It was, accordingly, with great pleasure that we read the incisive and constructive critique of our work by Upendra Baxi.[37] This critique itself suggests productive avenues for further theoretical exploration particularly through the writing of redemptive history which gives greater emphasis to the tradition of the oppressed.

CONCLUSION

Empirical research offers students challenges in terms of both practice and theory. It can be deeply frustrating and immensely rewarding. Despite the most careful planning, successful research is often dependent upon serendipity. Empirical research gives an opportunity to make a genuine contribution to the advancement of knowledge. Because it can never be exactly replicated but may constitute a precedent which is used to handcuff future researchers, it places grave moral and political burdens upon the individual researcher in respect of the terms on which funding is secured, dealings with prospective respondents, conduct of the field research and reporting of the findings.

In empirical research, choices must be confronted not only in the field but before any project is commenced. Whilst every researcher will be faced in the field with unforeseen challenges and choices, most issues are foreseeable and each researcher needs to have thought about and have answers to basic questions. These include whether the research is in any way likely to be compromised by the interests and concerns of the funding body and whether there are adequate guarantees for the independence of the researcher. The extent to which prospective respondents can be made 'insiders' to the research project will need to be resolved, especially where the findings are likely to be critical of those respondents or the institution to which they are affiliated. In terms of research methods, it is essential that the researcher decides whether partial disclosure or active deceit will ever be permitted.

I have found that it is idle to talk about the politics of research as if there was a choice. There is no choice: empirical research of any quality is necessarily political, and the only question, ethical and political, is whether to make explicit for the benefit of readers and future researchers what is deeply embedded in the undertaking.

The greatest art of the field researcher is the ability to talk to people and relate to their lives. Researchers must be able to get along with people at all levels in life not simply to gain acceptance and trust in the field but more importantly to see life from the perspective of respondents, to understand and identify with their lives without necessarily endorsing their behaviour.

And it is the duty of the researcher to try to make sense of what has been observed, a lesson all too often overlooked. Researchers need to bring to life the object of their interest, to give coherence and meaning to what may often appear disordered, disagreeable or even distasteful lifestyles. The task is to build, from the bits and pieces of data collected and isolated observations, a coherent picture held together by an over-arching theory in which the routines and rituals of daily practices and existence take on a meaning apparent only to the acute observer and not necessarily understood by those who are the object of inquiry. And in all of this, the researcher must retain a sense of humility as one singular perspective and one tiny endeavour is added to the ocean of information that marks humanity's past labours and, within that ocean, the isolated pools of knowledge to which we all aspire to add.

END NOTE

Whilst the focus of this chapter has been on the issue of plea bargaining, the same research issues arise in relation to work on empirical research generally, civil and criminal, and the same techniques and methodologies apply. For excellent accounts of empirical research in the area of civil justice, see, for example: Hazel Genn, *Hard Bargaining: Out of Court Settlement in Personal Injury Actions* (1987); Hazel Genn, *Paths to Justice: What People Do and Think about Going to Law* (1999); Hazel Genn and Alan Paterson, *Paths to Justice in Scotland: What People in Scotland Do and Think about Going to Law* (2001); T. Goriely, R. Moorehead, P. Abrams, *More Civil Justice?: The Impact of the Woolf Reforms on Pre-Action Behaviour* (2002); J. Baldwin, *Small Claims in County Courts in England and Wales: the Bargain Basement of Civil Justice* (1997).

FURTHER READING

J. Baldwin, *Small Claims in County Courts in England and Wales: The Bargain Basement of Civil Justice* (Oxford: Clarendon Press, 1997).

J. Barnes, *Who Should Know What?* (Harmondsworth: Penguin Books, 1979).

H. Becker, *Outsiders: Studies in the Sociology of Deviance* (New York: Free Press, 1963).

C. Bell and H. Newby (eds), *Doing Sociological Research* (London: George Allen & Unwin, 1977).

U. Baxi, 'The Craft of Disinterested History?' (2006) 17 *King's College Law Journal* 155.

R. Burgess, *In the Field: An Introduction to Field Research* (London: Allen and Unwin, 1984).

J. Flood, 'Researching Barrister's Clerks' in R. Luckham (ed.), *Law and Social Enquiry* (Uppsala: Scandinavian Institute of African Studies, 1981).

H. Genn, *Hard Bargaining: Out of Court Settlement in Personal Injury Actions* (Oxford: Clarendon Press, 1987).

H. Genn, *Paths to Justice: What People Do and Think about Going to Law* (Oxford: Hart Publishing, 1999).

H. Genn and A. Paterson, *Paths to Justice in Scotland: What Scottish People Do and Think about Going to Law* (Oxford: Hart Publishing, 2001).

T. Goriely, R. Moorehead and P. Abrams, *More Civil Justice?: The Impact of the Woolf Reforms on Pre-Action Behaviour* (London: Law Society and Civil Justice Council, 2002).

D. Hobbs and T. May (eds), *Interpreting the Field* (Oxford: Oxford University Press, 1993).

G. McCall and J. Simmons, *Issues in Participant Observation* (Reading, MA: Addison-Wesley, 1970).

M. McConville and C. Mirsky, *Jury Trials and Plea Bargaining: A True History* (Oxford: Hart Publishing, 2005).

M. Patton, *Qualitative Evaluation and Research Methods* (London: Sage, 1990).

M. Pogrebin (ed.), *Qualitative Approaches to Criminal Justice* (London: Sage, 2003).

G. Sjoberg (ed.), *Ethics Politics and Social Research* (London: Routledge & Kegan Paul, 1967).

M. Spector and J. Kitsuse, *Constructing Social Problems* (New Brunswick: Transaction Publishers, 2001).

G. Walford (ed.), *Debates and Developments in Ethnographic Methodology* (London: Elsevier Science, 2002).

NOTES

1. Sir Robert Mark, *Minority Verdict* (London: BBC Publications, 1972).
2. Morris Committee, *Jury Service* Cmnd. 2627 (London: HMSO, 1965).
3. Subject to various exceptions and disqualifications set out in the Act.
4. Implementation of the recommendations was delayed until the Juries Act 1973, by which time the requirement for unanimity had been abolished in 1967.
5. James' Committee, *The Distribution of Criminal Business between the Crown Court and the Magistrates' Court* Cmnd. 6323 (London: HMSO, 1975).
6. S. Cohen and L. Taylor, *Psychological Survival: The Experience of Long-term Imprisonment* (London: Penguin, 1972). Other examples of political interference in research include: T Morris and P. Morris, *Pentonville: A Sociological Study of an English Prison* (London: Routledge and Kegan Paul, 1963); and A. K. Bottomley, A. L. James, E. Clare and A. Liebling, *Monitoring and Evaluation of Wolds Remand Prison and Comparisons with Public-sector Prisons, in Particular HMP Woodhill* (London: Home Office Research and Statistics Directorate, 1997).
7. R. D. King and K. W. Elliot, *Albany: Birth of a Prison, End of an Era* (London: Routledge and Kegan Paul, 1978).
8. Despite our best efforts, we were unable to gain access to jurors themselves.

9. We soon found that prison officers would not allow prisoners to take away an unopened packet; we always removed one cigarette and left the packet on the interview table as an inducement for longer conversations than otherwise might have occurred.

10. H. Becker, *Outsiders: Studies in the Sociology of Deviance* (New York: Free Press, 1963).

11. Though this is not an axiom to which I have adhered throughout my research life. As I make clear later in the text, there have been occasions when I have consciously withheld information from respondents or undertaken research in a covert manner. Thus, for example, when working with Yorkshire Television on police practices in Birmingham, some of our filming was conducted without the informed consent of police officers who, as we filmed, were actively breaching the legal rules governing interrogation. See M. McConville, 'Videotaping Interrogations: Police Behaviour On and Off Camera' (1992) *Criminal Law Review* 532. My current empirical research on China's criminal justice system would not have been possible had it been predicated upon obtaining formal approval from all relevant authorities.

12. A practice that led the comedian Lenny Bruce to summarise the American system thus: in the Halls of Justice, justice is in the halls.

13. J. Baldwin and M. McConville, *Negotiated Justice* (London: Martin Robertson, 1977).

14. A number of my postgraduate students have been placed in even more difficult situations as, for example, one researcher who studied traffic policing was on a number of occasions witness to police illegality. Good sources for dealing with such dilemmas can be found in R. Luckham (ed.), *Law and Social Enquiry: Case Studies of Research* (Uppsala: Scandinavian Institute of African Studies, 1981).

15. Famous examples include S. Milgram, *Obedience and Authority* (New York: Harper Collins, 2004), and L. Humphreys, *Tearoom Trade* (New York: Aldine, 1975).

16. In a well-known example, after several years of negotiation, the Oxford University Centre for Criminological Research study into judicial sentencing was abandoned when the Chief Justice of the day pulled the plug on access.

17. P. Rock, *The Making of Symbolic Interactionism* (Totowa, NJ: Rowman and Littlefield, 1979). The categories may have changed but Rock's point remains valid.

18. See, for example, J. Baldwin and M. McConville, 'Plea Bargaining and the Court of Appeal' (1979) 6 *British Journal of Law and Society* 200–18; M. Zander and P. Henderson, *Crown Court Study*, Royal Commission on Criminal Justice Research Study No. 19 (London: HMSO, 1993); M.

McConville and C. Mirsky, 'Guilty Plea Courts: A Social Disciplinary Model of Justice' (1995) 42 *Social Problems* 216; M. Travers, *The Reality of Law: Work and Talk in a Firm of Criminal Lawyers* (Aldershot: Ashgate, 1997).

19. M. McConville, 'Plea Bargaining: Ethics and Politics' (1998) 25 *Journal of Law and Society* 562.

20. Some data had to be extracted the hard way. To get reliable information on 18-B earnings, we persuaded the appellate authorities to release into our custody the original bills submitted by lawyers. A battery of filing cabinets was thus transferred by us to the university on a Friday evening under a promise that they be returned by start of day on the following Monday morning, thereby enabling a team of researchers to trace the actual earnings of court-assigned lawyers over a ten-year period. Data on the Legal Aid Society was only released, however, when we initiated a suit under Freedom of Information legislation, the City authorities having earlier sought to suppress information on the actual financial support given to the Society and the Society's submitted budgets on the pretext that this was confidential.

21. Baldwin and McConville, see note 13 above.

22. Foremost among the reformers was Roscoe Pound who thought that adversary lawyering enabled 'those who habitually represent accused persons to study the weak spots in the system and learn how to take advantage of that' (see R. Pound, 'Criminal Justice in the American City', in R. Pound and F. Frankfurter (eds), *Criminal Justice in Cleveland* (Cleveland, OH: The Cleveland Foundation, 1922)).

23. L. Fabricant, 'The Voluntary Defender in Criminal Cases' (1924) *The Annals* 74.

24. See, M. McConville and C L. Mirsky, 'Criminal Defense of the Poor in New York City' (1986–7) 15 *New York University of Law & Social Change* 622.

25. *Gideon v Wainwright*, 372 US 335 (1963) establishing that state criminal courts were required under the Sixth and Fourteenth Amendments to the US Constitution to provide lawyers for those unable to afford counsel.

26. M. Galanter, 'Why the "Haves" Come Out Ahead: Speculations on the Limits of Legal Change' (1974) 19 *Law & Society Review* 95.

27. See, for example, D. J. Newman, *Conviction: The Determination of Guilt or Innocence Without Trial* (Boston, MA: Little, Brown, and Company, 1966); J. Eisenstein and H. Jacob, *Felony Justice: An Organizational Analysis of Criminal Courts* (Boston, MA: Little, Brown and Company, 1977).

28. A. S. Blumberg, 'The Practice of Law as Confidence Game: Organizational Co-optation of a Profession' (1967) 1 *Law & Society Review* 20.

29. Such lawyers would station themselves every day in the front row of the courtroom in the confident knowledge that the judge would assign them cases following a 'no-show' by a Legal Aid lawyer or upon the dismissal of any lawyer who displeased the judge.

30. See, for example, L. Zimmer, *Operation Pressure Point: The Disruption of Street-level Drug Trade on New York's Lower East Side*, Occasional Paper (New York: Centre for Research in Crime and Justice, New York University School of Law, 1987).

31. This model was further developed by S. Choongh, *Policing as Social Discipline* (Oxford: Clarendon Press, 1997).

32. See, for example, J. Langbein, 'Understanding the Short History of Plea Bargaining' (1979) 13 *Law & Society Review* 261; M. Feeley, 'Plea Bargaining and the Structure of the Criminal Process' (1982) 73 *Journal of Justice Systems* 338; and L. Friedman, *Crime and Punishment in American History* (New York: Basic Books, 1993).

33. See, for example, L. Mather, 'Comments on the History of Plea Bargaining' (1979) 13 *Law & Society Review* 282.

34. See, for example, G. Fisher, *Plea Bargaining's Triumph: A History of Plea Bargaining in America* (Stanford: Stanford University Press, 2003).

35. Friedman, see note 32 above, 67.

36. Feeley, see note 32 above, 349.

37. U. Baxi, 'The Craft of Disinterested History' (2006) 17 *King's College Law Journal* 155.

Notes on Contributors

Dr Satnam Choongh has been called to the bar since 1994, and has extensive experience in empirical research in the area of criminal justice with special emphasis upon policing and race as well as wide experience as a barrister at law. He has taught at the University of Warwick and is Adjunct Professor at the Chinese University of Hong Kong. He is author of *Policing as Social Discipline* (1997); *Review of the Delay in the Criminal Justice System* (1997); *Improving Custodial Legal Advice* (with L. Bridges, 1998) and *Ethnic Minority Defendants and the Right to Elect Jury Trial* (2000).

Dr Wing Hong Chui is Associate Professor, School of Law, The Chinese University of Hong Kong and formerly Senior Lecturer in the School of Social Science at the University of Queensland. He has published widely in criminology, particularly in the area of juvenile justice and probation studies. He is currently undertaking empirical research into criminal procedure in the People's Republic of China (with Professor Mike McConville) and litigants in person in civil proceedings in Hong Kong (with Professors Elsa Kelly and Camille Cameron). He is the co-editor of three books: *Moving Probation Forward* (with M. Nellis, 2003), *Social Work and Human Services Best Practice* (with J. Wilson, 2006), and *Experiences of Transnational Chinese Migrants in the Asia-Pacific* (with D. Ip and R. Hibbins, 2006). He is a member of the editorial boards of the *International Journal of Offender Therapy and Comparative Criminology* and *Social and Public Policy Review*, and is currently Book Review Editor of the *Asian Journal of Criminology*.

Ian Dobinson is Senior Lecturer, Law Faculty, University of Technology, Sydney, and previously Associate Professor, Law School, City University of Hong Kong. He has extensive teaching and research experience in the areas of criminal law, criminal justice and criminology and expertise in both quantitative and qualitative legal research methodologies. Past examples include a national survey of Australian judges and magistrates and their attitudes to sentencing and the relationship between heroin use and property crime, carried out in 1983–89. This latter study still stands as one of Australia's seminal works in this area. More recently he has carried out research on Chinese criminal law and the role of language interpreters in criminal trials in New South Wales.

Mark Findlay is the Professor of Criminal Justice and Director, Institute of Criminology, University of Sydney. Until recently he was Professor of International and Comparative Criminal Justice, Nottingham Law School. Since 2004 Professor Findlay has been a Senior Associate Research Fellow, Institute of Advanced Legal Studies, University of London, and was twice awarded the Inns of Court Fellowship from IALS. He has taught and researched in senior positions at Trinity College (Dublin), City University of Hong Kong, and the University of the South Pacific. He is author of sixteen books and over eighty journal articles and book chapters, including *The Globalisation of Crime* (1999) and *Transforming International Criminal Justice* (with R. Henham, 2005). Currently he is writing the monograph *Crime and Global Governance*, and with Professor Ralph Henham, *Beyond Punishment? Achieving International Criminal Justice*.

Stephen Hall is currently Professor at the School of Law, the Chinese University of Hong Kong. He is formerly Director of the European Law Centre at the University of New South Wales. He has been admitted as a barrister (High Court of Australia) and solicitor (Supreme Court of New South Wales), and practised law with the Australian Attorney-General's Department. His areas of research and teaching expertise are International Law, European Union Law, Contract Law, the traditions of Natural Law and the Common Law, and Administrative Law. His publications include *Nationality, Migration Rights and Citizenship of the Union* (1995) and *International Law* (2nd edn, 2006).

Ralph Henham is Professor of Criminal Justice at Nottingham Law School, Nottingham Trent University. He is an editorial board member of the *International Journal of the Sociology of Law, Howard Journal of Criminal Justice* and the *Nottingham Law Journal*. His research and teaching interests lie within criminology, criminal justice, legal theory and sentencing. His publications include *Sentencing Principles and Magistrates' Sentencing Behaviour* (1990); *Criminal Justice and Sentencing Policy* (1996); *Sentence Discounts and the Criminal Process* (2001); *Punishment and Process in International Criminal Trials* (2005); and *Transforming International Criminal Justice* (with M. Findlay, 2005), in addition to numerous articles on theoretical, comparative and policy-related aspects of sentencing.

Francis Johns is Lecturer, Law Faculty, University of Technology, Sydney (UTS). He has taught legal research at UTS since 2002 and also specialises in personal property. His previous experience and expertise in legal publishing includes: editing *Halsbury's Laws of Australia*, electronic product training and development, customer legal research support, and managing LexisNexis for the Australia and New Zealand market.

Mike McConville is Simon FS Li Professor of Law and Director, School of Law, the Chinese University of Hong Kong and formerly Head of the School of Law, University of Warwick. Mike McConville has been widely engaged in legal research in the area of criminal justice for some thirty years and has written extensively on such matters as legal representation, plea bargaining, juries, policing, neighbourhood watch and American legal history. His latest books, written with groups of colleagues, include: *Standing Accused*; *The Handbook of the Criminal Justice Process*; and *Jury Trials and Plea Bargaining*.

Dr George Meszaros is an Associate Professor at the School of Law, Warwick University. He holds a PhD in Sociology from the London School of Economics and Political Science and has taught research methods courses at the universities of London, Essex and latterly Warwick. Prior to this he was a freelance researcher working with a variety of organisations including the London Institute of Education's Thomas Coram Research Unit and the Public Law Project. Along with Professors Maurice Sunkin and Lee Bridges, he conducted large-scale empirical research into the scope and profile of judicial review in England and Wales. His teaching at Warwick has embraced both constitutional and administrative law as well as courses on its LLM programme in International Development Law and Human Rights. His research interests in Brazil date back twenty years, and he has recently completed a monograph examining socio-legal aspects of land reform struggles in Brazil. His publications include *Judicial Review in Perspective* (with L. Bridges and M. Sunkin, 1995).

Michael Pendleton graduated from the University of Sydney (1976) and the University of London (1980). He taught at the University of Sydney, University of Hong Kong, Murdoch University and presently at the Chinese University of Hong Kong. He was Chairman of the Law Reform Commission of Western Australia (1993). Michael is admitted as a solicitor in New South Wales, England and Wales and Hong Kong, China. He is a barrister and solicitor of the Supreme Court of Western Australia and the High Court of Australia. A mediator, arbitrator and domain name panellist of the World Intellectual Property Organisation (WIPO), Geneva, Michael has taught, written about and practised intellectual property law for the past twenty-five years. He has published eight books, and over 100 book chapters, refereed articles and published conference papers. According to Dr Stephen Stewart LLD QC, writing in (1985) 34 *International and Comparative Law Quarterly* 658, Michael was the author of only the second book on intellectual property (Butterworths, 1984) anywhere in the world (as opposed to just copyright, or just patents or just trademark texts). He was consultant to law firms including Deacons (Hong Kong), Blake, Dawson, Waldron (Australia), and Baker and

McKenzie (Hong Kong). He was Special Counsel to Deacons (Australia). He is presently consultant to Baker & McKenzie, Hong Kong. Among his publications are: *Intellectual Property Law in the People's Republic of China* (1986); *Intellectual Property and Technology Transfer Law* (1987); *Copyright Law in China* (1991); *Law of Intellectual and Industrial Property in Hong Kong* (2nd edn, with P. Garland and J. Margolis, 1994); *Intellectual Property – A Guide to the Law in Hong Kong with Reference to Developments in China* (with A. Lee, 2001); and *Intellectual Property Rights – Hong Kong SAR and People's Republic of China* (2003).

Geoffrey Wilson is Emeritus Professor of Law, University of Warwick and former Fellow of Queen's College, Cambridge. Professor Wilson pioneered the study of law in its social context and has written widely in the area of constitutional law and the English legal system as well as undertaking comparative research involving ancient civilisations. His publications include: *Cases and Materials on Constitutional and Administrative Law* (1966); *Cases and Materials on the English Legal System* (1973); and, as editor, *Frontiers of Legal Scholarship* (1995); *Challenges to European Legal Scholarship* (with R. Rogowski, 1996); and *The Handbook of the Criminal Justice Process* (with M. McConville, 2002).

Index